3

DATE DUE

JUL 2 5 2004			
AUG - 2 2004			

DEMCO 38-296

A SENTIMENTAL MURDER

ALSO BY JOHN BREWER

The Pleasures of the Imagination: English Culture in the Eighteenth Century

The Sinews of Power: War, Money and the English State 1688–1783

The Common People and Politics 1750–1800: Popular Political Participation Depicted in Cartoons and Caricatures

The Birth of a Consumer Society (with Neil McKendrick and J. H. Plumb)

Party Ideology and Popular Politics at the Accession of George III

A SENTIMENTAL
MURDER

Love and Madness

❧ *in the* ❧

Eighteenth Century

JOHN BREWER

FARRAR, STRAUS AND GIROUX

New York

Farrar, Straus and Giroux
19 Union Square West, New York 10003

Copyright © 2004 by John Brewer
Distributed in Canada by Douglas & McIntyre Ltd.
Printed in the United States of America
*Originally published in 2004 by HarperCollins*Publishers, *Great Britain, as* Sentimental Murder
Published in the United States by Farrar, Straus and Giroux
First American edition, 2004

Library of Congress Cataloging-in-Publication Data
Brewer, John, 1947–
    A sentimental murder : love and madness in the eighteenth century / John Brewer.
        p.   cm.
    Includes index.
    ISBN 0-374-26103-2 (hc. : alk. paper)
    1. Murder—England—London—Case studies.   2. Crimes of passion—England—
London.   3. Ray, Martha, d. 1779.   4. Hackman, James, 1752–1779.   I. Title.

HV6535.G6L525 2004
364.152'3'09421—dc22

                                                                        2003064345

EAN: 978-0-374-26103-0

www.fsgbooks.com

1   3   5   7   9   10   8   6   4   2

CONTENTS

ILLUSTRATIONS

vii

PROLOGUE

A Sentimental Murder began life as part of a review I wrote of G. J. Barker-Benfield's *The Culture of Sensibility* and has gone through several transformations before it found its present form. It started out as a more conventional historical account of James Hackman's murder of Martha Ray, the mistress of the 4th earl of Sandwich but, in large part because of questions raised in seminars and after lectures, I began to rethink how to tell the story. I'm especially grateful to Julie Peters for the remarks she made at a talk at Columbia University that brought out starkly (at least to me) the problems about how to handle this particular narrative. Thanks also to others at Harvard, Columbia, CalTech and Yale, for their help in shaping the book. I owe a special debt to my former colleagues at the University of Chicago, notably Jim Chandler, Katie Trumpener, Paul Hunter and Sandra Macpherson, all of whom probably heard the story more times than they cared to. Thanks to Donna Andrew, Claire L'Enfant, Max Novak, Roger Lonsdale, Peter Mandler, Helen Small, Kathleen Wilson, Angela Rosenthal, Martin Levy, Luisa Passerini, John Sutherland, John Wyner and Simon Schama for help, comments and support. Holger Hoock and Clare Griffith both provided invaluable research assistance, setting a high standard for me to follow.

The present Earl of Sandwich and Lady Sandwich generously afforded me access to the 4th Earl's private papers, gave me lunch and even allowed me briefly to exhibit my more than rusty cricketing skills. I have also to acknowledge the help of the librarian at Dove Cottage, and the kind permission of the Wordsworth Trust to quote from the papers about Basil Montagu in their collections at Dove Cottage, Grasmere. The staff at the Bodleian and Huntingdon libraries, so far apart yet so close in the high quality of their service, have made the research for this book a pleasure. I was fortunate in having a Moore fellowship at the California Institute of Technology, which gave me time to complete the book. Gill Coleridge, my agent, Arabella Pike at HarperCollins and Elisabeth Sifton at Farrar, Straus and Giroux have helped make this a better book by their constant critical support and vigorous editing. Special thanks to Stella, Grace and Lori for their constant support, love and forbearance.

This book is dedicated to the memory of Roy Porter, friend and colleague, who died in 2002. My first conversation with Roy took place in 1967 in the gate-house of Christ's College Cambridge. (We talked about seventeenth-century religion, sleep and his efforts to be a soccer goalkeeper.) Over the next thirty years or more our paths crossed in Cambridge, California and London. When I began this book I naturally turned to him – no one writing about love and madness in the eighteenth century would not have wanted to consult Roy Porter. No man knew more about love and libertinage in both the eighteenth and twentieth centuries. Characteristically, he plied me with references and information, quite a lot of it from his own work. Little did I know, when I began the project, that one of its incarnations would be the first Roy Porter lecture, established to commemorate him. Roy's absence has made me realize just how important he was to so many of us, not just as an endless source of gossip – no conversation was complete without a Porter anecdote – but as someone whose dedication and single-mindedness, expansive commitment to open-minded intellectual inquiry and to the best eighteenth-century values was (a sometimes intimidating) example and inspiration. He is sorely missed.

A SENTIMENTAL
MURDER

Preface

A *Sentimental Murder* investigates an eighteenth-century killing and attempted suicide. By tracing their changing interpretation over more than two hundred years, I want to explore the relations between history and fiction, storytelling and fact, past and present. I have adopted – and want to connect – two very different perspectives. On the one hand I examine in minute detail the events of a few crucial moments – it cannot have been more than a few seconds – between 11.30 p.m. and midnight on 7 April 1779, when, on the steps of the Covent Garden Theatre in London, a young clergyman, James Hackman, shot Martha Ray, the mistress of the Earl of Sandwich, and then tried to kill himself. On the other I consider a broad panorama that ranges over more than two centuries and is populated by journalists, doctors, novelists, poets, memoir writers, biographers, and historians who have tried to make sense (and sometimes art) out of the killing. My focus then is not just on what happened in 1779 but on the stories told about this event – who told them, how they were told, and what their tellers were up to in telling them.

Perhaps I have chosen this bifocal approach because, although I first came across the story of Hackman, Ray, and Sandwich when I was investigating the cultural life of eighteenth-century London, I learned about it from nineteenth-century sources: brief entries in the section on Covent Garden in histories of London, wedged between tales of great actors and lives of notorious whores; snippets in neatly arranged scrapbooks of newspaper cuttings about the theatre and music, crime and low life in the previous century collected by Victorian ladies and gentlemen; and anecdotes in popular histories based on eighteenth-century memoirs which first appeared in print in the mid-nineteenth century.

At first I ignored Martha Ray's story because I saw it through Victorian eyes as a simple moral tale. Covent Garden, with its theatres, wholesale grocery and sex trade, and the brutal crime of passion committed in its main square offered a snapshot of an earlier age, clinching evidence that the Georgians were sexier but less civilized, more glamorous but much less moral than their Victorian heirs. The incident seemed high on sensation but low on historical content – just a graphic anecdote about the seamier side of Georgian night life. But the peculiar insistence of the Victorian version of the story, the repeated stress on the moral distance between the crime of 1779 and the probity of the 1840s – the Victorian commentators worried over the story like a dog over a bone – made me curious to find out more. Eventually I was led back to the newspaper reports, trial and bits of surviving evidence at the time of the crime.

These revealed a different story – not a tale governed by moral distance and high-minded censoriousness but an account of a crime whose perpetrator and victim were obvious, but whose meaning was obscure. Of course Hackman killed Ray – a crowd of onlookers had seen him pull the trigger – but why? And who or what had led him to his crime? These were not just my questions; they were asked by many of Hackman's contemporaries.

Then, as now, crimes of passion, especially those committed by men against women, were not rare. But this particular killing attracted enormous attention and comment. No doubt this was because of the status and nature of the protagonists. A similar crime of passion committed by a drunken labourer who killed an impoverished girl-friend – the London courts handled many such cases – would have merited only a line or two, if that, in the London newspapers. But Hackman was a minister in the Church of England (albeit only recently ordained), and Martha Ray shared the bed of one of the most powerful and unpopular politicians of the day. Such a crime on the edges of high society was inevitably a good newspaper story, and a source of gossip and potential scandal, not least because the circumstances surrounding the murder were so obscure.

Few members of the public doubted that Hackman and Ray had become acquainted at Hinchingbrooke, Lord Sandwich's Huntingdonshire country seat, in 1775; no one doubted the killing (though some claimed it was not murder) four years later. But in the years between these two events almost nothing was known about Ray and Hackman's relations. Stories hate a hiatus. Unless it was filled, the tale of Hackman's crime would never be complete, much less understood. Into the empty space rushed all sorts of speculation: were they meeting secretly? Did they have an affair? Did they want to get married? Did Hackman press his attentions on an unwilling Ray? Were they intriguing together against the Earl of Sandwich? With the exception of Wordsworth's account of Martha Ray (discussed in chapter 7), which deliberately places her out of the context of her death, almost every version of the events of 1779 written over the next two hundred years, whether newspaper story, poem, novel or biography, offers answers to these questions. And they all took the form of particular types of story – sentimental tales of suffering, romantic stories of heightened male sensibility, scurrilous stories of libertine desire and female manipulation, tales of criminal turpitude, medical tales of love's madness, stories of female romance, tales for moral reflection on the dilemmas of women or speculation on the nature of history.

The earliest press coverage of the killing not only gave details of Hackman's crime but fostered public debate about its perpetrator. Within a year of Ray's death and Hackman's execution a Grub Street author, Herbert Croft, wrote an epistolary work, *Love and Madness*, which claimed to contain the correspondence of the murderer and his victim. Before the century was out, and in part because of the tremendous success of Croft's work, Hackman passed into medical history and Martha Ray into one of William Wordsworth's *Lyrical Ballads*. I'd already collected many fragmentary nineteenth-century accounts, but now discovered detailed discussion of the affair in such journals as the *Edinburgh Review*, provoked by the publication of the memoirs of two famous contemporaries of Hackman and Ray, Horace Walpole and George Selwyn. The story also lived on in the Victorian obsession with gruesome crimes, both past and present. In the second half of the nineteenth century interest in the trial seemed to peter out, but revived in the 1890s. The reprinting of a doctored version of *Love and Madness* put the story back in the public demesne and was the source for two twentieth-century versions of the story, Constance Hagberg Wright's *The Chaste Mistress*, published in 1930 and Elizabeth Jenkins's essay on Martha Ray in her *Ten Fascinating Women*, which first appeared in 1955.

I could have approached this large and growing body of material by asking the traditional question: what was the true story of what actually happened in those years between Ray and Hackman's first and final meetings? This would have meant that I was trying to 'see through' subsequent versions of the story in order to recover the 'real history' of the event. I would have had to reject a great deal of the material I had accumulated as inaccurate, irrelevant and obfuscating. But when you treat a novel or a poem, or even a polemical tract or a biographical apologia as if its aim was to be a work of history, you certainly sell it short. You lose what is most distinctive, moving, powerful and illuminating about a work by seeing it in only one dimension. You fail to appreciate both its purposes and its effects.

I was loath to do this and so I took another tack. I set out to write a history of the accounts, narratives, stories – call them what you will – that were built around James Hackman's killing of Martha Ray. The aim was to ask not 'is this story true' but 'what does this story mean, and why did it take a particular form at a particular time?' And, in order to answer these questions, I had to ask others: what does this story do? Or, to put it another way, what is the storyteller doing with this story?

Thus my account of the press reports of Hackman and Ray is as much about the nature of newspaper reporting as about murder and suicide; my analysis of the novel containing the so-called letters of Ray and Hackman is an investigation not of their veracity, but of the ways that fictional works played with different ideas of truth; the nineteenth-century version of Hackman and Ray is about Victorian ideas of morality and progress and their connection to a Victorian notion of real history; and the chapters on the twentieth century deal with the aims of women's writing and conservative politics in the inter-war period. Here history is not the history of a discrete set of past events, but a history of the changing ways in which past events have been understood. In this way history becomes not an anatomizing act, lifting the sheet to reveal the corpus of a distant and separate past, but an act of accumulation, in which the last historical account is seen (inevitably) to build upon its predecessors.

I want to stress that this does not mean that my interpretation is uncritical. On the contrary, a large part of my task has been to recover the aims, assumptions and prejudices (including my own) that shaped the different versions of the story. In this way accounts of the past are not separated from the dynamics of history, to be discarded or sacrificed as the historian sees fit, but are seen as an intrinsic part of them.

Inevitably I found myself writing not just about the events of 1779 but about eighteenth-century, Romantic, Victorian and twentieth-century attitudes to the events of 1779. In any historical period there are normally several different ways of thinking about earlier epochs, but almost every account of the events of 1779, whether supposedly factual or actually fictional, was shaped by a dominant narrative that placed the eighteenth century in relation to the time of its telling. The first accounts of Hackman and Ray were fashioned according to the eighteenth century's version of itself as a modern age of sentiment and sensibility, in which human (mis)conduct was the object of sympathy rather than censoriousness. The Victorians, by contrast, placed the incident in the context of aristocratic depravity and profound inequality that they thought modern material progress to have ended. Every era had its own 'eighteenth century', and each 'eighteenth century' shaped the way in which the story was interpreted.

I also learned that it was very difficult to distinguish fact and fiction in the work of writers who explored 'the truth' about Hackman, Sandwich and Ray. The first accounts of the crime purported to be factual, but they drew on the narratives and insights of popular fiction to make sense of the crime, and treated it as if it were the subject of a drama or a novel. It was only a short move for Herbert Croft in 1780 to turn the story of the crime into *Love and Madness*, a fiction, albeit one that claimed to be true. But the work of Croft's imagination was treated as fact in the medical literature on love's madness, even while Martha Ray's story was rewritten to place her in a literary tradition of lovelorn women. In the nineteenth century Hackman's killing of Ray became a factual anecdote, or a fictional tableau. In both cases the murder was intended to reveal a truth about an earlier age. In the 1890s, when *Love and Madness* was re-edited and reissued, it came to be seen not as a fiction but as a set of historical documents, a source for the historical reconstruction of a doomed love affair. As such it provided the material for two twentieth-century narratives, Wright's novel and Jenkins's biographical essay.

These many versions of Ray's killing showed that no story is innocent; all narratives involve plotting. To shape a set of events into a story is to exclude other possible narratives. This may sometimes be an unintended consequence, but in the case of the earliest versions of Ray's killing, it was deliberate. As we shall see, the Earl of Sandwich and his associates, together with the friends of James Hackman, agreed on a story about the crime that absolved the main participants of any blame. This was a whitewash, but it was also a cover-up designed to avert attention from stories about Sandwich and Ray that had been in circulation before her murder and that would have placed them in a poor light. The cover-up was never entirely successful – the repressed stories were to resurface again and again, and they re-emerge in my narrative as the two chapters on the 'missing stories' of 1779.

If we (including historians) are all implicated in the stories we tell, then I, too, have an obligation to explain my own narrative. What am I up to in writing about more than two centuries of stories about a crime of passion which, though terrible for those immediately involved – James Hackman, Martha Ray, the Earl of Sandwich and their children – hardly seems the stuff of 'history'? The answer to this lies, I believe, in my response to the sometimes rather brutal debates that have taken place over the last twenty years or so between two very different notions of history: one that emphasizes that history is the recovery of what actually happened in the past; the other that history is made in the present, the plotted and imaginative construct of a modern historical narrator. I leave these questions to my epilogue in which I try – doubtless disingenuously – to put my narrative in its turn-of-the-millennium context.

CHAPTER 1

Spring 1779

JOHN MONTAGU, 4th Earl of Sandwich, was a tall gangling man with 'strong legs and arms' and a ruddy appearance that led the novelist Frances Burney, when she first met him in 1775, to compare him with a rough-hewn Jack Tar: 'he is a tall, stout man & looks *weather-proof* as any sailor in the navy'. Portraits by Gainsborough and Zoffany reveal a large, hooked nose, thin, sensual lips and a long torso that makes his head seem unaccountably small. They also fail to conceal the clumsiness that led Sandwich's French dancing master to ask that 'your Lordship would never tell any one of whom you learned to dance'. 'Awkward' and 'shambling' were how his friends described him, one remarking to another as they spotted him from a distance, 'I am sure it is Lord Sandwich; for, if you observe, he is walking down both sides of the street at once'.

Sandwich had energy that more than compensated for his clumsiness. Despite his lack of polish, he had a reputation as a ladies' man. One anonymous female correspondent confided in him, 'you have it in your power to gain the affections of almost any woman that you study to please'. Women found him charming, and he pursued them relentlessly from his youth into middle age. In his sixties he admitted, 'I have never pretended to be free from indiscretion, and those who know me have been . . . long accustomed to

forgive my weaknesses, when they do not interfere with my conduct as a public man.'

For a peer, Sandwich was not wealthy, and from 1739, when he took his seat in the House of Lords at the age of twenty-one, he sought political office to increase his income. During a long career in government he served as Secretary of State, Postmaster General and as a diplomat, but the post that he saw as his own and for which he is best remembered was First Lord of the Admiralty, an office he held between 1747 and 1751 and again after his appointment by Lord North in 1770.

Waking on the morning of 7 April 1779 in the ample apartments in the Admiralty building that were one of the perquisites of his post, Sandwich faced a busy day of government business. The Admiralty gates in the Robert Adam screen that separated the offices from the street opened at 9 a.m., when four of the office clerks arrived to receive their instructions, began transcribing documents to captains and admirals, suppliers and politicians, and made neat copperplate copies in official letter books and ledgers. The eleven-hour day was one of the longest in any government office: all the clerks were in attendance between eleven in the morning and four in the afternoon, but a part of the staff kept the Admiralty open between nine and eleven, and between six and ten in the evening.

Though Sandwich had many political enemies, he was generally acknowledged to be a conscientious and industrious official. He was, as one contemporary put it, 'Universally admitted to possess eminent talents, great application to the duties of his office, and thorough acquaintance with public business . . . In all his official functions he displayed perspicuity as well as dispatch.' Normally his working day began even before the Admiralty opened: 'he rose at an early hour, and generally wrote all his letters before breakfast', and he frequently had no respite before taking a late evening meal. On one occasion he complained, 'I am fatigued to death having been with my pen in my hand [for] . . . thirteen hours.' The snack that bears Sandwich's name, and that was first made by slipping a slice of naval salt beef between two pieces of bread, was made to allow not, as legend has it, for longer hours at the gaming table, but more time at the office.

Admiralty business, of course, was not always so onerous, and the First Lord left much of the detailed work to his reliable and experienced Secretary, Philip Stephens, an official with more than twenty-five years' service for the Admiralty Board. But when the nation was at war and when parliament was in session, as it was in the spring of 1779, the office required constant attention. The nation was embroiled with its American subjects; France and Spain had just joined the rebellious colonists. Because of the weight of business the Admiralty had hired four additional clerks in the last year. The most recent appointment, Mr Hollinworth, had begun work the previous morning.

Yet there were additional reasons why the Admiralty was so frenetic on this warm spring day. For the Admiralty Board and especially Lord Sandwich were at the centre of a huge political row about the conduct of the American war. The parliamentary opposition, led by Charles James Fox in the Commons and the Duke of Richmond in the Lords, was determined to lay the blame for Britain's military failures at the door of the Admiralty, and had launched a determined attempt to drive Sandwich from office, if not to overthrow the government itself.

The squall had blown up more than a year earlier, when the war had been going particularly badly. Forced to maintain supply lines to Boston, New York and the Chesapeake, the navy was overstretched and undermanned. Encouraged by Britain's plight, and eager to revenge their previous defeats, France had pledged support to the Americans in the summer of 1778. One of Sandwich's spies, John

Walker, had been sending him alarming reports for several years of a major French naval build-up. Despite Sandwich's warnings to his colleagues, too little was done too late. Better equipped, the French battle fleet threatened to outnumber the British and to make possible a French landing on the south coast of England.

Sandwich and his colleagues had been bitterly attacked for their conduct of the war and their lack of preparedness for its escalation. Their hopes (like those of most Britons) had been pinned on an early and decisive naval victory against France that would have seen off the threat to Britain's supply lines and trade, and dispelled the threat of invasion. But when the two fleets met off Ushant on 27 July 1778, the French repelled the English attack and inflicted great damage before retreating to Brest. The threat of French superiority remained, and was soon compounded by the prospect of Spain's entry into the war on the colonists' side. On 15 October Sandwich wrote to the prime minister, Lord North, 'The situation of our affairs is at this time so critical and alarming that my mind will not rest, without I collect my thoughts and put on paper the ideas I have of the danger we are in, and what exertions we can use to guard against the storm that is hanging over us.'

On the same day an article appeared in the opposition newspaper, the *General Advertiser and Morning Post*, blaming Rear-Admiral Sir Hugh Palliser, a member of the Admiralty Board and a close ally of Sandwich's, for failing to follow an order of the fleet's leader, Admiral August Keppel, a political ally of the Foxite opposition, to engage the French more closely. The article provoked a huge row, which turned officers against one another and divided the navy into bitter factions (contemporaries talked of the Montagus and Capulets). Keppel and Palliser, both MPs, squabbled on the floor of the House of Commons; both were eventually court martialled. Throughout the winter and early spring of 1779 the Foxite opposition kept up the pressure on the government, proposing motion after motion attacking its policy in general and Sandwich in particular. In February it looked as if, for Sandwich at least, the game was up. King George III and Lord North decided to remove him from the Admiralty as a way of appeasing government critics. Only the failure of negotiations for a replacement kept him in office. On 11 February a court martial acquitted Keppel and dismissed Palliser's charges against the admiral as 'malicious and unfounded'. That evening a crowd of opposition supporters smashed the windows of Sandwich's lodgings, frightening his mistress, Martha Ray, who was staying there. The crowd tore off the Admiralty gates, looted Palliser's house in Pall Mall and attacked the homes of other Admiralty officials.

The government was losing its grip. Lord North sank into a depression that made business difficult to transact – on one occasion Sandwich was sent by the king to cajole him out of bed – while government supporters, thinking the administration doomed, began to absent themselves from important debates in parliament. In April the opposition's demand for an inquiry into the state of the British and French navies and into the Admiralty's preparedness for war placed an additional burden on Sandwich's officials, who had to assemble documents and statistics to be used in his defence. In the following week a debate was scheduled in the House of Lords in which Lord Bristol, a leading spokesman of the opposition, was expected to call for Sandwich's dismissal. On the afternoon of 6 April Sandwich met with the king to discuss the government's strategy.

While Sandwich laboured in the Admiralty Board room, struggling to salvage his career, other events that were to have a profound effect on his future were unfolding in another part of London. How much he knew of their background is difficult to tell, though he certainly did not know about the events that took place that day while he was at work.

Some time after the Admiralty gates had opened, a handsome young man knocked at the door of Signor Galli, in Jarvis Street, off London's Haymarket. The Reverend James Hackman, a tall, thin figure with a high forehead and fine, almost effeminate features, had only a week before been ordained as a priest in the Church of England and given the living of Wiveton, in Norfolk. But that morning he was not bent on clerical business. He demanded to see a letter that Galli had first shown him two days earlier. But the Italian turned him away, telling him that it 'was out of his power. The letter being no longer in his possession.' The letter had been written by Martha Ray, the thirty-five-year-old mistress of the Earl of Sandwich, and in it she pleaded with Hackman to 'desist from his pursuit' of her, refused to see him and told him she wished to cease all connection with him. Hackman left disappointed, unable to confirm what he did not wish to believe.

Martha Ray had been the mistress of the Earl of Sandwich for more than sixteen years and had borne him nine children, of whom five were living: Robert, born in 1763; Augusta, whose date of birth goes unrecorded; Basil, born in 1770; and two other brothers, William and John, whose birth dates were 1772 and 1773. With such a family it was obvious that Sandwich's relationship with Ray was no casual affair. She was effectively his common law wife and was known as his public consort. A contemporary described Ray as 'not what we would call *elegant*, but which would pass under the denomination of *pretty*; her height was about five feet five inches; she was fresh-coloured, and had a perpetual smile on her countenance, which rendered her agreeable to every beholder'. Others, especially those who heard her sing, were more impressed. The young clergyman Richard Dennison Cumberland, who listened to Ray's performances at Hinchingbrooke, spoke of her 'personal accomplishments and engaging Manner', describing her as 'a second Cleopatra – a Woman of thousands, and capable of producing those effects on the Heart which the Poets talk so much of and which we are apt to think Chimerical'. Her surviving portraits bear out this description showing a prepossessed and elegantly dressed woman with bright eyes, a slight smile and an expression that betrays considerable strength of character. Certainly James Hackman, who had met her at Hinchingbrooke, had been smitten with her since their first acquaintance in 1775. Nor did it seem likely, despite Ray's pleas, that the young man would desist in his pursuit of her.

Later that same afternoon Hackman dined with his sister, her husband, the attorney Frederick Booth, and a cousin at the Booths' house in Craven Street, off the Strand, a few doors down from Benjamin Franklin's lodgings; he left after eating, promising to return to the family for supper. Striding up Craven Street, he turned left into the Strand, walked through Charing Cross and down Whitehall towards the Admiralty, where Ray and Sandwich had their lodgings. When he arrived he saw the Earl's coach at the Admiralty's door. He guessed (rightly, as it turned out) that Martha Ray was going out, and he walked the short distance back towards Craven Street, and stationed himself at the Cannon Coffee House at Charing Cross, so that he could watch the passing traffic. His wait was not in vain. Shortly before six o'clock, Sandwich's coach swept by, carrying Ray and her companion, Signora Caterina Galli, up the Strand and past its many fine shops, with their first-floor displays of luxuries, cloth and jewels, before turning north into Covent Garden. Hackman followed hastily on foot, watching the two women enter the Covent Garden Theatre at about a quarter past six.

On that Wednesday the theatre was crowded. The star attraction was Margaret Kennedy, a statuesque if somewhat clumsy actress with a fine voice, famed for 'breeches' roles in which she played male parts. The evening's receipts were to go to her benefit, and she was to sing

Nathaniel Dance's portrait of Martha Ray which was engraved by Valentine Green and sold in many numbers after her death. She rests her right arm on the score of Handel's *Jephta*, in which she sang the role of Iphis, the embodiment of female sacrifice.

the part of Colin in *Rose and Colin*, a short comic opera by Charles Dibdin, and the male lead – Meadows – in Thomas Arne's extremely popular opera, *Love in a Village*.

Caterina Galli and Martha Ray were more than casual theatre-goers. They might have chosen that evening to go to Drury Lane to see a much-acclaimed production of Shakespeare's *Macbeth*, but they preferred comic opera and Mrs Kennedy because of their love of music. Caterina Galli was herself a famous singer and music teacher. A pupil of Handel, she had starred in his operas and oratorios in the 1740s and 1750s, usually singing male roles. After a spell back in her native Italy, she returned to London for two seasons before retiring in 1776. Martha Ray, though she had never performed professionally, was also a singer of great accomplishment, with a passion, shared by Sandwich, for Handel. Ray had been tutored by a number of musicians at Sandwich's expense, and Galli, as well as being Ray's companion, had sung with her at private concerts arranged by the Earl. It seems likely that Sandwich hoped to attend the performance at Covent Garden that evening – he had earlier cancelled a dinner with friends at the Admiralty – but was prevented from enjoying himself because of the press of Admiralty business.

Mrs Kennedy and *Love in a Village* were apt objects of Martha Ray's attention. Mrs Kennedy, like Martha Ray, had achieved success through the attentions of a male admirer: she had been spotted by Thomas Arne, singing songs in a pub near St Giles, one of the least salubrious parts of London. Ray, who had been a milliner's apprentice, owed her present station to the attentions of Lord Sandwich. And Isaac Bickerstaff's story, set to Arne's music, was about the perils of love and marriage, especially among social unequals, a topic that much concerned Ray, with her five illegitimate children by Sandwich.

Like most story-lines in comedy, the plot of *Love in a Village* enjoys a simplicity and happy resolution altogether unlike the unresolved complexities of relationships such as that between Ray and Sandwich. A young gentleman and -woman, Meadows and Rosetta, separately flee from marriage partners chosen by their parents but whom they have never seen. Disguised as a gardener and female servant, working in the same house, they soon fall hopelessly in love.

The couple try to resist their feelings, thinking that marriage – the proper consequence of true love – will be impossible. How could they marry someone whom they believed to be their social inferior? But, by an improbable contrivance typical of such comedies, they prove to be the very people their parents wished them to marry. Freed of their disguise, Rosetta and Meadows are united – duty and desire are neatly reconciled. The barriers of class and wealth are neither circumvented nor confronted but expelled through a twist in the plot.

Ray and Galli watched the performance from seats close to the royal box, where they not only had one of the best views of the stage but were easily seen by the rest of the audience. Accounts differ about who else joined them in the box. One, by a friend of Sandwich, speaks of their being accompanied by three young men belonging to Sandwich's circle of naval protégés; another singles out Lord Coleraine, a notorious libertine, who had been the keeper of the famous courtesan Kitty Fisher and of Sophia Baddeley, a stage beauty and singer. Whoever their companions were, Ray and Galli clearly enjoyed the evening, exchanging pleasantries with male friends and admirers when not engaged in watching the performance. James Hackman, who had entered the theatre, watched the two women across the pit.

Hastening to his lodgings in Duke's Court, St Martin's Lane, Hackman loaded two pistols, and wrote a suicide note to his brother-in-law:

My Dear Frederick

When this reaches you I shall be no more, but do not let my unhappy fate distress you too much. I have strove against it as long as possible, but it now overpowers me. You know where my affections were placed; my having by some means or other lost hers, (an idea which I could not support) has driven me to madness. The world will condemn me, but your good heart will pity me. God bless you, my dear Fred, would I had a sum to leave you, to convince you of my great regard. You was my only friend . . . May heaven protect my beloved woman, and forgive this act which alone could relieve me from a world of misery I have long endured. Oh! if it should be in your power to do her any act of friendship, remember your faithful friend.

Stuffing the note in one pocket together with one of the pistols, he put another letter in his other pocket with the second weapon. This letter, which Hackman had sent to Martha Ray but which she had returned unopened, offered to marry her and take her youngest child, John, off to a life of rural felicity in his country parish. The note concluded: 'O! thou dearer to me than life, because that life is thine! think of me and pity me. I have long been devoted to you; and your's, as I am, I hope either to die, or soon to be your's in marriage. For God's sake, let me hear from you; and, as you love me, keep me no longer in suspense, since nothing can relieve me but death or you. – Adieu!'

His pockets full of sentiment and violence, Hackman returned to the Covent Garden Theatre. He seems to have entered the theatre several times during the evening (a full night's entertainment lasted nearly five hours), retreating to the Bedford Coffee-house to strengthen his resolve with glasses of brandy and water. His friends claimed that he then tried to shoot himself on two occasions, first in the lobby – where he was prevented by the crowd from getting close enough to Ray to be sure that she would witness his death – and then on the steps of the theatre, where he was pushed by one of the Irish chairmen who carried the sedan chairs of the theatre's wealthy patrons.

At about a quarter past eleven Ray and Galli came out of the theatre, but the large crowd jostled them and prevented them from reaching their waiting carriage. John Macnamara, a young Irish attorney, saw the two women, 'who seemed somewhat distressed by the croud, whereupon he offered his service to conduct them to their carriage, which was accepted, and Miss Ray took hold of his arm'. Threading their way through the swirl of parting spectators and down the steps of the theatre, Galli entered the carriage first. Ray followed, putting her foot on the carriage step as Macnamara held her hand. At that moment a figure in black dashed forward and pulled Ray by the sleeve; she turned to find herself face to face with Hackman. Before she could utter a word, he pulled the two pistols from his pockets, shot Ray with the one in his right hand, and shot himself with the other.

As the crowd shrank back, Macnamara, unsure of what had happened, lifted Ray from the ground, and found himself drenched in blood. For years afterwards he would recall (somewhat hyperbolically) 'the sudden assault of the assassin, the instantaneous death of the victim, and the spattering of the poor girls brains over his own face'. According to Horace Walpole, Hackman 'came round behind her [Ray], pulled her by the gown, and on her turning round, clapped the pistol to her forehead and shot her through the head. With another pistol he then attempted to shoot himself, but the ball grazing his brow, he tried to dash out his own brains with the pistol, and is more wounded by those blows than by the ball.' Martha Ray died instantly, leaving Hackman on the ground, 'beating himself about the head . . . crying, "o! kill me! . . . for God's sake kill me!"'

With the help of a link-boy, Macnamara, shocked but with great composure, carried Ray's bloody body across the Square and into the nearby Shakespeare Tavern, where the corpse was laid on a table in one of the rooms usually hired for private supper parties. (The tavern was a notorious place of sexual assignation: in 1763 James Boswell took 'two very pretty girls' there and 'found them good subjects of amorous play'.) Hackman was arrested by Richard Blandy, a constable who had heard the shots as he was walking between the Drury Lane and Covent Garden playhouses: 'he came up and took Mr Hackman, who delivered two pistols to him . . . he was taking him away, when somebody called out to bring his Prisoner back; and then he took him to the Shakespeare Tavern, where he saw he was all bloody . . . he searched Mr Hackman's pockets, and found two sealed letters, which he gave to Mr Campbell, the Master of the Tavern'.

In the Shakespeare Macnamara angrily confronted Hackman, asking him, 'What devil could induce you to commit such a deed?' Hackman, 'with great composure', responded, 'This is not a proper place to ask such a question', and when asked what his name was and who knew him replied 'that his name was Hackman, and that he was known to Mr Booth in Craven Street whom he had sent for'.

Sir John Fielding, the blind magistrate and brother of the novelist Henry Fielding, was summoned and arrived at the Shakespeare at three o'clock in the morning. He examined the witnesses in the tavern and committed Hackman to the Tothills Bridewell, a gaol where prisoners were often held overnight. Before he was taken away Hackman asked to see Ray's body and commented, 'What a change has a few hours made in me – had her friends done as I wished them to do, this would never have happened.' One report described him as gazing 'upon the miserable object with the most deep attention and calm composure, instead of that violent agitation of spirits which every beholder expected, and exclaiming, *that he now was happy!*' In the Bridewell, and much to the surprise of many commentators, he fell into a deep and untroubled sleep.

Sandwich knew nothing of these events until some time around midnight. He had waited at the Admiralty, expecting Martha Ray to return for supper after the theatre. As she was late and he was tired, he went to bed at about half past eleven, only to be woken by his black servant James, who told him that Ray had been shot. A distraught James described the scene to Sandwich's friend, Joseph Cradock, the following day. At first Sandwich did not understand or believe what had happened. He thought James was referring to one of the many scurrilous ballads sung under the windows of the Admiralty. 'You know that I forbade you to plague me any more about those ballads, let them sing or say whatever they please about me!' 'Indeed, my Lord,' replied James, 'I am not speaking of any ballads; it is all too true.' Other members of the household then came in; 'all was a scene of the utmost horror and distress'. Sandwich 'stood, as it were, petrified; till suddenly seizing a candle, he ran upstairs, threw himself on the bed, and in agony exclaimed, "Leave me a while to myself – I could have borne anything but this".'

Whether James had been told the news by Caterina Galli or another messenger is not clear – 'all was confusion and astonishment'. Galli had fainted in the coach when Ray was killed and could not recall what happened thereafter, although we know she returned to the Admiralty in Sandwich's coach. Sandwich had enough presence of mind to dispatch a servant to the Shakespeare Tavern to watch over Ray's body and exclude prurient visitors. At seven the following morning he scribbled a hasty note to his friend Robert Boyle Walsingham, an aristocratic young naval officer, 'For gods sake come to me immediately, in this moment I have much want of the comfort of a real friend; poor Miss Ray was inhumanly murthered last night as she was stepping into her coach at the playhouse door . . . The murtherer is taken and sent to prison.'

Two hours later, Hackman was brought before Sir John Fielding at Bow Street. Fielding led Hackman to a private room 'in order to prevent, as much as possible, the unhappy prisoner from being exposed to the view of wanton, idle curiosity', and had the witnesses' testimony sworn before him. Hackman was no longer calm but visibly agitated: 'From the agonizing pangs which entirely discomposed and externally convulsed him, it was some time before the Magistrate could proceed.' Asked if he had anything to say Hackman replied that 'he wished for nothing but death; that nothing could be more welcome; that the sooner it came the better, for that alone would relieve him of the extreme Misery he laboured under'. Fielding committed him to Newgate, where he asked that he be granted his own room, a request that Fielding accepted on condition that he did not stay alone, as the court feared that he might again seek to take his own life. He was scheduled to be tried at the next sessions at the Old Bailey, set for 16 April.

That same afternoon the coroner's jury met at the Shakespeare Tavern in the room where Sandwich's servant still guarded Ray's body. The corpse was examined by two surgeons, Mr O'Brien and Mr Jarvis, who showed that the bullet had entered Ray's forehead on the right side, causing massive damage, and then exited near the left ear. Hackman who, at five foot nine, was several inches taller than Ray, must have been pointing his pistol downwards when he fired; this would also explain why Macnamara believed that the blow he felt to his arm was caused not by Ray's fall but by the spent bullet that had killed her. During the inquest, against the advice of Mr O'Brien and much to the distress of Sandwich, it was decided to open Ray's skull in order to trace the trajectory of the wound. The doctors 'owned that they never saw so dismal and ghastly a fracture'; the inquest brought in a verdict of wilful murder.

That day all of Lord Sandwich's servants 'out of livery' changed into mourning clothes. In the evening Sandwich had Ray's body removed to an undertaker's near Leicester Fields. One paper reported that she was wrapped in a sheet or shroud and that she would be buried wearing the valuable clothes and jewels she wore at the moment of her murder, 'so that property to the amount of near £2000 will be deposited in her coffin'. On 14 April, Ray was interred in a vault in Elstree church, where her mother, who had died three years previously, was also buried.

Sandwich's grief did not stop him taking decisive action in the days after Martha Ray's murder. He employed Walsingham and two lawyers, Mr Balding and Mr William Chetham, to take depositions and informations from Signor Galli, his wife Caterina and Macnamara; they also questioned Hackman and discussed the case with Sir John Fielding. Sandwich himself questioned Signor Galli on the day after Ray's death. He learnt that Hackman had contacted Ray about a week earlier. (A scribbled note from Ray to Caterina Galli of 30 March – 'My Dear Galli I am in open distress I beg you come immediately to me' – possibly refers to the contact.) Ray gave the Gallis her letter to Hackman asking to be left alone, and they read it to Hackman on the evening of 5 April. Galli assured Sandwich that there had been no assignation or meeting between Ray and Hackman at his house, and that, though he had seen Hackman walking in St James's Park, he had avoided him.

The same day Sandwich sent a message via Walsingham to Hackman telling the murderer of his forgiveness, though the press reported that the Earl also claimed that Hackman 'has disturbed his peace of mind for ever'. Hackman, on his part, told Walsingham 'upon his word as a dying man, that he has never spoken to Miss Ray since the beginning of the year 1776, at which time he had proposed marriage and was rejected'. The murderer was pleased to be assured that his victim had no other special admirer: 'poor Miss Ray was innocent. He lays the whole on Galli' – and expressed his determination to die. 'He is desirous to dye by the hand of the law . . . he wishes not to live himself, he told me today,' wrote Walsingham to Sandwich, 'he hoped to suffer as soon as possible.'

The agreement between Sandwich and Hackman that Martha Ray was innocent of any wrongdoing placed Caterina Galli in a difficult position. A day after the murder a story was already circulating that Hackman's decision to kill Ray, and not merely to end his own life, was explained by a stratagem of Galli's: to get Hackman to leave Ray alone, she had told Hackman that Ray had tired of him and had a new secret lover. Seeing Ray with male companions at the play, he had been driven into a frenzy of jealousy.

The papers reported that Sandwich offered to secure a pardon for Hackman if he were convicted. (As a member of the cabinet, which determined such matters, Sandwich would certainly have been able to exert great influence on Hackman's behalf, and he clearly did not relish the role of sitting in judgment on a person's life. Years earlier, commenting on this cabinet function, he had written to a friend, 'you can't think how it distresses me to be put to a momentary decision where a man's life is concerned'.) But as early as two days after the murder Hackman seems to have rejected the Earl's aid, an act that was rightly interpreted as a determination on his part to die. For, as Fielding explained in a letter to Sandwich on 10 April, Hackman's conviction seemed inevitable:

> I am clearly of opinion that the evidence against Hackman is full and compleat to the last degree and that he can make no defense that would not aggravate his guilt and tend to his conviction; but will not neglect any hint your Lordship gives. As to Insanity it cannot be offered as an excuse as it appeared and can be proved

that he was rational and sensible of his Wickedness at 4 in the morning, when I examined him, and has been so ever since.

At first Hackman said that he would plead guilty as charged of Ray's murder. But in the days after the crime, his sister, his brother-in-law, Booth, and the lawyer who was acting on his behalf, Manasseh Dawes, persuaded him 'to avail himself of the plausible plea of temporary insanity'. The trial came on at 9.30 on the morning of 16 April. Hackman was defended by Davenport and Silvester, the prosecution conducted by Henry Howarth and Sir John Fielding. The courtroom was packed with fashionable society, the same sort of people who had witnessed the murder the week before. James Boswell, who had visited Hackman's brother-in-law on a number of occasions and seen Hackman himself in prison, was sitting at the table of defending counsel. John Wilkes, the radical libertine who was one of Sandwich's most bitter political enemies, was also present, as were a number of famous aristocratic beauties. (Boswell was shocked when Wilkes passed him a note during the trial that said, 'I always know where the greatest beauty in any place is when Mr Boswell is there, for he contrives to be near her, but does not admire the first grace more than Mr Wilkes does.') Frederick Booth, who had worked so hard to help his brother-in-law, felt unable to watch the proceedings and awaited the verdict outside the court.

The trial opened with the prosecution, which called witnesses to prove the facts of the case. Macnamara's was the chief testimony. He was followed by 'Mary Anderson, a fruit girl' who had also seen the killing, and by an apothecary, Mr Mahon, who had seized one of the pistols from Hackman and helped the constable Blandy make his arrest. The final witness was Mr O'Brien, one of the surgeons who had given evidence at Ray's inquest. None of the facts were contested by the defence. Sir William Blackstone, who chaired the bench, invited Hackman to offer anything material in his defence. Reading from a prepared statement, the young man admitted the crime, professed himself ready to die, but explained his act as a brief moment of madness: 'I protest, with that regard for truth which becomes my situation, that the will to destroy her who was ever dearer to me than life, was never mine, until a momentary phrenzy overcame me, and induced me to commit the deed I deplore.' Hackman's counsel, Davenport, one of the most famous lawyers of the day, argued the case for insanity, maintaining that Hackman's suicide note, in which he had asked Booth to take care of Ray after his death, showed that he had not originally intended to kill her.

But the court was not persuaded of the defendant's case. Blackstone argued that the presence of two pistols showed felonious intent. He added that 'the prisoner has rested his defense upon a sudden phrenzy of mind; but the judge said, that it was not every fit, or start of tumultuous passion, that would justify the killing of another; but it must be the total loss of reason in every part of life'. The jury was instructed to convict the accused, and Hackman was condemned to death. Boswell hurried from the courtroom to tell Booth, who received the news with 'mains serrees' (clenched fists).

Eighteenth-century justice was swift. Three days later Hackman woke a little after five in the morning, and spent two hours in private prayer, before taking communion in the chapel in Newgate prison. At nine 'he came into the press-yard, where a great croud of persons assembled to satisfy their curiosity, at the expense of one shilling each. That all might have an equal share of the sight, a lane was formed by the multitude on each side, through which Mr Hackman passed, dressed in black, leaning on the arm of his friend the Rev. Mr Porter, whose hand he squeezed as he muttered the solemn invocation to Heaven, not to forsake a sinner of so enormous a degree, in the trying hour of death.' Haltered with the rope with which he would be hanged, Hackman was reported as exclaiming, 'Oh! the

sight of this shocks me more than the thought of its intended oper-
ation.' Driven in his mourning coach to Tyburn, jeered and cheered
by a group of building workers in Holborn, he spent his final minutes
praying for Martha Ray, the Earl of Sandwich and their children,
before being 'launched into Eternity' at about ten minutes past eleven.
James Boswell, who witnessed the hanging, and asked the executioner
if he had heard Hackman's last words ('No. I thought it a point of
ill manners to listen on such occasions'), ended the day drunk: 'Claret
h<urt>. Very ill.'

Hackman's body, like that of all murderers, was then sent to
Surgeon's Hall for dissection. On the day after the execution the
nineteen-year-old fencing master Henry Angelo went with a friend
to Surgeon's Hall to view the corpse. 'Having been placed on a large
table, an incision had been made on his stomach, and the flesh was
spread over on each side.' Angelo's next stop was Dolly's Chop House,
but the memory of Hackman's flesh was too much. He was unable
to eat his pork chops and never touched the dish again.

The press reckoned that Hackman's execution attracted the largest
crowd since the hanging of another clergyman, William Dodd, for
forgery three years earlier. (Such was the press that two members of
the crowd died, trampled after they fell.) But Dodd had been a public
figure: the chaplain of the Magdalen Hospital for penitent prostitutes,
author of a successful Shakespeare anthology, the friend of literati
like Dr Johnson, and the client of a number of prominent aristocrats.
Hackman was a nobody before he murdered Ray. Now he was an
object of public fascination. When he had dropped his handkerchief
to signal he was ready to die, the hangman got down from the cart
and pocketed it; the souvenir was very valuable. On the day after his
execution, a crowd pressed into the Surgeon's Hall to see the body:
'Soon after the doors were opened, so great a crowd was assembled
that no genteel person attempted to gain admittance, as it was

observed that caps, cardinals, gowns, wigs and hats, &c. were destroyed, without regard to age, sex or distinction.' In death, as in life, Hackman was able to cause mayhem.

After the first few days of frenzied activity that followed the murder, Sandwich left the Admiralty office and retreated to a friend's house in Richmond. From there he wrote an importunate note to Lord Bristol, asking him to postpone the opposition's motion in the House of Lords for his removal as First Lord of the Admiralty:

> It is understood that navy matters are to be discussed in the House of Lords on Thursday or Friday next. I am at present totally unfit for business of any kind and unable to collect any materials to support the side of the question that I must espouse. I perceive impropriety in putting off the business by a motion from anyone with whom I am politically connected; I have therefore recourse to your humanity, to request that you would contrive that this point is not brought on till after this day sevennight, by which time I hope to be fit for public business as I ever shall be.

Bristol promised to ask for a postponement, using the excuse that he was suffering from gout, and he ended his reply, 'No-one can be more concerned than I am for any interruption to your domestic felicity.'

Sandwich received many letters of advice and condolence. Aristocratic friends like Lord Hardwicke praised Martha Ray and reassured the Earl of their faith in her virtue: 'From what I have heard of her Conduct I never doubted but it had been entirely irreproachable.' Even the prudish George III, who had once argued that Sandwich should not hold political office because of his notorious private life, offered the Earl his sympathy, using a stilted formula that ensured that he did not have to mention Ray's name: 'I am sorry Lord Sandwich has met with any severe blow of a private nature. I flatter myself this world scarcely contains a man so void of feeling as not to compassionate your situation.' One of his colleagues urged on Sandwich the stoicism he had shown in political adversity: 'You have suffered much and the utmost exertion of your fortitude is now required. Show yourself in this my Lord, as you have done in most other things equal if not superior to the rest of mankind.' Others took a less sympathetic view. As George Duke Taylor remarked, 'Enemies more inveterate than the rest make no scruple to affirm that they look upon these things are come down upon you as judgments, for your private and public conduct during these ten or twelve years past, which in their language have been both wicked and arbitrary.' Over the next few years Sandwich's opponents would occasionally refer to Martha Ray's murder, but on the whole they respected his privacy.

It did not take long for Sandwich's life to return to its old routines. He was back in the Admiralty office in the week after Hackman's execution. He managed to survive the attempt to remove him from office, and was soon deeply involved in plans to thwart the French invasion and keep the government in power. He remained a key political figure until the British surrender at Yorktown effectively ended the American war and brought down Lord North's government; even after he left the Admiralty, he had a small group of followers in the House of Commons and took an active interest in politics.

Ray's death was clearly a great loss for Sandwich. His friend Joseph Cradock recalled the period after her murder in his *Memoirs*. He tells the story of his embarrassment when he first visited Sandwich after Ray's death. Entering the Earl's study 'where the portrait of Miss Ray, a most exact resemblance, still remained over the chimney-piece', Cradock rather clumsily 'started on seeing it'. Sandwich 'instantly endeavored to speak of some unconnected subject; but he looked so ill, and I felt so much embarrassed, that as soon as I possibly could,

I most respectfully took my leave'. A similar incident occurred some time later when Sandwich was invited to dine with a few friends at the house of 'our open-hearted friend Admiral Walsingham'. The evening went well, and Sandwich seemed to regain his spirits, until one of the guests put Sandwich in mind of Ray: 'one of the company requested that Mrs Bates would favour them with "Shepherds, I have lost my Love". This was unfortunately the very air that had been introduced by Miss Ray at Hinchingbrooke, and had been always called for by Lord Sandwich. Mr Bates immediately endeavored to prevent its being sung, and by his anxiety increased the distress; but it was too late to pause.' Sandwich was mortified. He struggled to overcome his feelings, 'but they were so apparent, that at last he went up to Mrs Walsingham, and in a very confused manner said, he hoped she would excuse him not staying longer at that time, but that he had just recollected some pressing business which required his return to the Admiralty; and bowing to all the company, rather hastily left the room'.

Yet, within a year, Sandwich had a new mistress, Nelly Gordon, who was to remain his consort until his death in 1792, and who also bore him children. (In his will he arranged an annuity of £100 a year for life for her – in addition to another he had given her in her lifetime for the same sum – and a further £25 a year for life for her child.) Nor was he a recluse. The end of the American war and his active political career enabled him to indulge his passion for music, and he was the key figure behind the enormously popular concerts held to celebrate Handel's Centenary in 1784.

Apart from Ray's children – young Basil was soon in all kinds of trouble at school – Ray's companion Caterina Galli suffered the consequences of her murder more than anyone else. Deprived of her position in Sandwich's household, she was ostracized from polite society, and could no longer make a living by teaching rich young

girls to sing. The Duchess of Bedford wrote to her that she was 'sorry
to inform Signor Galli that she made a determination, at the time
the unfortunate affair happened in which she was concerned, never
to take notice more of her in any way'. The Duchess did so because
she was sure that 'whatever appearances being against her if she was
blameless her good protector would never let her want a proper
maintenance without applying to the public'.

Galli wrote a succession of letters to Sandwich in her native Italian
complaining of her plight. A month after the murder she told Sandwich, 'I am ill and afflicted to see myself exposed in a book and in
the papers so unjustly wronged as well as my character ruined that
I don't know how I can live in the world.' Nine months later her
situation was even worse:

> I cannot assist myself in my profession, being badly liked by
> everyone who believe me to be guilty; I have lost my reputation
> in the face of my protectors being sufficient to madden any person
> ... Where can I look for assistance? They all tell me I should
> defend myself against the charges and that my silence makes me
> more culpable and that they will know that your excellency does
> not admit me and that you dislike me. Lord I believe I have given
> you sufficient proofs of my innocence at not having taken any part
> of deceit, I have taken in due time my oath. I have been by orders
> of your excellency to the court, did not hide myself or otherwise
> flee. I have always been prepared to go before any judge and prove
> my innocence. I have lost both my health and reputation as well
> as money through me not defending myself and punishing the
> culpables, and all this I did through the certainty that your excel-
> lency will be my protector as you sent me information both by
> word and letter that you would always help me.

Impoverished, Galli was forced to return to the stage, though her
voice had gone. She made a number of concert appearances in the
1790s, when she was deemed to cut a pathetic figure, and was given

money by the Royal Society of Musicians. We know Sandwich donated twenty guineas to her and may have given her more. But she remained in sad circumstances, and when her husband died she had to borrow the money to bury him. As a result of Martha Ray's murder she had lost her employment and could no longer work in the job she knew best and loved.

These, as far as I can tell, are the 'facts' of the murder by James Hackman of Martha Ray. They make up the story that almost all commentators, both at the time and subsequently, agree on. But they leave much unanswered. No one doubted that Hackman killed Ray, that he was the black figure who came out of the crowd and shot her to death before a shocked public. But what lay behind the murder? Why did he kill her? What was their relationship like? Was Hackman demented, or did he have understandable reasons to shoot her? Such a brutal killing, like any act that temporarily tears the social fabric apart, called out for explanation. But the facts alone could not provide an answer. Evidence about motive was hard to come by, not least because, as we shall see, there were interested parties concerned to keep the case under wraps. The vacuum created by a lack of information was, however, quickly filled by supposition, speculation and interpretation. For plenty of people, for many different reasons, wanted to publicize their own versions of the lives of Hackman, Ray and Sandwich.

The murder was, of course, a personal tragedy, but it was also a public event. Public, not only because it involved one of the most prominent households in the land and one of the nation's most important political figures, but because it received so much publicity. In the 1770s London boasted a thriving press with five daily and eight or nine triweekly papers that were widely circulated in London and in many provincial towns. By the time of Ray's death newspaper proprietors were paying the government an annual stamp duty for more than 12.5 million papers. The provinces also had their own papers – nearly forty by the 1770s – that shamelessly plundered news and information from the London press, adding vignettes of their own. Within days of Hackman's crime accounts of the murder, commentary on its significance and speculation about why it had happened flowed out from the newspaper printers' offices in the vicinity of St Paul's Cathedral and spread across the nation, as news and stories were duplicated in local papers, then in magazines and periodicals. Readers of the *Public Advertiser*, the *Gazetteer*, the *St James's Chronicle*, *Lloyd's Evening Post*, the *London Evening Post*, the *Norwich Mercury*, and the *Newcastle Chronicle* – in fact of every London paper and most of those in the provinces – were regaled with the unfolding story of Hackman's crime. The flow of information explains why in his Norfolk parish Parson Woodforde broke off his usual culinary catalogue – no diarist has devoted so much space to the joys of the table – to bewail the fate of Hackman, a fellow man of the cloth, while at Salisbury the gentleman musician and young lawyer John Marsh tut-tutted in his journal about the fate of a young man he had known at school.

The eighteenth-century press made Hackman's crime into a 'media event' both because it was a sensational crime and because the events of 7 April were so obviously connected to stories that the print media in general had been telling the public for the last twenty years. These were tales of political corruption and moral depravity in high places, of male aristocratic debauchery, and of the growing power and influence of beautiful and intelligent women who used their charms for their own ends. This culture of scandal, propagated by the press, thrived on supposition, rumour, and speculation. It took 'the facts' and wove them into a variety of seamless narratives that opened up all sorts of possible interpretation. Such stories were designed to sell newspapers and magazines, attack the government, traduce and shame individuals, and settle personal scores.

The press of the 1770s is not therefore a place we should go in pursuit of 'the truth' about Hackman and Ray's relationship, but it does show how the different versions of Hackman's crime were shaped and fashioned. The aftermath of Ray's death saw a struggle conducted in the press to form and even to determine how the public viewed the affair.

CHAPTER 2

---·❦·---

The Press: A Case of Sentimental Murder

THOUGH THERE WAS plenty of pressing news for the papers to cover in the spring of 1779 – the failing war with the American colonists and the internecine political battles in parliament – the newspapers devoted a great deal of space to the killing of the Earl of Sandwich's mistress and the subsequent conduct and execution of her murderer. Between the night of Martha Ray's murder and Hackman's execution on 19 April daily items about the case appeared in many London papers. At first these were dominated by detailed accounts of the events of 7 April, reconstructions that culminated in the evidence offered at Hackman's trial on 16 April. But there was also an obsessive interest in Hackman himself. Papers reported on his moods and comments, trying to understand what had led this handsome, respectable young man to commit a crime of such enormity. They published many tantalizing vignettes of Hackman, Ray, and Sandwich both before and after the crime. And many speculated about the circumstances that had led to the crime and offered comments on its moral import.

To the untutored eye these items can seem to be little more than the fumblings of an unsophisticated news media trying to piece together a story. But, as we shall see, the coverage of the Hackman/

Ray affair was part of a more complex plot that involved attempts on the part of the Earl of Sandwich and the friends of James Hackman to shape and control public response to the sensational killing. This was possible only because of the peculiar state of the newspaper press at the time. Since the accession of George III in 1760 the rapid expansion of the press had produced a new kind of newspaper, more opinionated than ever before, fuller of comment and criticism, yet not governed by what today we would consider the professional protocols of impartial reporting and editorial control. As the press grew, so papers changed in size and content. A loophole in the 1757 duties on paper made it cheaper for printers to make their papers larger and increase the number of their pages. They needed more copy. Newspapers had always carried many advertisements (their key source of revenue) as well as official government information, commercial news, and items gathered from coffee-houses and interested readers. Though many had a political bias – like the notoriously anti-government *London Evening Post* – most were primarily advertisers and purveyors of information. Opinion – on matters political, commercial, social and cultural – was found in pamphlets or weekly papers, like *The Test* and *The Contest*, that were editorial rather than informational. But with the change in the law, newspapers began to publish political commentary and essays on subjects ranging from taste to science, theatrical, music and art reviews. And, in some cases, they printed lots of gossip and scandal.

Where did this news and commentary come from? Most papers were owned by consortia of businessmen – theatrical proprietors, booksellers, and auctioneers – who considered papers chiefly as advertising vehicles. They were put together by a printer, who may have had strong opinions but was not a journalist, and the few part-time news-gatherers whom the papers employed could hardly be described as reporters. What few experienced journalists there were, were employed to cover politics, reporting parliamentary debates or such sensational events as the court martial of Admiral Keppel, whose trial ended just a few months before Ray's murder. Henry 'Memory' Woodfall, whose amazing recall was vital, as note taking was prohibited during parliamentary debates, was the most celebrated of this small group of reporters. Papers therefore relied on the public for their information and commentary. Most of what appeared in the press was either unsolicited information and commentary from interested parties or news sold by peddlers for a profit. Above all, the paper relied on its correspondents, publishing huge numbers of letters submitted by its readers. *The Gazetteer*, one of the first papers to speculate on the causes of Hackman's crime, received no fewer than 861 letters in one four-month period, publishing 560 of them 'at length' and a further 262 in abbreviated form under the heading 'Observations of our Correspondents'. Long articles, masquerading as correspondence and signed by such figures as 'Honestus', 'A Friend to the Theatre', 'Cato', 'Old Slyboots', and, most notoriously, 'Junius' fanned the flames of controversy, offering views on politics, religion, taste, novels, painting, the state of nation and the nature of crime. Anonymity and pseudonyms protected the authors, who included leading politicians, playwrights, artists, magistrates and doctors as well as opinionated readers.

James Boswell, who found his métier and his fame with his *Life of Samuel Johnson* published in 1791, was for much of his London life a typical newspaper correspondent. He wrote to the papers to puff his works, denigrate rivals, and comment on the issues of the day. On the afternoon of Hackman's trial on 16 April, for instance, he strolled into the office of Henry Woodfall, the publisher of the *Daily Advertiser*, offering him an account of the trial, only to discover that 'A blackguard being was writing a well-expressed account of the trial'. Nothing daunted he went on to the managers of the *St James's*

Chronicle, who inserted his anonymous piece in the paper of the following day. This essay contained a long quotation and a puff for an essay in *The Hypochondriack* on the nature of love that Boswell himself had written and published earlier. Boswell then wrote a highly personal account, which Woodfall printed in the *Public Advertiser* for 19 April, of Frederick Booth's reaction to his brother-in-law's conviction – '"Well", said Mr Booth, "I would rather have him found guilty with truth and honour than escape by a mean evasion".' 'A sentiment', Boswell commented, 'truly noble, bursting from a heart rent with anguish!' When a false report appeared in *Lloyd's Evening Post* that Boswell was in the coach that had taken Hackman to his death at Tyburn Tree, he rushed off to the offices of the *St James's Chronicle*, and the *Public Advertiser*, as well as *Lloyd's Evening Post* to get them to insert a paragraph to correct the story.

Boswell did not expect to be paid for his letters and paragraphs, but many who dealt with newspaper proprietors were in it for the money. A German visitor to London was surprised by the 'prodigious multitude of persons' engaged in collecting news. 'Among these', he wrote, 'may be reckoned the paragraph writers, who go to coffee houses and public places to pick up anecdotes and the news of the day, which they reduce to short sentences, and are paid in proportion to their number and authenticity.' Some papers had receiving stations for contributions. The *Gazetteer*, for instance, used J. Marks, a bookseller in St Martin's Lane, paying him sixpence 'for every letter or article of intelligence transmitted to the paper'.

This informal process of news-gathering supposed a very different relationship between the press and its readers than the print media have today. Those who read the papers – a broadly based group that extended well beyond the aristocracy, even if it did not include a great many of the poor – were also those who wrote them. The newspaper was not an authoritative organ, written by professionals to offer objective information to the public, but a place where public rumour, news, and intelligence could circulate as if it were printed conversation. Freedom of the press in this period meant not only freedom from government control but freedom of access – not just to information, but to the pages of the press itself in order to transmute opinions into news. The producer of a paper was not so much an editor, shaping its opinions, as a technician, making available a new means of transmitting the disparate opinions of the public at large. The press was thus very open to manipulation.

Many commentators believed that the enormous growth in news, fuelled by the business interests of the newspaper proprietors and lacking any check on its veracity, created a climate of scandal and sensation. Collecting so-called news, which newspapers quickly took up, copied and stole from one another, was often indiscriminate. Paragraph writers created press stories that played fast and loose with the facts and were frequently embellished. As one critic complained:

> The general run of readers have not seen the *paragraphical drudges*, hurrying over the town for malicious materials, and eves-dropping at every door of intelligence; while another *tribe of slaves*, sit *aloof*, at the task of improvement and invention . . . nor are they perhaps aware that other *inferior agents* are constantly employed in picking up invidious anecdotes of *domestic misfortune;* and *private imprudence.* These hint-catchers have no sooner filled the budget to the brim, than their labours are delivered to the *embellisher*, by whom they are finished and arranged, and sent into the world.

Commentators were especially concerned at how personal matters and private lives had become a staple of the press. Some blamed this new fashion on the political journalism of the 1760s, first perfected by John Wilkes in his weekly paper *The North Briton*, which combined political criticism with highly personal attacks on such figures as the Princess Dowager, George III's mother, and the king's favourite, Lord

Bute, who was accused of being the Princess's lover. Wilkes mixed sexual scandal with government policy. This was a familiar tactic in the histories of royal courts where women were often said to have had excessive influence because of their hold over male rulers. But Wilkes and his followers extended this tactic by attacking ministers and leading aristocrats for their private moral conduct, maintaining that this made them unfit for public office. This led to unprecedented exposure of the private lives of public figures. One critic of the 'new journalism' complained to the *Morning Post*:

> The Political Controversy at the beginning of the Present reign, taught printers to feel their Power: we then first find Personal Abuse, unrestrained, stalk abroad, and boldly attack by Name the most respectable Characters. Your brethren were not idle in taking the hint: from that Period we find a material change in the stile of every News-Paper; every Public Man became an object of their attention; and many a sixpence has a Patriot earned, by Paragraphs, which a few years before, would have brought the Printer unpitied to the Pillory.

The advent of the newspaper editor in the 1770s led to little change. The first major editor, the Reverend Henry Bate, used his *Morning Post* simply to perfect existing journalistic practices. He extended the coverage of his paper to include boxing and cricket as well as theatrical and art reviews; most notoriously, he made a part of the paper into a satirical scandal sheet, attacking individual men and women of fashion, hectoring his theatrical opponents (Bate was a minor playwright), and peddling the latest gossip. He was one of the models for Snake, the purveyor of poisonous rumour who inserts anonymous paragraphs in the newspaper in the opening scene of *The School for Scandal* (1777), Richard Brinsley Sheridan's pointed satire of a society obsessed with 'inventing, adding and misrepresenting everything they hear, or their rage, folly, malice or prolific brains

Petticoat government: The Princess Dowager leads her son, George III, by the nose, watched by her supposed lover, Lord Bute.

can suggest'. Bate deliberately cultivated notoriety, and fought a number of duels with readers who believed themselves maligned or libelled by his publication. Eventually he was imprisoned for accusing the Duke of Richmond of consorting with the enemy during the American war. Bate was said to take fees for publishing some paragraphs and agreeing to suppress others. He was also a client of the government. He had a pension of £200 a year from the secret service funds in return for keeping his 'Newspaper open for all writings in favour of Government'. In 1781 he was finally paid off with a gift of £3,250, so that he could purchase a handsome clerical living for himself.

Bate made little attempt to conceal the *Morning Post*'s connection with Lord North's administration, frequently beginning reports, 'As well as our government can judge', or 'the government says' or 'we are authorized to say'. Bate knew Sandwich and seems to have dealt with him directly on a number of occasions. Lord Bristol, who led the attack on Sandwich in the House of Lords on 23 April, wrote on the following day to an opposition publisher, John Almon, asking him to insert his version of the debate in a number of newspapers 'with[ou]t saying you had it from me', to counter the influence of what he described as 'Ld. SANDWICH'S Morning Post'. It is not surprising that the most sympathetic portrayal of Sandwich in the aftermath of the murder came from the pages of Bate's paper. Conversely, the accounts of Hackman's crime in the *Gazetteer,* the *London Evening Post* and the *London Chronicle* – all papers with which John Almon was connected and all associated with the parliamentary opposition – were markedly less sympathetic to Ray and Sandwich.

All the political parties tried to influence the press. Sandwich had been doing so for many years. In the 1760s he employed his chaplain, Dr James Scott, to write newspaper letters under the pseudonyms 'Anti-Sejanus' and 'Old Slyboots', that were some of the most successful political polemics of the decade. And he was not averse to planting paragraphs of news (as opposed to pieces of political commentary) in the newspapers, not as pieces of information but as ways of influencing opinion. Newspapers in the 1770s were halls of mirrors in which partial views and tendentious opinions were refracted so as to appear as transparent 'facts'. As we enter them, we have to remember that nothing was quite what it seemed.

On 20 April 1779 the *Gazetteer* interrupted its report on Hackman's final hours and execution to speculate on the nature of and motives for his crime. The author of this mélange of reporting and reflection was probably a Mr Newman of Guiltspur Street, who was paid occasional fees for items about trials and executions. 'There is evidently a *something*', he mused, 'hangs suspended in doubt, and remains unrevealed' about the case. Hackman's suicide note to his brother-in-law Booth, he remarked, 'pours the Blessings of heaven on the murdered lady, and avows an intention of the murderer to kill *himself only*'. Why, then, did he change his mind? 'Love could not be the impulse – that passion might have led him to act the hero before his mistress; but the fondness, which dictated the affectionate sentence in his letter, and breathed *preservation* to the lady, can never be supposed to turn into resentment without a cause, and operate to her *destruction*.' Perhaps the sight of Ray on Mr Macnamara's arm drove him into a jealous rage. 'But if so,' the article asked, 'why did he not confess it?' The evidence of the two pistols was ambiguous, since the unreliability of firearms meant that many suicides armed themselves with more than one weapon. 'There is certainly a part in his defense that requires explanation', it concluded.

The *Gazetteer* then shifted from speculation to titillating gossip. 'Besides many other cogent reasons, which it may not be proper to disclose, the talkative part of mankind say, that a certain noble lord had his doubts of the true motives that actuated the perpetrator in this extraordinary transaction.' Perhaps, the paper surmised, Martha Ray had had enough of Sandwich and really wanted to leave him. The rumour was 'That Miss Ray was satiated with the vicious enjoyment of splendour, and desirous to enter the Temple of Hymen with a man who had given every proof of affection; but that there was some barrier started to prevent the union, and she absolutely refused to marry him, though in the hour of reciprocal tenderness she had promised'. Even if this were untrue, the paper concluded, Sandwich had gone to great lengths to find out Hackman's motives: 'it is certain, that the Noble Lord himself, or one of his friends, questioned Mr Hackman in prison when the solemnity of the sentence was fresh on his mind, as to the inducement for committing the crime'. Yet much remained obscure. 'In short', the article ended, 'there is so much to be said on both sides of the question that arises on a review of the circumstances, that it might seem premature, as it is certainly difficult to form an opinion.'

Such difficulties certainly did not inhibit the press from reporting details of the murder, the interrogation, trial and execution of Hackman, or from speculating about the love triangle. As early as the following day the *St James's Chronicle* sketched in the background to the affair:

> Upon Enquiry into the Cause of this desperate Action, we learn that it was occasioned by an unhappy Passion which the Prisoner had entertained for the Deceased. This Gentleman, whose name is Hackman, was formerly an Officer in the Army, and being upon a Recruiting Party at Huntingdon, in the summer of 1775, saw Miss Ray first at H———ke, to which he had been invited by his Lordship. After that he saw her several Times both in Town and Country, in one of which Visits, it is said, he proposed Marriage to her, which she very genteelly declined; and to prevent any disagreeable Consequences, never after admitted him to her Presence. This, it is supposed, driving him to Distraction, induced him

to commit the bloody Act above-mentioned, which he meant also
to have been fatal to himself.

Over the following weeks more and more detail was published about
Hackman and his victim.

We can be sure that most of the items appearing in the press were
planted either by Sandwich and his supporters or by the friends of
James Hackman, notably his brother-in-law and the young lawyer
Manasseh Dawes who took it upon himself to be the chief apologist
in the press for the murderer. Many readers were aware that what
they were reading was *parti pris*; indeed, the *Gazetteer* recognized this
when it wrote of 'both sides of the question'. The difficulty for readers
was how to interpret the different accounts.

The *Gazetteer* had been right about the questioning of Hackman:
Walsingham, acting on Sandwich's behalf, had spoken at length with
him the day after the crime. But the fragments that survive make
the two men's conversation appear more like an attempt to agree on
a story than an effort to investigate the truth of the matter. Both
sides seem to have been seeking common ground, searching for a
version of events they could agree upon. Their first concern was to
establish Martha Ray's innocence. Hackman, wrote Walsingham, 'is
desirous to dye by the hand of the law and says he is happy to know
that Miss Ray was innocent . . . Her innocence being cleared up and
your forgiveness as a Christian is all he wishes for.' But Hackman
and Sandwich differed over what Ray's innocence consisted of. For
Hackman it was that she had not taken a new lover, as he claimed
Caterina Galli had told him; for Sandwich it was that she had not
been carrying on an illicit affair with Hackman. Thus the Earl was
relieved to report to his lawyer that 'Mr H has since declared to
Captain Walsingham upon the word of a dying man, that he has
never spoken to Miss Ray since the beginning of the year 1776, at
which time he had proposed marriage and was rejected' and he told

at least one newspaper, the *General Advertiser*, that he was sure that Hackman and Ray had not been with one another since their earlier meetings at Hinchingbrooke. Quite apart from their undoubted affection for Martha Ray, both men had strong reasons to assert her innocence. It meant that Hackman could place the blame for his actions on Galli – 'he lays the whole on Galli' – and it stood to prevent Sandwich being ridiculed as an old roué cuckolded by a younger man.

With the help of Sandwich and Hackman's friends, the papers gradually sketched in a story about the three protagonists, with both plot and characters. They told a tale of two attractive young people – a dashing young army officer and an aristocrat's mistress of great accomplishment – who meet by chance. The mistress has a keeper who is almost twice her age and with whom she has had five children. The young man falls in love, asks for the mistress's hand in marriage, but is forced to leave his loved one and join his regiment in Ireland. Eager to return to the object of his affections, he leaves the army, takes holy orders, and asks Ray once again for her hand in marriage. Rejected by her, he is driven first to plan suicide and then to commit murder.

This story opened with richly detailed (though sometimes contradictory) accounts of Hackman and Ray's first meeting. Several papers portrayed the two on romantic rides in the Huntingdonshire countryside: 'It was Miss Ray's custom, at that time, for the benefit of air and exercise, to ride out on horseback behind her servant. Undeniable it is, that Mr Hackman took frequent opportunities of riding out at the same time; and being a good horseman, and dexterous at a leap, was sure to afford no small diversion to the lady.' Others spoke of Hackman as 'being of a facetious, agreeable turn of conversation' which secured him a place at Sandwich's table and a place close to Martha Ray. Joseph Cradock later recalled the first time that Hackman appeared at Hinchingbrooke, when he was asked to dinner and ended the evening unpacking a telescope, newly arrived from London, to look at the stars.

Sandwich's house parties in Huntingdonshire were jolly and roistering, attended by musicians and naval explorers, Admiralty officials and minor literati, as well as other aristocrats and rakes. John Cooke, Sandwich's chaplain, recalled that

> The earl of Sandwich was one of the few noblemen, who spend a considerable portion of their time at their country-seats; where he usually resided whenever he could gain a vacation from the duties of his office, and attendance on parliament. His house was at all times open for the reception of his friends and neighbours; and distinguished for the generous, truly hospitable, and liberal entertainment which it afforded.

Another of Sandwich's friends put it more pithily: 'Few houses were more pleasant or instructive than his lordship's: it was filled with rank, beauty and talent, and every one was at ease.' Charles Burney, the music scholar and father of the novelist Frances Burney, found the parties so boisterous that they gave him a headache. There must have been many witnesses who noticed the handsome young man who paid Martha Ray such attention. The beginnings of Hackman and Ray's relationship were neither unknown nor obscure, for it had not been difficult for paragraph writers frequenting the fashionable coffee-houses of St James's to pick up details from former guests at Sandwich's country house.

Thereafter the story became more shadowy and suppositious. Attempts to find out what had occurred between Hackman's departure from Hinchingbrooke and his presence on the steps of the Covent Garden Theatre four years later were met with silence and prevarication. 'The lady's [Ray's] friends do not know that there has been any intercourse whatever since', reported the opposition *General*

Evening Post. Lord Sandwich, as we have seen, took a similar line. The papers all agreed that Hackman had gone to Ireland, had exchanged his red coat for a clerical habit, and returned to London in the hope of persuading Ray to marry him. Many papers believed that Hackman's clerical preferment to the living of Wiveton in Norfolk was obtained with the help of Sandwich, probably because of Ray's solicitation for her friend. All of the press suggested a sudden change in Ray's attitude towards Hackman, whom she pointedly refused to see.

The papers were perplexed by the nature of Hackman and Ray's relationship – were they friends or lovers? Was their affection mutual or was Hackman enamoured of a woman who did not care for him? How often did they meet, and how intimate were they with one another? The *General Advertiser*, after reporting that 'Lord Sandwich says he does not know there has been any intercourse' since Hackman's visit to Hinchingbrooke, confidently asserted, 'We however hear that he [Hackman] renewed his addresses to her some time ago now at Huntingdon, and received some hopes, which her future conduct had entirely disappointed.' The *General Evening Post*, though it shifted the venue of the intrigue to London, was also sure that Ray had continued to meet Hackman: 'his visits became frequent to the Admiralty . . . The Tables, however, afterwards turned in his disfavour; for, from whatever cause, he was certainly forbidden the house.' Whatever the papers said, they all agreed that the story ended tragically: Hackman was rejected and his final actions were prompted by terrible feelings of unrequited love.

In these versions of the drama, the characters were all portrayed sympathetically. Hackman was always an accomplished, handsome and admirable young man. On the day of his trial, he was described in the *General Advertiser* as 'The unfortunate Mr Hackman', who 'was esteemed one of the most amiable of men. When in the army, his company was courted by all who knew him; his readiness to oblige, by every act of kindness in his power, endeared him to every body.' The *General Evening Post*, the *London Evening Post* and the *Gazetteer* each printed a report describing him as 'descended from a very reputable family; he is a person of a lively disposition, and was esteemed by his numerous acquaintance, and his character was never impeached until the unhappy catastrophe on Wednesday night'. Hackman's respectable origins and his station in the middle ranks of society made his crime more extraordinary and his fate more sympathetic.

Much was made of the honourable nature of Hackman's obsession. A correspondent who called himself 'PHILANTHROPIST' in the *St James's Chronicle* of 10 April pointed out that 'Mr Hackman, so far from being an abandoned and insensible profligate, was rather distinguished for taste and Delicacy of Sentiment', while James Boswell wrote in the same paper a few days later:

> As his manners were uncommonly amiable, his Mind and Heart seem to have been uncommonly pure and virtuous; for he never once attempted to have a licentious connection with Miss Ray. It may seem strange at first; but I can very well suppose, that had he been less virtuous, he would not have been so criminal. But his Passion was not to be diverted by inferior Gratifications. He loved Miss Ray with all his soul, and nothing could make him happy but having her all his own.

Writers thought it important to establish that Hackman was no sexual predator – a rake or libertine – who lashed out in anger because of thwarted desire, but merely a young man hopelessly in love.

Martha Ray, 'the lovely victim' as she was described in the *London Chronicle,* was given a similarly good press. The PHILANTHRO-PIST who praised Hackman described her as 'irreproachable in her conduct, any otherwise than what perhaps was not well in her power to prevent, that she was unprotected by the legal Marriage ceremony'.

A poor girl who became a rich man's mistress was hardly culpable. The *General Evening Post* assured its readers that 'the memory of Miss Ray, with respect to Mr Hackman, stands clear, at present, of every imputation'. He may have loved her, but she remained true to her keeper. The *St James's Chronicle* saw her as a female paragon. It glossed over the potentially sordid origins of Ray's relationship with Sandwich, alluding only to her being 'under the protection of the noble Peer'. It lauded her looks and accomplishments: 'Her person was very fine, her face agreeable, and she had every Accomplishment that could adorn a woman, particularly those of Singing, and Playing most exquisitely on the Harpsichord.' And it placed her in the bosom of the family: 'She was also highly respected by all those who knew her, especially all the Servants, and her death is most sincerely regretted in the Family.'

Several papers dwelt on Ray's virtues as a companion and parent. Her fidelity to Sandwich, the *General Evening Post* reported, 'was never suspected'. In return for his 'protection' Ray gave Sandwich a 'life of gratitude and strict fidelity'. Her five surviving children were raised, according to the *London Chronicle*, with the 'strictness of motherly attention'. Several papers reported on her concern for the financial well being of her much-loved but illegitimate children. 'Miss Ray made it a rule, on the birth of every child,' they wrote, 'to solicit her noble admirer for an immediate provision for it, which was invariably acquiesced in.' Her children were therefore provided for after her death: 'the issue of this lady will have nothing to lament from her sad fate . . . but the circumstance of having lost a tender mother'.

In the eighteenth century charity came high among the concerns of virtuous women, and Ray was seen as no exception. She was 'liberal in a high degree, and the bounty of her noble Lover enabled her to indulge benevolence, in becoming the patroness of the poor'. One of the objects of her charity, it was said, was her elderly and poor parents who lived in Elstree. She could not refuse them aid though, in line with her reputation for moral scrupulousness, she refused to see her father because of the way he had encouraged her to become a mistress or a courtesan.

Ray's most remarked upon quality was her having mastered the skills of an elegant lady. Sandwich, the papers said, had spent lavishly to refashion a milliner's apprentice as a lady. The *London Chronicle* waxed lyrical on her accomplishments:

> There was scarce any polite art in which she was not adept, nor any part of female literature with which she was not conversant. All the world are acquainted with the unrivalled sweetness of her vocal powers, but it was the peculiar pleasure of a few only to know that her conversation, her feelings, and indeed her general deportment, all participated of an unparalleled delicacy, which had characterized her through life.

No doubt the shocking manner of Martha Ray's death prompted a surge of sympathy for her. The *General Advertiser* commented on how 'all ranks of people drop the tear of pity on her bier, while the sharp tooth of slander seems for a time to have lost its edge'. Even the author of one of the most vicious attacks on Ray, a mock opera published in 1776 that had portrayed her as an unfaithful greedy harridan who twists a besotted but impotent Sandwich round her finger, was heard 'to describe in the most pathetic terms, the amiable qualifications of her head and heart'. Sympathy for Ray stemmed equally from admiration for a poor, fallen woman who had successfully transformed herself not into a flamboyant courtesan, but into a respectable mother who could pass for a lady.

Sandwich was the least likely of the three victims of Hackman's crime to be treated kindly in the press, but even he was accorded an unusually sympathetic reception. Naturally enough the government-subsidized *Morning Post* pleaded his case:

> Is there any one so obdurate, however party may have warped or blunted his affections, as not to feel some little concern for a man, who, in the course of one month, has had a personal accusation adduced against his honesty as a man – several vague imputations, and the measure of a direct charge against his character, as a Minister – a daughter dead [his daughter-in-law had just died], and a beloved friend most bloodily assassinated?

But even the opposition papers were willing to acknowledge Sandwich's dignity in his suffering. Several articles emphasized his benevolence towards Martha Ray – his willingness to pay for her education and to provide for their offspring. His performance as a good father and spouse matched the domestic virtues of his murdered lover. Others praised his remarkable action in being willing to forgive James Hackman for his terrible crime. 'We are assured from respectable authority, that a noble Lord, much interested in the death of the late unfortunate Miss Ray, pitying the fate of the unhappy Hackman, sent a message to him after condemnation by the Honourable Captain W—— [Walsingham], informing him, "that he would endeavour to get him a pardon;" but that unhappy man replied, "he wished not to live, but to expatiate his offence, if possible, by his death".'

Above all, reports of Sandwich's suffering at the news of Ray's death made the man who was regularly depicted in the opposition press as a political monster appear altogether more vulnerable and human. He was 'inconsolable' . . . 'he wrung his hands and cried, exclaiming – "I could have borne anything but this; but this unmans me".' The *General Advertiser* suggested that Sandwich was so stricken that his servants feared that he might kill himself, while the *Gazetteer* depicted his situation as 'deplorable' and portrayed him as withdrawn and wounded, seeing 'no one but his dearest friends'. The *St James's Chronicle*, no special admirer of Sandwich as a politician, summarized the prevailing sentiment:

From [Ray's] having lived so long with his Lordship, there is no Doubt but his feelings on this Occasion must be such as the most lively Grief can inspire. Indeed, we are told, that his Lordship's Sensations expressed the greatest Agonies; and that whatever may be his sentiments on political Matters, in this affair he has shown a Tenderness which does the highest Credit to his Heart, and the warmth of his Friendship.

Thus all three of the main parties were victims, united in their common suffering. Ray and Hackman excited the most sympathy, because they both lost their lives, but even Sandwich was given his share. The press portrayed them all as suffering from forces beyond their control and for which they bore little or no responsibility. Hackman was driven to his crime by feelings that overpowered him; Ray was unable to escape his unwanted attentions; and Sandwich was suddenly and unexpectedly deprived of the woman he loved deeply. So the early newspaper reporting, strongly informed by the friends of Sandwich and Hackman, was remarkably free from acrimony and blame; it invited readers to sympathize with the victims, to understand their plight and, more generally, to interpret the sad events as a consequence of natural desires and feelings, 'the common passions of Humanity'. As PHILANTHROPIST put it in the *St James's Chronicle*, 'let us endeavor therefore to trace this rash and desperate Action, from some cause in human Nature equal to the Phaenomenon'.

Though the majority of newspaper reports encouraged readers' sympathy, a few were overtly censorious. Several news commentators (as well as writers of unpublished, anonymous letters to Sandwich) interpreted Ray's death as the result of the Earl's profligate and immoral life, and urged him to see the error of his ways and to reform. In the days just before Hackman's trial the *London Evening Post* – an old enemy of Sandwich's – published a number of items attacking the Earl. These included a long letter upbraiding the public for extending too much sympathy to Ray, Hackman and Sandwich and blaming the murder on the moral failings of all three of them. 'The public', it began, 'at present give way to a strange kind of sympathy, whilst they shed tears of condolence with one of the vilest of men, to alleviate his distresses for the loss of his mistress.' What about the victims of the American war, it asked its readers, people who had suffered because of the benighted political policies of Sandwich and his colleagues? Should we not be more concerned about 'the many thousand widows and orphans, who rend the continent of America with piercing lamentations for the loss of their husbands and fathers who were murdered in cold blood, or slaughtered in the field by the emissaries of despotism'? After damning Sandwich as a 'man who, by his voice and counsel, had drenched whole provinces with murdered blood', the author turned to Martha Ray. Unfortunate as she was, 'we should not forget what she was; we should not lament her as a spotless, or amiable character, but as a deluded woman cut off in the midst of her days, without any previous warning'. Her fate should not obscure the moral lesson of her life: 'We should rather point out the impropriety and wickedness of such connections as she formed, which, through a variety of complicated circumstances, laid the foundation of her untimely death, and which frequently, almost always, in one way or another, terminate fatally.' 'Had Miss R— been virtuous', the writer concluded, 'she had not fallen as she did.' Similarly, Hackman's fate was explained by his moral failings: 'had the wretched assassin cultivated that delicacy of sentiment which abhors impurity, and suffered no criminal passions to influence his conduct, he would never have found himself within the walls of Newgate, and might have attained an honourable old age, and gone down to the grave in peace'.

But, on the whole, it was unusual for the three protagonists to be portrayed as so morally reprobate. Hackman was repeatedly characterized as 'unfortunate' and as having 'delicacy of sentiment', a quality he shared with Ray; even Sandwich was complimented for his tenderness. The press reporting of the case was designed to elicit sympathy not censoriousness. No doubt, as I have explained, this was partly because Sandwich's and Hackman's friends worked hard to shape the newspapers' response to the case. But it is worth asking why this was possible, and why there was so little attempt to offer an alternative version of the events of the spring of 1779. Why, to put it in modern terms, was Sandwich and Hackman's *spin* on the murder and its aftermath so successful?

The love triangle of Ray, Hackman and Sandwich was shaped as a *sentimental* story, designed to reveal the feelings of the protagonists and to excite the feelings of readers. Reporting and commentary were less concerned with what had happened, though trying to establish the facts of the case was important, than about a mystery of the human heart, an effort to understand the motives and feelings of those involved. Did Ray really love Hackman? Was Hackman justified in feeling that Ray had led him on with false promises, or was he suffering from a sort of delusion, what contemporaries called 'love's madness'? Similarly, the aftermath of the crime was described indirectly through the feelings of Lord Sandwich, of Hackman and, perhaps most prominently, of the public. The responses to the bloody murder, affecting trial and the murderer's execution were covered as extensively as the crime itself. The newspapers pulled readers into a wide circle of sympathy. The press largely avoided the blood-and-gore variety of crime reporting, which had hitherto been common. Its accounts were neither sensational nor melodramatic. Readers were made to understand events through the emotive responses of participants by a form of indirect narration. They were invited to share in the distresses of the victims, to express their sympathy, to establish an emotional closeness rather than a moral distance.

This sort of complicity has to be understood in the light of prevailing ideas about human sympathy and sensibility. Eighteenth-century human sciences, which embraced physiology, psychology, sociability and morality, had created a new way of looking at, depicting and judging human conduct which was less concerned with its strict conformity to a universal moral law than with its social and psychological complexity. We cannot understand the story of Hackman and Ray unless we take some time to explore the values and ways of seeing that informed how contemporaries understood those events.

Eighteenth-century sentimentalism, the understanding that people were first and foremost creatures of feeling, considered sympathy as the key human quality. As the philosopher David Hume put it, 'No quality of human nature is more remarkable, both in itself and its consequences, than that propensity we have to sympathize with others, and to receive by communication their inclinations and sentiments, however different from, or even contrary to our own.' Sympathy was the means by which sentiments were communicated; it was the psychological and emotive transaction that placed them at the heart of social life. Sensibility, in turn, was the ability to feel and exert sympathy; it was, according to *The Monthly Magazine*, 'that peculiar structure, or habitude of mind, which disposes a man to be easily moved, and powerfully affected, by surrounding objects and passing events'.

But sensibility, though seen as a psychological phenomenon, was also viewed as an ethical response. Sentimental feeling, the exercise of sympathy, was a form of moral reflection, for which some people had a greater capacity than others. To be able to express sympathy was to be a better moral being. The key physical sign of sensibility – a spontaneous tearfulness – also became a sign of humanity. As *Man: a Paper for Ennobling the Species* (1755) commented: 'it may be questioned whether those are properly men, who never wept upon any occasion . . . What can be more nobly human than to have a tender sentimental feeling of our own and others' misfortunes?'

The periodical essayists, critics, doctors and natural philosophers who examined sensibility believed it was a general feature of man, and one that was especially encouraged by the conditions of modern life. As the physician Thomas Trotter put it, 'The *nervous system*, that organ of sensation, amidst the untutored and illiterate inhabitants of a forest, could receive none of those fine impressions, which, however they may polish the mind and enlarge its capacities, never fail to induce delicacy of feeling, that disposes alike to more acute pain, as to more exquisite pleasure.' Acute sensibility was the result of modern commerce, urban life and the manners they promoted – Montesquieu's *doux commerce* – which created new, peaceful forms of mutual dependence among strangers, led to the better treatment of and greater regard for women, and encouraged the arts of politeness and refinement. Commercial society, the argument went, encouraged greater sympathy and sensibility; this distinguished modern societies from both the ancients and the primitives. As Sandwich's friend and memorialist Joseph Cradock put it, 'How much soever the ancients might abound in elegance of expression – their works are thinly spread with sentiment.'

Though the ability to sympathize with others was a sign of modern refinement and virtue, it was also, as many verses and essays on sensibility commented, a source of distress, a sign of moral superiority but also of weakness. As a contributor to the *Lady's Magazine* in 1775 exclaimed: 'Sensibility – thou source of human woes – thou aggrandiser of evils! – Had I not been possessed of thee – how calmly might my days have passed! – Yet would I not part with thee for worlds. We will abide together – both pleased and pained with each other. Thou shalt ever have a place in my heart – be the sovereign of my affections, and the friend of my virtue.'

Women, young people of both sexes, and those connected to the fine arts and literature were all believed to be especially susceptible to sensibility, prone to virtuous feeling and to excessive sentiment that made them melancholic (in the case of men) or hysteric (in the case of women). Expressions of sympathy, though praised as *the* great virtue of modern life, indeed as its defining social characteristic, could also be pathological and crippling.

Critics quickly recognized that sentimentalism supposed a different sort of writing and storytelling, one that in the words of the cleric and scholar Hugh Blair 'derives its efficacy not so much from what men are taught to know, as from what they are brought to feel'. The sympathetic moral response that sentimental literature evoked in the reader depended on particularity, a sense of intimacy that engaged the reader rather than on moral lessons or grand abstractions that appealed only to their intellect. The interior feeling of characters had to be explored and not just their external actions. Memoirs, biographies, collections of letters and verses, histories and, above all, novels portrayed the quotidian, ordinary, private and mundane because it was more likely to excite the reader's sympathy, being close to their own experience. In Blair's words, 'It is from private life, from familiar, domestic, and seemingly trivial occurrences, that we most often receive light into the real character.'

Sentimentalism was best staged in the intimate theatre of the home and family, and its most characteristic plots concerned the joys and misfortunes of everyday life – romantic and conjugal love, amatory disappointment, misfortunes brought on by intemperance and improvidence, the pleasures of familial companionship in a circle of virtue. A sentimental story was, in the words of the novelist William Guthrie, 'an *Epic* in lower Life', a story, in other words, exactly like that of Sandwich, Ray and Hackman.

Sentimental writing spread with astonishing swiftness in the second half of the eighteenth century. Newspaper reporting, pamphlets advocating reform and improvement such as Jonas Hanway's *A Sentimental History of Chimney-sweepers* (1785); biographies and memoirs like Oliver Goldsmith's *Life of Richard {Beau} Nash* (1762) or Joseph Boruwlaski's *Memoirs of the Celebrated Dwarf* (1788) – 'I not only mean to describe my size and its proportions, I would likewise follow the unfolding of my sentiments, the affections of my soul'; travel literature such as John Hawksworth's account of Captain James Cook's voyage; histories such as those of David Hume; and sermons, of which the most popular were those of Hugh Blair; literary forgeries, advice literature, plays, periodical essays, as well as a raft of sentimental novels and verses – all these used the techniques of literary sentimentalism to capture the hearts of their readers.

The cult of sensibility reached a peak in the 1770s, around the time of Ray's murder. It was not therefore very difficult to present the tragedy of Hackman and Ray as a sentimental story and to expect that the terrible tale would provoke the sympathy of those who read about it. Sentimental literature, especially the sentimental novel, was filled with stories of virtue in distress, a description that was easily applied to all three figures in this love triangle. Hackman after all was a victim of his amatory passion, Ray was a fallen woman who had achieved some respectability only to be murdered, and Sandwich was a former rake whose domestic felicity had been shattered by Hackman's bullet. The lovelorn youth, the fallen woman who nevertheless retained some virtue, and the reformed rake were all familiar figures in the many sentimental novels that were commissioned, published, sold and loaned by publishers like the Noble brothers, who ran 'novel manufactures' and circulating libraries to distribute this extremely popular form of fiction.

A sentimental account of the affair suited Sandwich and Hackman's followers because it depicted all three as blameless. But it fell on fertile soil because the case seemed such an obvious one of life imitating art. Readers were likely to respond as if the story was a sentimental fiction, because to do so was an obvious way to make sense of the events surrounding the crime. It gave Sandwich, Hackman's friends and the public what they all wanted – closure, a way of making the case understandable by placing it in a familiar light. We all know the pleasures of recognizing the familiar – 'ah! It's one of that sort of story'. We can wrap it up and put it away and, in doing so, perhaps hide the parts of the story that are troubling or disturbing, or suppress other ways of telling it. In the spring of 1779 the protagonists' desire to end speculation and the public's desire for assurance were at one, but it proved rather more difficult than might at first have been supposed to keep the story under wraps.

CHAPTER 3

The Killer as Victim:
James Hackman

IN THE SPRING OF 1779 Dr Johnson and his close friend Hester Thrale, whose own intimacy has long been a source of speculation, discussed relations between the sexes. Mrs Thrale was all for woman-power: 'It seems to me that no Man can live his Life thro', without being at some period of it under the Dominion of some Woman – Wife Mistress or Friend.' Nevertheless she found it hard to fathom Hackman's passion for Ray. It was, she said, 'the strangest thing that has appeared these hundred years'. Boswell had told her that his last words on the scaffold were *'Dear Dear* Miss Ray'. *'Here* was Passion for a Woman neither young nor handsome; whose eldest son was eighteen [sic] years old & a sea officer when she was shot by her Lover, & a woman not eminent as I can find for Allurements in the Eyes of any Man breathing but himself, & Lord Sandwich, who 'tis said had long been weary of her, though he knew not how to get free.' But Dr Johnson took a very different view. 'A woman', he said, 'has *such* power between the Ages of twenty five and forty five, that She may tye a Man to a post and whip him if she will.'

While Mrs Thrale pondered the powers of middle-aged women and Johnson surrendered to his masochistic fantasy, all over London people of fashion gossiped about the murder and its motive. In the twelve days between the killing of Martha Ray and the execution of James Hackman, the crime was on everyone's lips. Sandwich's colleagues from the Admiralty chatted at court with Lord Hertford about the tragedy. Ladies and gentlemen exchanged notes and items of news. 'For the last week', Horace Walpole wrote to his friend in Florence, Sir Horace Mann, 'all our conversation has been engrossed by a shocking murder.' Lady Ossory concurred, writing to George Selwyn, 'I found Miss Ray, or at least her unfortunate admirer, occupied everybody.' But if Johnson and Thrale's discussion was one of many that took place in the few weeks after Martha Ray's murder, it had a rather unusual feature: it was about Martha Ray, and not about her murderer. Lady Ossory's mid-sentence switch from the victim to her 'unfortunate admirer' perfectly captured the public's changing preoccupations. Ray was dead, Sandwich had retired from the public eye first to a villa at Hampton and, 'when every thing there brought her to his remembrance', to a house in Blackheath. This left Hackman as the focus of public attention: the extensive newspaper reports of his interrogation by Sir John Fielding, his trial at the Old Bailey, and his execution on 19 April less than two weeks after the killing made him, as one news report put it, 'the topic of conversation'.

Naturally enough, much of this gossip took the form of speculation about Hackman's motives for the crime. Many, like Mrs Thrale, were puzzled about the strange affair. As Horace Walpole commented to a friend, 'Now, upon the whole . . . is not the story full as strange as ever it was? Miss Wray [sic] has six children, the eldest son is fifteen, and she was at least three times as much. To bear a hopeless passion for five years, and then murder one's mistress – I don't understand it.'

This curiosity about the love of a young man for an older kept woman manifested itself in a preoccupation with Hackman's conduct after the murder. It was as if the means of understanding him and his bloody crime lay not in a forensic investigation (which, as we have seen, Sandwich tried to stifle), but in evidence offered in the person of Hackman himself. The key to the crime lay in Hackman's character. What he said was less important – though this mattered – than his entire bodily comportment. True feeling, in any sentimental story, was often beyond words. It could be seen in involuntary (and therefore authentic) physical expression: shudders, blushes and blanching, and, above all, spontaneous tears. Such bodily signs were clues to character and evidence of refinement and sensibility. As Samuel Richardson put it, 'the man is to be honour'd who can weep for the distresses of others'. Tears told observers about the person who wept but they also excited powerful sympathetic feelings in the viewer. Indeed, the response that a character's palpitations and weeping provoked was itself an indication of what the responder was like. Thus after the murder both press coverage and private correspondence were preoccupied with Hackman's public conduct, and with the powerful feelings aroused among those who witnessed his trial and execution.

All the newspapers reported that when Hackman was questioned by Sir John Fielding the day after Ray's shooting, he found it hard to answer the questions. 'From the agonizing pangs which entirely discomposed, and externally convulsed him,' reported the *London Chronicle*, 'it was sometime before the magistrate could proceed.' Onlookers were moved by his distraught behaviour, the papers noted: 'His manifest agitation, contrition, and poignant grief, too sensibly affected all present, to wish to add to such heart-felt misery by judicial interrogations during such keen distress of mind.' An unexpected delay in proceedings made him worse, and it took him a while to recover his composure and display 'the utmost steadiness'. During Fielding's questioning Hackman 'wept very much and was entirely convulsed each time the name of the deceased was mentioned. He did not palliate his offence, and said he eagerly wished to die.' The *London Evening Post* recorded that when Fielding presented him with evidence of the shooting, 'he sank into a grief which is impossible for the power of words to paint'. But by the end of the proceedings, he had become 'quite composed, and at present appears perfectly resigned to meet his approaching fate with a becoming fortitude'. 'His sighs and tears', the paper concluded, 'added to his genteel appearance, made most people give way to the finest feelings of human nature.'

The *General Advertiser* of 13 April drew a general moral lesson from this piece of sentimental theatre: 'The very humane behaviour of Sir John Fielding on a late melancholy occasion, and the tender constructions of a pitying audience on the conduct of the unhappy subject, does infinite honour to the laws of our country, and displays the humanity of our nature in the most beautiful and lively colours.' People may have been shocked by the crime, 'but who will say that the author of the shocking tragedy of Wednesday last is not amply punished? Who can picture to himself the misery that must penetrate and fill the deepest recesses of his mind, who has suffered himself to commit the horrid crime of murder, through the dire excess of a passion the most admirable that can fill the heart, while within the pale of reason?' As another press item concluded, 'the tear of compassion should not be withheld from him in the moment that *Justice* demands *an exemplary expiation of the deed*'.

A similarly powerful sympathetic response dominates the press accounts of Hackman's trial, which contrast strongly with the formal record of the court proceedings which was remarkably prosaic. Most of the proceedings were taken up with establishing the facts of the case, calling successive witnesses to satisfy the law by confirming what everyone already knew. Hackman's counsel did not dispute the facts, and asked witnesses very few questions. What would have been of most interest to modern legal scholars – Davenport's speech at the end of the trial arguing that Hackman was innocent on the grounds of temporary insanity, or 'irresistible impulse' – was not even recorded by the shorthand writer. Given that one of the perquisites of the recorder's job included the profits from the publication and sale of the trial's transcript, it would seem that there was very little interest in the *legal* deliberations of the trial.

Blackstone, like most judges at the time, was strongly opposed to pleas of temporary insanity, and he made it clear that such a plea had no legal status (English law does not recognize anything like *crime passionnelle*) and that insanity pleas in general were admissible only if strong evidence of the defendant's history of madness were presented. But no one seems to have thought that Hackman would be acquitted. Commentators as diverse as Horace Walpole and Sir John Fielding concurred in Hackman's inevitable fate. There was little interest in the trial's outcome, in the possibility of a surprise verdict of innocent. What mattered was Hackman's performance in justifying his actions and contemplating his fate.

This is clear from responses to the trial. For Lady Ossory, Hackman's conduct in court 'was wonderfully touching'. The news reports agreed. 'The prisoner by his defence drew tears from all parts of the Court; so decently and properly he conducted himself.' 'The behaviour of this unfortunate criminal', ran another item, 'was in every respect descriptive of his feelings. When the evidence related the fatal act, his soul seemed to burst within him. His defence was intermixed with many sighs and groans, and the trickling tear bespoke penitence . . . and remorse. The letter to his brother melted the most obdurate heart, and whilst the horror of the deed shocked the understanding of the audience, there was not a spectator who denied his pity.' 'However we may detest the *crime*,' wrote the *London Evening Post*, 'a tear of pity will fall from every humane eye on the fate of the unhappy *criminal*.' Witnesses, or – as it was more usually said – the *audience* was preoccupied with Hackman's performance. Boswell was pleased that the killer never tried to palliate his crime: 'He might have pleaded that he shot Miss Ray by accident, but he fairly told the truth: that in a moment of frenzy he did intend it.' When Boswell left the courtroom to tell Frederick Booth of the verdict, the first question Booth asked him was about his brother-in-law's behaviour. 'As well, Sir,' responded Boswell, 'as you or any of his friends could wish: with decency, propriety, and in such a manner as to interest every one present.' 'Well,' said Booth, 'I would rather have him found guilty with truth and honour than escape by a mean evasion.' Boswell thought Booth's reply 'a sentiment truly noble, bursting from a heart rent with anguish!'

Three days later, when Hackman went to the gallows, Lady Ossory described his conduct as 'glorious'. One paper commented, 'He behaved with a most astonishing composure, with the greatest fortitude, and most perfect resignation.' In the chapel in Newgate prison his conduct reduced spectators to tears. In his last hours, 'he collected his fortitude, he employed every moment of life to the worship of the Almighty, and prepared himself to meet the awful Judge of the World by prayers, and the overflowings of a contrite heart'. He died, remarked several commentators, as he should have done. The *Gazetteer* wrote, 'He behaved as a man should in such a situation.'

In the eyes of most observers Hackman's conduct was redemptive. His spontaneous grief affirmed the authenticity of his love for Martha Ray. The press invariably interpreted his lachrymose conduct as being prompted by her death and not by thoughts of his impending execution. He wept not for himself but, more nobly, for his dead lover.

Hackman's stoicism before the law and on the gallows showed

James Hackman, sentimental murderer, as he appeared in his *Case and Memoirs* and in a print sold separately. His head wound is covered with a black spot which looks more like a love patch than a dressing and he holds a handkerchief. This is a reminder both of his tearful contrition and of his fate: he dropped a handkerchief to signal the hangman to do his duty.

him to be a person in command of his faculties. Nearly all the papers characterized his conduct in the same way: it showed his contrition and grief about what he had done, and re-established a sense of himself as a sane man. 'He repeated that affecting acknowledgement of his guilt . . . and seemed in a state of composure, unruffled with the idea of punishment . . . His whole behaviour was manly, but not bold; his mind seemed to be quite calm, from a firm belief in the mercies of his Saviour.' Commentators spoke of Hackman's manliness, which they contrasted with his behaviour in killing Ray when, as they saw it, he suffered 'a momentary frenzy' that 'overpowered' him. The rhetoric was one in which Hackman lost his masculine identity in committing the murder, but recovered it through his stoic conduct during the trial and at the execution. The murderer was now himself cast as a victim, constantly referred to as 'the unfortunate' Mr Hackman. Though Hackman's lawyers had failed to persuade Blackstone and his fellow judge of the defence's case, their client's speech and conduct were readily accommodated within a sentimental story in which the life of an otherwise virtuous young man was destroyed by a love affair that had gone catastrophically wrong. Ray's story ended with her murder, but Hackman's spectacle of suffering continued to the gallows.

Hackman's repeated enactment of his exquisite sensibility, the legibility of his feelings as they manifested themselves in his conduct, fashioned bonds of sympathy, despite the crime he had perpetrated. As Boswell had written in *The Hypochondriack*, a year before Hackman's execution, 'the curiosity which impels people to be present at such affecting scenes, is certainly a proof of sensibility not of callousness'. Or as Adam Smith explained it in *The Theory of Moral Sentiments*, published in 1759, 'We all desire . . . to feel how each other is affected, to penetrate into each other's bosoms, and to observe the sentiments and affections which really subsist there. The man who indulges us in this natural passion, who invites us into his heart, who, as it were, sets open the gates of his breast to us, seems to exercise a species of hospitality more delightful than any other . . . How weak and imperfect soever the views of the open-hearted, we take pleasure to enter them.' Smith, in fact, had specifically cited a murderer as a person with whom one could not establish bonds of sympathy, whose actions could not be understood sympathetically. But Hackman was thought to be no ordinary killer. He was a man who slayed his lover and was himself destroyed not by his wickedness but by his overwhelming affection for Martha Ray. His conduct after Ray's death redeemed him. Like Martha Ray, he became a sacrifice to love.

The horror provoked by Hackman's crime combined with the sympathy excited by his obvious infatuation and contrition made him an object of public fascination. Many in libertine circles concurred with James Boswell's view – 'Natural to destroy what one cannot have' or, as he later put it in conversation with the notorious roué Lord Pembroke, 'Natural to <shoo>t mistress'. Such views were unsurprising among the young bloods of St James's and the Strand, but even women like Lady Ossory, who had more sympathy for Martha Ray, were moved by Hackman's intensity of feeling. Though there was some talk of Hackman being insane in the first few days after the murder, it soon dwindled away. True, his action was frenzied, his mind temporarily disordered by jealousy, but it seemed understandable in a young man hopelessly infatuated with an unattainable woman. And the source of his crime was not malevolence or depravity but the positive impulse of love.

The Hackman case was used, particularly by young men like James Boswell and the anonymous author of *The Case and Memoirs of James Hackman*, to explore their own feelings about romantic love and its perils, hazards that were understood not as a threat to women but as a challenge to a man's ability to govern his feelings. This was more than sympathy for Hackman; it was a positive identification with him. Boswell was particularly explicit about this. In a letter published in the *Public Advertiser* he wrote, 'Let those whose passions are keen and impetuous consider, with awful fear, the fate of Mr Hackman. How often have they infringed the laws of morality by indulgence! *He,* upon one check, was suddenly hurried to commit a dreadful act.' He elaborated on this theme in another letter, printed in the *St James's Chronicle*. 'Hackman's case', Boswell maintained, 'is by no means unnatural.' Citing an earlier essay he had written in *The Hypochondriack,* he pointed to the selfishness of romantic love; 'there is no mixture of disinterested kindness for the person who is the object of it'. 'The natural effect of disappointed love', he concluded, 'is to excite the most horrid resentment against its object, at least to make us prefer the destruction of our mistress to seeing her possessed by a rival.' Adopting a biblical tone, Boswell drew a moral from Hackman's story based on his close identification of all young men of feeling with the killer: 'Think ye that this unfortunate gentleman's general character is, in the eye of Heaven or of generous men in their private feelings, worse than yours? No it is not. And unless ye are upon your guard, ye may all likewise be in his melancholy situation.' Hackman had shown that he was capable of manly composure, but it had come too late.

Hackman's conduct after the murder reinforced his claim that he had been tricked into believing that Ray had a new lover. Surely a man who behaved with such dignity after his crime could not have been crazed, nor could he have plotted or planned to kill his lover. (Boswell never even considered the possibility that Hackman might have set out on the night of 7 April to murder Martha Ray.) Some other, outside circumstance must have pushed him over the edge. As we have seen, Hackman told Walsingham that he blamed it all on Galli, and rumours to that effect were soon in circulation, though they did not feature much in the newspapers. Hackman did not press the point and did not mention it at his trial. He had strong reasons not to antagonize Sandwich. Blaming Galli would not have helped his defence at the trial – indeed, it would have supplied a stronger motive for premeditated murder – and any vindictiveness would not have sat well with his determination to die with dignity. But once Hackman's body had been sent to Surgeon's Hall his supporters and critics of Sandwich were free to attack the Earl and Martha Ray's chaperone.

Soon after Hackman's execution most London papers ran advertisements for a new pamphlet entitled *The Case and Memoirs of James Hackman* written by 'A PARTICULAR FRIEND' and published, it was claimed, in order to prevent other 'spurious publications'. *The Case and Memoirs* was an immediate success. Within two weeks of its first appearance, the publisher was announcing its fifth edition, promising a large print run so that eager readers would not be disappointed. The tenth and final edition appeared in early June.

The Case and Memoirs was certainly the most eloquent defence of James Hackman, an apology that used the sympathy that Hackman had excited during his trial and execution to place his conduct in the most favourable light. In many ways it trod familiar ground. It emphasized Hackman's 'manly and collected behaviour' and how 'his deportment was noble, and gained him the admiration of his judge and jury in the course of his trial'. It framed the entire story as one of Hackman's heroic, eventually successful struggle to tame his passions. It was a saga about how a man was able to recover from a momentary act of madness.

But the publication of *The Case and Memoirs* also marked the breakdown of the consensual view of the murder that had been shaped and shared by the friends of Hackman and Sandwich. The author of *The Case and Memoirs*, confronted by public scepticism of his interpretation of events, grew progressively more outspoken and altered the fourth edition in early May to make his picture of Hackman even more sympathetic. Eventually, in the seventh edition, he placed the blame for her death squarely on the shoulders of Martha Ray. He even tried to blackmail Caterina Galli into implicating the Earl of Sandwich, offering to absolve her from blame in the affair, if she would pin the blame on Ray's keeper.

The Case and Memoirs was published by George Kearsley, the former publisher of John Wilkes's *North Briton*, one of the men who had been arrested in 1763 when the government had tried to put a stop to Wilkes's acerbic and very popular periodical. Kearsley, threatened with prosecution by the Secretary of State's office, had reluctantly – and much to the disgust of Wilkes – revealed all he knew about the *North Briton* and its author's publishing activities. In 1764, possibly as a result of his difficulties during the Wilkes affair, he was declared bankrupt, though he was soon back in business. Embarrassed and humiliated, Kearsley was full of resentment against members of the government, including Lord Sandwich who had played a major part in his prosecution.

Kearsley was a general bookseller who had first started publishing books, pamphlets and papers in the late 1750s in Ludgate Street, moving to new premises in Fleet Street, opposite Fetter Lane, in 1773. Though he had no particular speciality, throughout the 1770s he published pamphlets and poems attacking the moral depravity of the aristocracy, as well as political tracts attacking the government and supporting the American colonists. He had close connections with John Almon, Wilkes's publisher and friend, who had been behind the attack on Sandwich and Martha Ray for corruption in 1773, and he was connected to the group of booksellers who took a consistently critical line on the government throughout the 1770s. He had no love for the Earl of Sandwich. So he was an obvious figure for an author to approach if he were bent on publishing a defence of Hackman. But even if Kearsley had not had reasons to dislike Sandwich and Ray, he would have jumped at the chance of printing the life of such a notorious and controversial figure.

The anonymous author of *The Case and Memoirs* was in fact a young barrister of the Inner Temple, Manasseh Dawes, who had assisted in Hackman's defence. Though he occasionally makes a brief appearance in the press reports of 1779, very little is known about him apart from his fame for legal erudition and what can be gleaned from his published work. His preoccupations in print are revealing. His first books – *Miscellanies* and *Fugitive Essays* both of which Kearsley published in 1776 – mixed poems and stories of the trials of love with short political essays supporting the opposition, political reform and the American colonists. His subsequent writings tackled such issues as libel, crime and punishment, the extent of the supreme power, and the nature of political representation. His position, though sometimes eccentric, followed a consistently reformist line.

If we read Dawes's first writings – his poems and stories of romantic love – autobiographically, then it is not hard to see why he took up Hackman's cause. His verses are full of the irrational power of love. Love is a source of woe, a wound, a form of possession that takes hold of its victim: 'What tho' I once resolv'd and strove/To quell and spurn the force of love,/I then could not my mind controul,/While such fond pangs were in my soul'. In his stories Dawes was much exercised by the tension between sexual passion and proper conduct, especially among young men. He seems to have accepted that sexual desire (and its fulfilment) was natural outside wedlock, but to have worried about how illicit sexual practice, the guilt and perplexity it produced, affected relationships. His first publications are full of youthful ardor and confusion, as well as a passionate adherence to political probity and the reform of the law.

Dawes claimed to know Hackman and his brother-in-law Frederick Booth well, but in the controversy that blew up about the authenticity of his pamphlet he was forced to concede in the press that he had known neither of them before the notorious case. So Dawes chose to intrude himself into the story – to offer Hackman legal advice, to explain his turbulent feelings, and to act as his public apologist. Certainly he was Hackman's visible supporter. The *St James's Chronicle* reported that 'Mr Hackman was attended into and out of court by his friend, Mr Dawes, a Gentleman of the Bar, who has kindly attended him in his Confinement, and endeavoured to give him all the Counsel and Satisfaction in his power'. (It is worth bearing in mind, however, that Dawes probably got this item inserted into the paper.)

Dawes went to great lengths to give his pamphlet the authority of being Hackman's version of why Ray had died. The advertisements for *The Case and Memoirs* claimed its swift publication was intended to pre-empt less reliable accounts that might place Hackman in an unfavourable light. And in the pamphlet's dedication to the Earl of Sandwich Dawes makes the claim to be acting as Hackman's spokesman clear: 'the following pages . . . are authentic, because they are taken from the mouth of Mr Hackman while in confinement, and reduced to writing by a person who . . . knew him, and respected his very amiable and fair character'.

But from the outset there were doubts about the authority of Dawes's apologia. The day before *The Case and Memoirs* was published Frederick Booth printed a notice in the newspapers reminding readers that only he had the documents to produce an authentic 'case': 'I think it necessary to be known, that no Materials for such a Publication are or can be in any Hands but my own; and that if ever it should seem to me proper to give any Account to the Public, it will be signed with my own name.' Later apologists for Martha Ray claimed that Booth denounced Dawes's writing as a self-interested fraud, but Booth may just have wanted to make clear that he was not, as many might suppose, the author of *The Case*.

Even though – or perhaps because – *The Case and Memoirs* was such an extraordinary success, Dawes was forced on the defensive. When the fifth edition was published in early May, he inserted a notice in the papers indignantly asserting his probity and veracity:

There being some doubts with the public of the truth of this publication, the Author of it declares, on his honour and veracity, (which he hopes are unimpeachable) that the facts contained in it are genuine, he having presented it to the public for the purpose expressed in the dedication, and no other, which he is ready to testify, if necessary, on an application to him at Mr Kearsly's, who knows and believes him incapable of the mean artifice of obtruding on the public any thing with a view to catch the penny of curiosity.

In June, a verse appeared in the *Public Advertiser* mocking Dawes and identifying him as the author of *The Case*:

> The Rope, the penalty of broken Laws,
> Is not more shocking than the pen of D-ws.
> Both to deserve no Crime can be so great;
> Yet both to suffer was poor Hackman's fate.

What made Dawes's account so controversial? First and foremost he categorically asserted that Hackman and Ray had been not only friends but lovers. From the outset he described the two as 'revelling in all its [loves] rites by stealth', and enjoying 'stolen bliss'. Because of 'the indulgencies she had . . . with him', Ray and Hackman had 'unlimited (though illicit) gratification'. This contradicted everything the press had been told before Hackman's death. He also claimed that Sandwich had learned of the affair and confronted Ray, who had promised to end her relationship with Hackman. But, he claimed, her passion for him was too great and she even agreed to marry her young lover. Only his departure to Ireland delayed the ceremony, and while they were apart, 'they corresponded in the most affectionate manner by every post'. So Dawes depicted Hackman and Ray as being bound by mutual love and destined for conjugal felicity. Hackman's expectations of Ray were portrayed not as delusional but as eminently reasonable.

What, then, had gone wrong? In his dedication to Lord Sandwich and in the main body of his narrative Dawes placed the blame on Galli and Sandwich. Galli, according to him, had taken money from Hackman so that the couple could continue to meet without Sandwich's knowledge. But, after a while, Galli '(whether under the management and direction of his Lordship, who wished to break off the connexion at all events, or otherwise, we do not know) informed Mr Hackman that all future visits from Miss Reay would be dispensed with, for that Lord S—— was too well acquainted with their amour to bear with it longer'. She is also reported as adding, 'That Miss Reay had tired of him, and had resolved to quit him for the sake of another gentleman, who was much more dear to her'. Here was the full-blown version of Galli's betrayal.

In the early editions of *The Case and Memoirs* Dawes says nothing about Ray's own view of the matter. The reader is left to assume that she still loved Hackman, even when temporarily unable to see him. Perfidy perhaps lay with Sandwich and certainly blackened the character of Galli. But no matter where responsibility was placed, the act of warning off Hackman was the turning point in the plot. It triggered 'his despair and grief', transforming his character: 'he was an altered man . . . he was agreeable, sprightly and affable; but on a sudden he changed himself to a pensive and grave deportment'. He grew increasingly subject to a melancholy 'originated on that occasion, which, by continually brooding over, increased and inflamed his wretched mind'.

Dawes included in his account a letter from Hackman to Ray which, 'with one other, (a copy whereof is in the hands of his brother-in-law) is the only one he did not cancel'. In it Hackman pleaded with Ray to relieve him of 'his pleasing pain'. He mentions their meeting secretly 'at Marylebone, and other places'. He calls on her to honour her promise of marriage, urging her to bring her youngest child with her to live a life of rural felicity as a cleric's wife. 'I know you are not fond of the follies and vanities of the town. How tranquil and agreeably, and with what uninterrupted felicity, unlike to anything we have yet enjoyed, shall we then wear our time away together on my living.' Full of despair, he threatens Ray with the prospect that if she does not marry him he will die: 'For God's sake let me hear from you; and as you love me, keep me no longer in suspense, since nothing can relieve me but death or you.'

The deception of others, continued Dawes, plunged Hackman into this melancholia, but only when he saw Martha Ray with another man in the playhouse on the night of the murder did he decide on suicide. 'Gloomy, melancholy, and outrageous, at the injuries he had conceived, which exceeded all human knowledge to explain', he determined to shoot himself 'in the presence of a woman, whose supposed infidelity had brought him to a misery and despair not to be described by words'. And only when he looked into Ray's face as she tried to enter her coach did he think of killing her – 'he concluded it would be best for both to die together'. This was no premeditated crime but an act of 'momentary phrenzy [sic]'.

The lawyer in Dawes wanted to acquit Hackman of murder, though he could not, of course, deny the killing. In his long 'Commentary on his Conviction', Dawes absolved Hackman of any felonious intent to kill Martha Ray. Murder, he reminded the reader, is distinguished as a crime by proof of prior intention and malice: 'It is the wickedness and malignity of the heart which raises the crime of murder, and not simply the act that kills.' Yet Hackman's suicide note, with its request to his brother-in-law that he care for Ray after Hackman's suicide, showed 'that he did not kill her with an *express* or previous intention, but from a momentary phrenzy, which overpowered him, after he had resolved to destroy himself *only*'. His intent to do away with himself, Dawes conceded, was 'a felonious action and disposition of mind' and it was on these grounds that Blackstone in his summary of the case pressed for Hackman's conviction. But Dawes argued that 'as he was found guilty of murder by malice implied and not expressed, he deserves not to be classed among common assassins and murderers'. He also pointed out that if Hackman had succeeded in killing himself, he would have been condemned for an act of lunacy. If he tried to kill himself in such a state, did not this condition apply as much to his killing of Ray, which was thus not a responsible act, and therefore not murder? In his conclusion, Dawes blamed the whole affair on Hackman's passion: what began as a virtue 'hurried him, when born down by disappointment, ingratitude and inconstancy, to the vice that concluded his unconquerable misery, while either himself or Miss Reay were living'. Only after the crime was he able to recuperate, struggling successfully to control his feelings and face his fate.

In *The Case* the murderer is lost in the lover. Dawes was at pains to emphasize Hackman's youth and inexperience, the way he was led on by a passion he could not control: 'he has fallen a sacrifice to love and an unguarded moment, when reason driven from his mind gave way to a deed, which he not only deplored, but for which he has forfeited his life according to law'. In case his readers did not grasp his point, Dawes inserted a character sketch of Hackman in the fourth edition in which he pleaded for their sympathy: 'he was a lover . . . He was a slave to its influence, and sought a cure in death, when a supposed contempt from her, on whose account he had long been miserable, robbed him of his reason, and in his phrenzy compelled him to execute that deed, which, peculiar as it was, will be remembered with compassion, not remorse; with pity, not abhorrence; with charity, not indifference; and whenever we think of the man we shall exclaim – Alas! Poor Hackman!' Hackman's case was one of 'imprudence, impolicy and folly . . . powerful ingredients in love' as opposed to 'the colder considerations of lucre, rank, and fortune'.

This was a sentimental tale but, like Thomas Day's later *History of Sandford and Merton* (1783–9), one with a political twist. Hackman emerges as a sincere, ordinary man caught up in the intrigues and moral depravity of a vicious aristocratic milieu of which he has little understanding. His innocence explains his guilt or, as James Boswell had put it in his letter to the *St James's Chronicle*: 'had he been less virtuous, he would not now have been so criminal'.

Dawes's interpretation of events was corroborated in a number of newspaper items published in late April, about the same time as the appearance of the fourth edition of *The Case and Memoirs*, with its new character sketch of Hackman. The first, dated 26 April, revealed the discovery of new letters. 'The Council who pleaded for Mr Hackman on his trial', reported the *Gazetteer*, 'had really in his pocket, besides the letter he produced, two others; one from Mr Hackman to Miss Ray, and another from Miss Ray to him.' The second letter, it reported, 'confessed, that having far exceeded in her expenses the bounty of her Lord, a connection in marriage must, with respect to Mr Hackman, prove ruinous, and therefore not to be insisted upon'. This may be the letter that Dawes referred to in a new footnote to the fourth edition of *The Case and Memoirs* as 'entreating him [Hackman] not to think of marrying her, as they might be happier as they were'. Two days after the first report, the *Gazetteer* followed up with an item that paraphrased and reinforced Dawes's view of Hackman's plight, confirming that Ray had promised to marry him, outlining the betrayal of Galli, and blaming Sandwich for forcing her to tell Hackman that Ray refused to 'have any connection with him'.

At about the same time Dawes sent a letter to Galli offering to tell her story and to clear her character:

> The author of Mr Hackman's case and memoirs having concealed the particulars of Mrs Galli's conduct towards that gentleman and thinking that it will be very proper for her to make it known in

answer to a letter in the newspapers; he will (if agreeable) to her make the same public, as her friend, in order that she may avoid every imputation of having behaved improperly between Mr Hackman and Miss Ray – her silence may otherwise condemn her undeservedly.

Dawes followed this offer with a detailed account of Galli's dealings with Hackman, claiming that, though she had known the young man only for a few months, she had acted as an intermediary between the couple. He claimed that Martha Ray had been angry when Galli, her curiosity piqued by the affair, asked her if she had really promised to marry Hackman. He also asserted that Hackman had seen Galli at noon on the day of the murder and that when they parted he had 'said to her three times *God bless you Galli*'.

Dawes seems to have wanted Galli's co-operation because it would have enabled him to show conclusively that it was Sandwich's interference that had driven Hackman to melancholia and to plan suicide. But to judge by the presence of Dawes's letter to Galli in Lord Sandwich's papers, Galli must have taken it to the Earl, and he probably instructed her in her reply: 'She will not enter into any correspondence with any person on that head, nor will she allow any mention to be made of her name.' Dawes remained persistent. Just as the seventh edition of *The Case and Memoirs* went to press in mid-May he urged Galli to go to Kearsley's shop to read and endorse its contents. She sent back a curt note saying 'she was out of town'. Dawes's attempts to win over or blackmail Galli were thwarted by her loyalty to Sandwich. They make all the more poignant her successive pleas to the Earl asking him to help her.

At this point Dawes shifted his position, adding to the seventh edition of the *Case and Memoirs* a new 'Address to the Town', in which he placed the blame for Hackman's conduct firmly on the shoulders of Martha Ray. He began by once again defending Hackman's love for Ray. 'Some of you', he conceded, 'may however say that he never loved Miss Reay.' Perhaps this was true at the moment when he shot her. 'But that he had long previously loved her there are ample proofs.' 'It is wrong', asserted Dawes, 'to say he could not love her, because she was the mistress of another. It is wrong to say that his love was impure, because he wished to marry her.' 'The passion of love', he reiterated, 'is headstrong; it sets reason at defiance.' Once Hackman's motives were understood, so would be the true nature of his crime. He was certainly at fault: 'to give a loose to passions the order of society requires to be submitted to rules is a blemish in any character' but 'it is not so great as to call down the odium of good men, or to merit the implacable vengeance of eternal punishment'. 'His capital crime', Dawes concludes, 'was principally to love, and that, when hurried to madness by its consequences, he sought death as a relief, with her who alone had made it preferable to life.'

Thus far the later editions of *The Case and Memoirs* seemed merely to reiterate the story of Hackman's love, as Dawes desperately tried to convince his readers of the truth of his version. But they did more. For now Dawes blamed a new scapegoat – neither Sandwich nor Galli – but Martha Ray herself, whom he depicted as a skilled manipulator of men. Hackman was first encouraged and then 'ruled' by her. 'The passion of love is headstrong; it sets reason at defiance; it gives an artful woman an opportunity which she seldom fails to embrace, of governing a fond affectionate man in an arbitrary way.' Ray was not a loving partner, torn between her passion for Hackman and her prudent concern for her children. She was a well-known type, the scheming mistress whose success is a result of her ability to manipulate men. Ray, Dawes says, was 'a capricious and an ungrateful woman'. And we should remember Hackman 'as an unhappy example, that however unworthy a woman may prove, a man may be sincere enough to prefer death to her ingratitude, and violent enough in the moment to plunge her into eternity with him'. So not only was Hackman's crime not murder, but Ray was responsible for her own demise.

As Dawes wrote and rewrote *The Case and Memoirs*, and as he realized that not everyone saw Hackman as the unfortunate victim of youthful and inexperienced love, he looked for someone else to blame. Despite his efforts, he was unable to obtain the evidence that could incriminate either Galli or Sandwich. He became more and more convinced that someone other than Hackman himself was responsible for the young man's woes, and he was led inexorably to blame the object of Hackman's affections. In so doing he drew both on a sense that the innocent Hackman was entering a world of (aristocratic) sexual depravity and on the notion that a successful mistress was necessarily, by virtue of her station, a powerful manipulator of men. As we shall see, he was drawing on stories about Sandwich and Ray with a long pedigree, even if the Earl and his supporters managed to keep them out of the papers after Ray's death.

Dawes's case did not remain unanswered. Shortly after its last edition an anonymous tract appeared, *The Case and Memoirs of Miss Martha Reay, to which are Added Remarks, by way of Refutation on the Case and Memoirs of the Rev. Mr Hackman*. We do not know the author or provenance of this pamphlet, but its contents make clear that it was written by a sympathizer of Sandwich, and it may even have been published at his request. It sets out a completely different version of events, contradicting Dawes in almost every particular. It begins by categorically denying that the relationship between Hackman and Ray was 'criminal'. They had not, in other words, enjoyed a sexual relationship. Hackman was both a venal and a skilful young libertine. In a clever twist to the plot, the author of this new version explained Hackman's interest in Ray as growing from his wish to share the money she had been given by her keeper. Sandwich's generosity fuels Hackman's greed. 'It is much to his Lordship's honor, that the settlement which was made in case of any accident, was a spontaneous offer of his own, without a single solicitation on the part of Miss Reay.' This settlement, the author added, 'was the motive that first induced Mr Hackman to make the offer of marriage'. Far from being naïve, Hackman was a seducer who needed all his skills to take Ray away from Sandwich: 'to disturb the tranquility of two persons so peculiarly fashioned for each other, it was necessary that the adventurer should possess a competent knowledge of intrigue'. His eventual failure to win Ray, her calm refusal to accept his overtures, drove him to a frenzy and thence to his crime, 'an act that would disgrace the hand of a barbarian'. This was not a love affair; it was murder: 'He deprived the King of a subject, Lord S— of a friend, her tender innocents of an affectionate mother, and the community of a valuable member.'

The author of this new pamphlet rehearsed Martha Ray's virtues, denied her corruption, and appealed for sympathy for her children. The work challenged Dawes to donate the earnings from his own publication to the 'unoffending innocents' who survived their mother. It reminded Dawes and his readers that Ray was truly a victim:

> Thus in an unsuspecting moment, when perhaps she was but little prepared for the awful event, the late unfortunate Miss Reay, who only in one instance transgressed the most rigid virtue, and who had a thousand amiable qualities to atone for it, was summoned to give an account of her life, her enemies have so much laboured to traduce.

The Case and Memoirs of Martha Reay condemned Dawes's tract as yet another crime against poor Martha Ray, impugning her character and conduct when she was no longer able to defend herself. It is also, concluded Ray's defender, a work of fiction. 'You subscribe yourself the Author.' 'Author, and Inventor, according to my idea of the words, are synonymous, . . . the inference is this, and indeed it cannot be any other, that the pretended intrigue between the late Mr Hackman and Miss Reay, is the wanton production of a Luxuriant imagination.'

The conflict between *The Case and Memoirs of Martha Reay* and *The Case and Memoirs of James Hackman* was posed as one between fact and fiction. But it was more that what had once been one consensual sentimental story, in which everyone was a victim, divided into two competing stories in which the misfortunes of either Ray or Hackman bore the responsibility of the other. Yet what both these stories concealed, though they sometimes hinted at alternative ways of understanding the events of 1779, were two powerful interpretations of what was at stake in the triangle of Sandwich, Martha Ray and Hackman. These narratives were concerned less with sentiment and sensibility than with the material world of sex and power.

CHAPTER 4

Missing Stories:
Lord Sandwich and
the Making of a Libertine

THE PRESS COVERAGE after Martha Ray's murder was remarkably reticent about Sandwich's reputation as a libertine and about the nature of his relationship with Ray. No doubt his efforts to control coverage of such a sensational story partly explain this omission, as does the wave of sympathy for a man whose misfortune temporarily outweighed his public unpopularity. But the Earl had influence only on the daily press. He could not suppress discussion of his affairs in pamphlets and magazines. Tales of his libertinage and of Martha Ray's career as a successful mistress had been in circulation long before the murder. And the reading public's interest in the demi-monde that Sandwich haunted, a world imagined as full of intrigue and deception, had been fed by a prurient literature that vividly described – and usually condemned – a sexual economy that linked titled older men with poor, young and beautiful women.

These tales of intrigue took many forms: magazine articles about the moral failures of the rich and famous; kiss-and-tell memoirs that named names and promised to reveal all; biographies of famous courtesans and rakes; guides to the brothels and bath-houses that were the staple of the sex industry; and sentimental short stories and novels about the rise and fall of libertines and whores. They created a fantastic world of money and sex – 'Two fiends with joint and sovereign sway shall reign,/The love of pleasure and the love of gain' – in which duplicity and deception were rife, and fact and fiction almost impossible to untangle. Libertines bent on seducing virgins invented stories of marital felicity, procurers metamorphosed experienced whores into innocent virgins, courtesans told tales of financial misfortune to extort money and gifts from their clients. Sexual intrigue thrived on a mix of fiction, fantasy and mendacity.

The same was true of the literature that brought it to the reading public. What, after all, was a reader to make of a memoir written by a woman (or an author posing as a woman) who had devoted her life to dissembling and deception? Some accounts referred to or were supposedly written by living persons, but this was no guarantee of their veracity. Others were fictions in which living persons occasionally had walk-on parts. Almost all contained stories within stories, tales told by jilted men and fallen women about how they had come to their present condition. All were written for profit; most were not what they seemed. Some, like *The Honest London Spy, Discovering the base and subtle intrigues of the Town* (1724), posed as warnings to the innocent but offered titillating detail. Others, such as *The Genuine Memoirs of Miss Faulkner* (1770), the life of the mistress and eventual wife of the Earl of Halifax, ostensibly praised but actually besmirched their protagonists. *The Genuine Memoirs of the Celebrated Miss Maria Brown* (1766), sometimes attributed to John Cleland, was one of several palpable fictions that posed as nothing 'but plain truth'. There were also personal apologetics and works written as blackmail.

During the 1760s and 1770s these stories of moral depravity and misfortune were taken up by social satirists and politicians and shaped into an indictment of the aristocracy in general and of government ministers in particular. Fears of corruption, vice and luxury were commonplace in social commentary throughout the eighteenth century, but they were now focused on the sexual conduct of high society and the nation's political leaders. As the young sailor poet Edward Thompson put it, contrasting the virtuous ancients with the depraved moderns:

> Ye Gods! When future ages read this o'er,
> Will they believe, to keep a painted whore,
> A thousand Nobles of the *British* line,
> Of diff'rent ages, could promiscuous join?
> Peruse the Antients, nothing could employ
> So many tails [sic], unless the siege of *Troy*.

Thompson was the friend of the poet and libertine clergyman Charles Churchill, the co-author, with John Wilkes, of the *North Briton*, and the most important political satirist of the 1760s. If Thompson, Churchill and other commentators were to be believed, the nation was awash with sexual licence and Britain's leaders more attentive to the needs of their mistresses and whores than to the good of the nation. The production and exploitation of scandal became a political weapon.

A typical example of this genre was an attack mounted on Colonel Henry Lawes Luttrell, later Lord Carhampton, a government supporter, client of Lord Bute and political ally of Sandwich who had replaced the radical John Wilkes as MP for the constituency of Middlesex, after Wilkes had been removed from his seat by a vote of the House of Commons in 1769. Opposition papers and periodicals were full of a story, fleshed out in *The Memoirs of Miss Arabella Bolton* (1770), that claimed Luttrell had seduced and abandoned the beautiful young daughter of a gardener who tended a family friend's estate. According to the *Memoirs* – and this was supported by documents included in the text purportedly submitted by the physician who attended Miss Bolton – Luttrell drugged and seduced the girl, then left her both pregnant and riddled with venereal disease. Despite earlier promises to do so, he refused to pay for her medical treatment or for the treatment of a wet-nurse, who became infected from the child. The baby died of the disease it was born with; the physician, encouraged by the government's opponents, continued to sue for his fees; and Miss Bolton died prematurely in 1769. For the author of *The Memoirs of Arabella Bolton*, published just after her death, the moral was clear:

> The man who can with deliberation, and cool pursuit of an innocent, virtuous, though obscure girl, by long persuasion, and false promises, seduce and rob her of her chastity and reputation, and afterwards abandon her to the world, covered with shame, infamy, and dreadful disease, would not hesitate one moment to blast the reputation, or destroy the peace, honour and happiness, of the first or most respectable character of the nation.

Personal depravity rendered Luttrell unfit for office, unworthy of public trust, as likely to betray a true patriot as a young girl. This sentimental story had a political message hostile to the government.

That so many politicians of the 1760s lived openly with their mistresses – not just Sandwich with Ray, but Lord Halifax with Mary Anne Faulkner, John Calcraft with the actress George Ann Bellamy and, most notoriously, the Duke of Grafton with Nancy Parsons – laid them open to a rather different charge: it enabled opponents of successive governments to claim that the depraved appetites of ministers led them to neglect their public duties or, worse, to be influenced in their policies and patronage by their mistresses. According to these stories, the women were not victims but manipulators, exercising 'petticoat' government.

All these tales of debauchery and intrigue followed standard plots, usually about seduction, and involved stock characters: the libertine against whose schemes almost no woman was safe; the roué in thrall to women, led by his jaded desires to obey their every whim and desire; the fallen woman, forced to fend for herself because of the loss of her virtue; the perfidious procuress who betrayed her female friends and acquaintances; and the scheming woman who used her sexual wiles in pursuit of money and pleasure.

Such was the context in which people thought about Sandwich's relationship with Martha Ray. So, while the newspapers euphemistically glossed over it, describing her as 'a favourite friend and confidante', 'connected with a noble Lord', and as someone who 'went into his Lordship's keeping', authors less sympathetic to the Earl or more interested in exposing the sexual mores of a depraved aristocracy for either political, pecuniary or prurient ends were not so discreet in their accounts of the menage at the Admiralty and at Sandwich's country seat at Hinchingbrooke, which one critic described as 'the scene of your youthful debaucheries, the retreat of your hoary licentiousness.'

Sandwich's notoriety as the very personification of aristocratic libertinage was the starting point of all such stories. His life had certainly not been blameless. In 1755 he had separated from his wife, Dorothy Fane, who for some years had been mentally ill (she was probably suffering from manic depression), a condition that became so severe that she was made a ward of the Court of Chancery in 1767. But even before their separation Sandwich had been carrying on a passionate and illicit affair with his sister-in-law, Sarah Nailour, in Huntingdonshire. For three years the couple kept up a secret correspondence, exchanged love tokens – handkerchiefs, a portrait and a lock of hair – and quarrelled over petty jealousies. Nailour lived in perpetual fear of discovery by Sandwich's brother or, even worse, by Lady Sandwich, and constantly urged her lover to burn her letters (which still survive today). Sandwich was bolder: when in his coach with his 'Sally' he sat with his hands up her coat, and he did not hesitate to send his servants directly to his mistress, which she felt sure would lead to their detection.

Once on his own in 1755, Sandwich enjoyed the pleasures available to an aristocratic man about town, and for the rest of his life, including the years when he lived with Ray and her children, he continued to have sexual relations with prostitutes and young girls. After his separation from Dorothy Fane, his friend the Duke of Cumberland wrote to warn him of his conduct: 'as you are now a single orphan I fear you have thrown aside all decency and endeavour to prove your youth by your deeds; take care they don't betray your age instead of proving your youth'.

There was much for someone in Sandwich's position to enjoy. The sex industry of London was as flourishing as it is today, catering for different tastes and to rich and poor alike. The area that ran from St James's Park, past Charing Cross, down the Strand and past Covent Garden into the City – the route followed by Martha Ray on the last evening of her life – was full of young prostitutes, poor girls plying their pitch and selling themselves for a shilling. Women like Nanny Baker, 'a strong, plump good humoured girl', Elizabeth Parker, who offered 'the lusty embraces of a young Shropshire girl, only seventeen', and Alice Gibbs, a girl who James Boswell described as 'a very agreeable congress'. The poorest girls worked on the street itself – Boswell slipped with one girl into a court off the Strand, and copulated with others in St James's Park, the Privy Garden and even on Westminster Bridge – others plied their trade in taverns and brothels. In the nine years before Martha Ray's death, more than two hundred keepers of bawdy houses were arrested in the parishes of St Martin-in-the-Fields and St Paul's Covent Garden; more than forty more had been bound over to keep the peace at the more up-market houses they ran in St James's and St Ann, Soho. There were clusters of brothels in Covent Garden and off the Strand, in Johnson's Court off Charing Cross (close to the Admiralty), in Wardour Street and Meard's Court in Soho and in St James's, Princes, King and Jermyn Streets in Westminster. Covent Garden, whose courts and terraces the aristocracy had deserted for the newly fashionable squares in the West End, had become the most notorious centre of prostitution. As the magistrate Sir John Fielding, who examined Hackman after he had killed Ray, complained

> One would imagine that all the prostitutes in the kingdom had picked upon that blessed neighbourhood for a general rendezvous, for here are lewd women enough to fill a mighty colony, and . . . here is a great quantity of open houses, whose principle employment is to minister incitement to lusty rakes and shameless prostitutes. These and the taverns afford ample supply of provision for the flesh, while others abound for the consummation of desires which are thus decided. For this design the bagnios and lodging houses are near at hand.

For a predatory aristocrat, richly dressed and obviously affluent, the pickings were easy; the choice of partners as varied as genteel and respectable 'ladies' or the poorest whores who worked the alleys. A woman wrote to Sandwich a few months after Ray's death reminding him that two years earlier he had accosted her in Bedford Street, Covent Garden, and taken her into a house round the corner in Chandos Street where, 'we had some conversation then Your Lordship did me the honour to call me by the tender name of wife and I were to call you by the name of husband and Your Lordship took out of your pocket ten guineas'. The woman claimed that at first she was confused and therefore did not take the money, which Sandwich prudently returned to his pocket. 'Then Your Lordship began to take liberties with me which I never had taken with me since the death of my husband and after what passed Your Lordship told me that you would provide for me but it could not be done all at once.' Whatever may or may not have happened that night, it is clear that the woman was proposing that she might take the place of the recently murdered Ray.

Sandwich might have taken this widow to a bagnio like the one used by his friend Robert Boyle Walsingham, who took his lover, Ann Sheldon – a courtesan who had a string of lovers rumoured to include Sandwich himself – to 'a Mansion where parties of any relation may sleep together, *except* that of man and wife, and that was the *Bagnio* in Leicester Fields'. This type of make-shift arrangement was available to illicit lovers, but houses also kept lists of working prostitutes. At Tom's, a bagnio to the north in Soho Square, women who wanted to use the house entered their names and addresses in a book, were sent for when needed and paid the proprietor five shillings a time for the use of a room. Sandwich could have gone to the notorious Shakespeare Tavern, where Ray's body was taken on the night of 7 April 1779, to examine Harris's Lists, which provided detailed information on the available whores. Or, if he was of a voyeuristic turn of mind, he could have visited other houses where naked 'posture girls' were paid to adopt lewd poses for the paying clientele. (Many of these young women distinguished themselves from common whores by refusing to have sex with their patrons.)

But it was more likely that Sandwich's tastes would have been best met by a visit to one of the new sorts of brothel that were first set up in the 1770s by women like the notorious Charlotte Hayes and that catered exclusively for the most wealthy and aristocratic clients. These were clustered in Westminster, just north of St James's Park, in King Street, St James's Place and, above all, King's Place off Pall Mall, close to the clubs and assembly rooms patronized by rich young men, and just around the corner from where Sandwich sang in his all-male Catch Club. Certainly, Sandwich was blackmailed by an acquaintance of the well-known courtesan 'Miss Polly Hermitage', whose other lovers included Lord Robert Spencer, Lord Deleraine (whose name she assumed for a while) and the son of the Tripoline ambassador, and who worked in one of these houses in St James's Place. The blackmailer forced Sandwich to pay for letters that he had foolishly written to her arranging assignations: 'she throws [them] about in a very careless manner so that I as well as other visitors can peruse them'. On a number of occasions Sandwich used a similar up-market house in Berkeley Row, Mrs Jane Price's. Here the famous beauty Grace Dalrymple Eliot committed her first infidelity with Arthur Annesley, Viscount Valentia. Here also Sandwich brought the teenage virgin Edith Williamson after he had picked her up in Ranelagh Pleasure Gardens in 1759.

In the year of Ray's death no fewer than five of these brothels were operating in King's Place alone. They claimed to model themselves on the best French houses in their atmosphere of luxurious domesticity. All had girls in residence, rather than having girls on call, were furnished like aristocratic town houses and offered fine wines and food. Most had female proprietors who provided their clients with fancy beds and condoms as well as special forms of entertainment.

Charlotte Hayes of King's Place was the most notorious of the brothel-keepers, famous for her genius for self-advertisement. The notorious survey of these brothels, *Nocturnal Revels* (1779), claimed that on one occasion she invited her most favoured clients – twenty-three guests, all nobles and baronets except for five commoners – to witness a re-enactment 'of the celebrated rites of VENUS, as practised at *Otaheite*'. There is no evidence that Sandwich was present at this event, much less that it ever took place, but as the patron of Captain Cook's expeditions, the collector of Tahitian artefacts, and the protector of Omai, the South Sea Islander who visited England between 1774 and 1776, he would have made the perfect guest. It was reported that under the watchful eye of Hayes, who acted the role of Oberea, a Tahitian princess, a dozen young men and women enacted the Tahitian rites, a performance supposedly also modelled after the classical pornographic poses of Aretino. When it was over the young men retired and 'the females remained, and most of them repeated, the part they had so skillfully performed, with several of the spectators'.

The young women who worked in these houses were supposedly sober and free from disease. Despite the sex shows, the proprietors cultivated a relaxed atmosphere like that of a rich private house. Ann Sheldon knew several of the houses and worked in them. (She was first seduced by Sandwich's young friend, Boyle Walsingham, in a King's Place house known as Kildare's, and she returned there with him on many other occasions.)

Sheldon described the girls who worked in these houses as young, poor and virtual prisoners of their keepers, who catered for the aristocratic libertines' preoccupation, which Sandwich shared, with young virgins and pubescent girls. As one libertine put it, 'The time of enjoying immature beauty seems to be a year 'ere the tender fair find the symptoms of maturity . . . Before the periodical lustration hath stained her virgin shift, whilst her bosom boasts only a general swell rather than distinct orbs.' More prosaically virginity was a guarantee of chastity and freedom from venereal disease. Accordingly, the girls at Mrs Mitchell's King's Place house were aged between thirteen and seventeen. Charlotte Hayes recruited her young girls by advertising for servant girls under twenty and 'not long in town'. Another famous bawd, Mrs Goadby, was said to have control of register offices, where servants went to seek employment, so that she could recruit young innocents. Certainly the press was full of stories like the account that appeared in the *Covent Garden Magazine* in 1774 of an innocent servant girl, accosted in a registry office by a woman of genteel appearance who took her to a house off Pall Mall with sumptuous fittings and a couch with a magnificent canopy where she was raped by a nobleman.

Miss Jones, the child of a hawker and pedlar, who eventually became the mistress of the Duke of Cumberland, George III's miscreant brother, was taken into Mrs Mitchell's house:

> the poor girl was stripped naked, put into a large tub of water, when after having been cleansed from the dirt and defilement of her situation, she was handsomely clothed, and at night consigned to a defilement of another and more fatal species, in the arms of a gentleman, who gladdened Mrs Mitchell's heart with the sum which he gave her for the prize she had so luckily procured him.

She was later spotted by the Duke of Cumberland at Vauxhall Pleasure Gardens; the king's brother paid Mrs Mitchell £70 for her. This was the ideal career move for the young girls who worked in these expensive up-market brothels: to find a single keeper, set up an independent household in some style and even acquire a less tarnished reputation.

The system of aristocratic libertinage depended upon an informal network of male procurers and female bawds. Many were up-market trades people, like Mrs Pike of Swallow Street off Piccadilly, whose business selling silk bags for wigs and hair brought her into contact with rich young men. The standard guide to London trades defined the term milliner – the trade in which Martha Ray was apprenticed – as 'a polite term for bawd'. Most procurers were women, usually former or still practising but more experienced *filles de joie*, but a few were men. Ann Sheldon was approached by Andrew White, 'well known in the purlieus of low gallantry, and who, after having passed through a variety of infamous characters, had settled, at last in that of Procurer-General for the public brothels, and private gentlemen'.

The readers of Ann Sheldon's *Memoirs* must have felt that in London procurers were everywhere. Sheldon met her first bawd when a Mrs Horsham, a very respectable-looking woman, engaged her in polite conversation on a bench in St James's Park. She also became friendly with the fruit-seller who worked in the lobby of the House of Commons and took fees from MPs in return for girls' names and addresses. But then, as Robert Boyle Walsingham once complained to her, 'I suppose madam . . . you mean to engross the whole House of Commons, for here have been six of its members within this hour at your door.' In later years she turned bawd herself. (When a courtesan grew older, and if she had failed to find a faithful keeper – no easy task – she could either turn to procuring or threaten to write her memoirs – blackmailing her former clients – or, like Sheldon, she could do both.) She worked for Lord Grosvenor, 'who wishes to engage me in the number of those who furnish novelties for his seraglio', but was shocked by his taste for low life. She brought him poor girls from Westminster Bridge covered in vermin and was astonished at the medley of mistresses that filled his house: 'the garret was inhabited by pea-pickers, – the first floor by a woman of elegance, – the parlour by women servants – and the kitchen by a negro wench'.

Lord Halifax first set up his mistress, Miss Faulkner, by paying an intermediary to approach her. Sandwich also used an emissary to carry on an intrigue with a young girl, Laetitia Smith, whom he helped set up as a milliner's apprentice in the summer of 1779, less than three months after Ray's death. Another woman, 'Anna De Blessell', who managed a house in Hammersmith, 'the green door', acted as his procurer. She arranged for Sandwich to meet a sixteen-year-old girl – 'she was *then* a virgin' – in Green Park; Sandwich took the girl to the house in Berkeley Row.

In the histories and fictions of gallantry and seduction, bawds, procurers and the proprietors of brothels are always depicted as hard-nosed traders in the commerce of a commodity called sex. The bawd in *The Honest London Spy* bemoans the ageing of her girls:

> these *stale commodities* will never do: I see there is no carrying on of Trade without *fresh Goods* to please my customers: I know there's many of my customers hankering after M*aiden-heads,* and had I but such goods as those, I quickly should have Customers to take them off.

When Maria Brown is forced to work in a brothel she is told by her keeper that 'our prostitution is founded on base interest', and that 'every woman that is desirous of making her way into the world . . . should imitate the tradesman and have no other object in view but interest and gain'. Her keeper forces her to lift her skirts and examines her, for 'you know that a merchant cannot deal in a commodity without he is acquainted with its goodness'. Such women operate in a world of economic rationality; they seek to pass as respectable – the best bawds have a sober and genteel appearance – and they justify their business in the language of free trade: 'I'll have you do nothing, but what is honest . . . To steal, or take that which is none of your own from another body, that's dishonesty, and you must by no means do it: But . . . she that is single, and lies with another Man, can't be called Dishonest; for she disposes of nothing but what is her own.'

In the fallen woman's memoir, or in the prurient stories that told of female seduction in novels and magazines, the bawd and madame depend for their trade on female innocence but above all on the desires and skills of the libertine. For it is he who debauches young women, forcing them out of respectability and towards prostitution, and he whose jaded appetites demand constant satisfaction. In the annals of seduction the rake is an absolute monarch, whose will is law and cannot be resisted. Almost every tale involves a man whose powers of attraction are irresistible, figures like Lord Kingsborough in *The Genuine Memoirs of Miss Faulkner* who are 'completely versed in all the arts of seduction, intrigue and gallantry'. Kingsborough never forces himself on a woman but uses his manifold charms to seduce her, then abandons her after a single night. Such were his appetites that 'it was not uncommon with him, *in one night*, to debauch two or three of these deluded wretches'. And his country house is portrayed as a seraglio of fallen women – 'there were seldom less than fifty or sixty unfortunate girls contained in it'.

Sandwich's appetite apparently never quite reached the proportions attributed to Lord Kingsborough, but along with the prostitutes he paid for, he maintained a similar reputation as a rake of irresistible charm. As one of his admirers, seeking to resist him, wrote, 'Your assurance that you wish to render yourself agreeable to me flatters me but little, as I know your principles too well not to be convinced that your *Heart* has no share in your wishes.' But having shown she knows he is a libertine, the woman feels it necessary to placate Sandwich: 'excuse this appearance of severity you know the world too well, and our sex in particular not to be certain that you have it in your power to gain the affections of almost any woman that you study to please'.

There was little doubt that Sandwich was a rake and he never pretended otherwise. But his modern biographers, seeking to exonerate their subject, have tended to point out that, though no saint, he was little better or worse than many of his aristocratic contemporaries. Certainly, within the private circles of rakish men – many of whom were army and naval officers – who frequented the clubs, brothels and houses in Westminster and Covent Garden, he was no more notorious than the military hero the Marquis of Granby, who kept a stable of young girls for his delectation – 'the Marquis was not to be disappointed of a Virgin', or Field Marshal Ligonier, who kept four mistresses in his house and who, 'now he is near eighty gives it as his opinion, that no *woman* past fourteen is worth the trouble of pursuing'. Sandwich's conduct was no more egregious than that of Lord Masham, who offered Ann Sheldon an annuity provided she was prepared to engage in certain sexual acts, a proposal she declined because she believed sodomy to be unnatural. He was no more libidinous than Lord Harrington, 'lecherous as a monkey', a follower of 'the lowest amusements in the lowest brothels', or than Lord Grosvenor, whose preference for what was seen as the lowest of low life – lice-covered girls off the streets and women of colour – was regarded as distasteful even by his libertine friends. Any of these men could have been singled out to embody the depraved habits of a decadent ruling elite but none suffered such ignominy as Sandwich. Why, then, was he picked out as the embodiment of aristocratic sexual vice?

Sandwich was first stigmatized as a libertine in the early 1760s at about the time that he set up his menage with Martha Ray. Sandwich became notorious because he roused the anger and became the victim of the most brilliant political satirist of his day, John Wilkes. In 1763 Sandwich made a catastrophic error of judgment that gave him a short-term political advantage over Wilkes but only at a very high price.

The accession of a young new king in 1760 and the difficulties of adapting to peace after Britain's huge successes of the Seven Years' War inaugurated almost a decade of vicious political infighting and controversy. Sandwich, whose promising political career had been cut short in 1751 when he had been pushed out of office, was eager to re-establish himself as a government servant and to refurbish his dwindling family finances by getting back into power. In 1763 he got his wish, being appointed briefly to his old post at the Admiralty before becoming Secretary of State for the Northern Department in George Grenville's ministry.

The duties of this office brought him into direct conflict with the greatest thorn in the government's side, John Wilkes, brilliant adventurer, MP and journalist whose enormously popular weekly paper, *The North Briton*, had poured scorn on successive governments, poked fun at the young king and his Scottish favourite, Lord Bute, and castigated the terms of the peace that ended the Seven Years' War. Despite being political opponents, Wilkes and Sandwich knew one another, moved in the same rakish circles and may even have been friends. Wilkes, like Sandwich, wished to profit from the turbulent times, but as an opposition polemicist, not a servant of the crown. The government, for its part, was eager to have him silenced. Sandwich's predecessor, Lord Halifax, had had Wilkes arrested in the spring of 1763, using a 'general warrant', which did not specify the accused but permitted the arrest of anyone thought to be connected with the writing, printing and publishing of the 'Seditious and Treasonable Paper, intitled, The North Briton, Number 45'. Government officials arrested forty-seven people thought to be connected with the paper and took Wilkes off to the prison in the Tower of London. Employees of the Secretary of State then ransacked Wilkes's apartment in Great George Street, broke into his locked desk and carted off his papers in a large sack.

This heavy-handed attempt to silence Wilkes turned the tables against the government. Bold as always, Wilkes struck back, secured his release, counter-sued government officials and challenged the legality of general warrants. Instead of remaining under lock and key in the Tower Wilkes returned to his apartments in Great George Street, set up a printing press and ran off a collected edition of *The North Briton* and a dozen copies of his *Essay on Woman*, an obscene parody of Alexander Pope's *Essay on Man*. He then left for Paris to visit his daughter, to try to seduce her chaperone and console himself, as the French police reported, in the arms of 'Mlle L'Etoile' and 'Mlle Sainte-Foix'.

With the king's favourite, Lord Bute, driven from office and in self-inflicted exile, the parliamentary opposition gaining ground, and a new administration trying to find its feet, George III and his senior ministers planned a new attack on Wilkes during the summer and autumn of 1763. Sandwich, who had taken over the Northern Secretary of State's job after the death of Lord Egremont, directed operations. The government planned to get the House of Commons to condemn the *North Briton* as a seditious libel and then to eject Wilkes. They were in a hurry, eager to secure Wilkes's political condemnation before he appeared before a probably sympathetic London jury on charges of seditious libel. But they also had another stratagem, one that Sandwich, who was almost certainly its originator, pushed forward with exceptional zeal.

Sandwich had obtained a copy of *The Essay on Woman.* In this he was abetted by the Revd Kidgell, the disreputable chaplain of Sandwich's friend and fellow rake the notorious Earl of March, later Duke of Queensberry. The plan was to discredit Wilkes by exposing *The Essay on Woman* in the House of Lords. The plot depended on subterfuge: Kidgell secretly obtained a copy of *The Essay* from the foreman supervising the 'devils' manning Wilkes's printing press, and before the debate Sandwich spirited witnesses who might be called by the Lords out of London to prevent them leaking the plot.

Wilkes had foreknowledge of moves to expel him from the Commons, but he was taken totally unawares when Sandwich rose to read out the poem in the Lords on 15 November. The Secretary of State planned to use the fact that Wilkes attributed the notes in *The Essay on Woman* to William Warburton, Bishop of Gloucester, to justify raising the matter in the House. (Citing the bishop's name without permission was a breach of parliamentary privilege.) Sandwich began his speech with an apology: 'he had a paper in his hand abusing in the grossest manner, the Bishop of Gloucester. It was so infamous, so full of filthy language as well as the most horrid blasphemies that he was ashamed to read the whole to their lordships.' But it only took a moment for him to overcome his scruples and to recite the verse:

> Awake, my Fanny, leave all meaner things,
> This morn shall prove what rapture swiving brings.
> Let us (since life can little more supply
> Than just a few good Fucks, and then we die)
> Expatiate free o'er that lov'd scene of Man;
> A mighty Maze! For mighty Pricks to scan:

Lord Lyttelton apparently covered his ears, but the rest of the House cried out, 'Read on! Read on!' It took a little while for their lordships to condemn *The Essay on Woman* as blasphemous and to decide that using the name of Bishop Warburton was a breach of parliamentary privilege.

But Sandwich paid a high price for his brief victory. He had always insisted that private morality and public duty were two separate spheres, justifying his own free ways by insisting that 'they do not interfere with my conduct as a public man'. On these grounds he had every reason to attack Wilkes's political tactics of mixing personal and political grievances. Yet in using a work of pornography, never published but stolen from a private house, to smear Wilkes, Sandwich had used precisely those tactics that he and other government ministers had always condemned.

Wilkes was furious and quickly began spreading stories about Sandwich's own licentious and libertine ways. As Horace Walpole reported to Lord Hertford three days after the debate, 'Notwithstanding Lord Sandwich's masked battery, the tide runs violently for Wilkes . . . One hears nothing but stories of the latters impiety, and of the concert he was in with Wilkes on that subject.' The day before,

Walpole had written to Sir Horace Mann in Florence describing Wilkes's claim that he had never read *The Essay on Woman* publicly to anyone except Lord Sandwich and Lord le Despencer (formerly Sir Francis Dashwood and an ex-Chancellor of the Exchequer). Nor could he resist adding another piece of gossip: 'the wicked even affirm that very lately at a club with Mr Wilkes, held at the top of the playhouse in Drury Lane, Lord Sandwich talked so profanely that he drove two harlequins out of company'.

Writing again to Hertford in the following week, Walpole concluded 'The blasphemous book has fallen ten times heavier on Sandwich's own head than on Wilkes's; it has brought forth such a catalogue of anecdotes as is incredible'. Among these was the (false) rumour that Sandwich had been expelled from the Beefsteak Club for blasphemy. In the next few weeks, during a London run of John Gay's *The Beggar's Opera*, Sandwich acquired the nickname that stayed with him for the rest of his life – 'Jemmy Twitcher', the man who in the play betrays his companion in crime and hero of the piece, the highwayman Macheath.

There has been much speculation about Sandwich's motives in pursuing this attack on Wilkes. It is sometimes said that the Earl was angry at what he found when sifting through Wilkes's confiscated papers. Though he probably was not offended at the lewd parody entitled 'Instructions to Lord Sandwich', despite its description of the Earl's 'eternal dangler' as a 'little short rapier', and its hints at sodomy, he cannot have been happy to read the attack on his character in the unpublished copy of the *North Briton* No. 46. Describing the members of Grenville's new government, Wilkes had written:

> Of these men the most infamous in every respect was the earl of Sandwich. He had passed his youth in so abandoned and profligate a manner that when he arrived at the middle age of life, he did not, in the opinion of the world, remain in possession of the

smallest degree of virtue or honour. His conduct with respect to women was not only loose and barefaced, but perfidious, mean and tricking . . . With respect to men he had early lost every sentiment of honour and was grown exceedingly necessitous from the variety of his vices, as well as rapacious from the lust of gratifying them. Nature denied him wit, but gave him a species of buffoonery of the lowest kind, which was ridiculous in a man of fashion and fit only for the dregs of the people.

The attack was typical of Wilkes's writing. It was personal and exaggerated, but it embellished what was commonly known – that Sandwich was a libertine, was miserly (in the view of his friends), liked practical jokes and was physically clumsy – so that it both stung its victim and seemed plausible to its readers. It cannot have been welcome, but it is just as likely that Sandwich, who was famous for shrugging off hostile criticism, pursued Wilkes because he saw this as his obligation as a loyal and efficient servant of the crown.

Whatever his motives, Sandwich's action laid him open to the charges of hypocrisy and personal betrayal. According to Horace Walpole's *Memoirs* Sandwich read *The Essay on Woman* in the House of Lords 'with more hypocrisy than would have been tolerable even in a professed Methodist'. This hypocrisy was both individual and collective. Sandwich probably had already seen, even if he had not read *The Essay* and so had a good many others, including members of both houses of parliament. First written in 1754, it had been circulated within libertine circles and had even been read by the former prime minister, the elder Pitt. Such works were common fare, not often printed, but passed around by hand or read aloud at club dinners and parties. The twelve printed copies of *The Essay on Woman* were probably intended for the twelve members of Sir Francis Dashwood's Monks of St Francis at Medmenham, a libertine group whose members included both Sandwich and Wilkes. They met periodically at a house on the site of an old Cistercian monastery on the banks of the Thames not far from Dashwood's house at West Wycombe.

Because Sandwich and Wilkes moved in the same circles and belonged to the same clubs of rakes and libertines, it was easy for Wilkes to stigmatize the Earl both as a hypocrite and as a perfidious friend. It also palliated Wilkes's own vice: he may have been a rake, but he was certainly no dissembler (a feature often ascribed to government officials and courtiers), nor would he dream of betraying his companions in vice. The historian Edward Gibbon understood Wilkes well. 'I scarce ever met', he commented, 'with a better companion. He has inexhaustible spirits, infinite wit, and humour, and a great deal of knowledge.' But, he went on, 'he is a thorough profligate in principle as well as practice; his character is infamous, his life stained with every vice, and his conversation full of blasphemy and bawdy'. As if this was not enough, Gibbon concluded, 'these morals he glories in – for shame is a weakness he has long surmounted. He told us himself, that in this time of public dissension he was resolved to make his fortune.' Charming and opportunistic, Wilkes flaunted his vices, parading a succession of mistresses and lovers in public – including Marianne Genevieve Charpillon, the woman who so ruined Casanova's health that he claimed he never properly recovered, and Gertrude Maria Corradini, who, Wilkes wrote in his incomplete memoir, 'had the divine gift of lewdness'.

While parading his libertinism before the public, Wilkes continued to attack Sandwich's character. As Nathaniel William Wraxall, who knew both men, put it, 'At an early period of His Majesty's Reign, Wilkes and Churchill combined their Powers, in order to expose his [Sandwich's] Character to universal Condemnation.' In his *Letter to the Electors of Aylesbury*, Wilkes described Sandwich as 'the most abandoned Man of the Age', while Charles Churchill's

William Hogarth portrays the libertine Sir Francis Dashwood in monk's robes worshipping female flesh. The face looking down above his head is said to be of the Earl of Sandwich.

bestselling poem, *The Candidate*, contains line after line of vitriolic condemnation of the Earl he calls Lothario:

> LOTHARIO, holding Honour at no price,
> Folly to folly added, Vice to Vice,
> Wrought sin with greediness, and sought for shame
> With greater zeal than good men seek for fame.

It concludes:

> Search Earth, search Hell, the Devil cannot find
> An Agent, like LOTHARIO, to his mind.

Edward Thompson, another member of Churchill's circle, was equally scathing, harping repeatedly on Sandwich's false piety and perfidy:

> Come Jemmy Twitcher, whose adult'rate fame,
> Makes thee distinguish'd 'mong the sons of shame; . . .
> This is the man who first impeach'd his friend,
> And on his ruin rose, yet could not lend
> One cobweb virtue from his scurvy soul,
> Which sinned by study, and without control;
> This is that Jemmy Twitcher, whose pretence
> Is pure Religion, and state innocence:
> Yet mid'st these royal virtues, he defil'd
> The mother, and seduced her only child:

Tales of Sandwich's debauchery, miserliness and lack of good faith were endlessly repeated, inexorably corroding his reputation. One of the most notorious examples was a biography published in the late 1760s that depicted Sandwich as an arsonist and thief as well as a libertine with a predilection for drugging young women before raping them. Wraxall knew what Wilkes and Churchill were up to, but this did not prevent him being affected by the remorseless chipping away at the Earl's integrity. 'His licentious mode of life', he wrote, 'seemed more befitting a Minister of Charles the Second, than a confidential servant of George the Third.' Nor was Sandwich helped by his financial difficulties. 'His Fortune, which did not altogether correspond to his high rank, and habits of gratification or expence, was supposed to lay him open to seduction.' And as a result, 'His enemies, who were numerous and violent, maintained that even Official Appointments were sometimes conferred under conditions not honourable to the First Lord of the Admiralty.' Wraxall took these allegations to be 'improbable' and 'unproved', the results of 'party malevolence' but he also recognized that 'as Names and minute Particulars were added or invented, they obtained general credit, and made a deep impression'.

As they blackened Sandwich's character, so Wilkes and his friends teased the public with enticing snippets of information about the debaucheries that Sandwich and Wilkes had shared together at Medmenham. But the fullest revelations and most often repeated stories about the libertine fraternity and its members were made in the 1765 continuation of a novel first published in 1760 and written by Charles Johnstone, a Scottish lawyer and friend of Charles Churchill whose deafness had forced him to give up the bar and take up writing for a living. *Chrysal, or the adventures of a guinea* is told from the point of view of a coin that circulates from one pocket to the next, a device that enables the author to wander at will and depict a variety of fashionable scenes and scandals. Johnstone always claimed that his satire was general and did not single out particular persons, but it is not difficult to identify the members of the Order of St Francis and Sandwich himself in the graphic accounts of their blasphemous debauches.

The Medmenham depicted in *Chrysal* is a place of luxurious libertinism: 'The cellars were stocked with the choicest wines; the larders with the delicacies of every climate; and the *cells* were fitted up, for all the purposes of lasciviousness, for which proper objects were provided.' The chapel, where the monks enact their blasphemous rituals, is richly decorated, its ceiling 'covered with emblems and devices too gross to require explanation' and its walls 'painted with the pourtraits [sic] of those whose names and characters they assumed, represented in attitudes, and actions, horrible to imagination'. Kneeling before the altar, Sandwich and Wilkes are admitted to the fraternity, after reciting parodies of the Anglican creed: 'even the most Sacred rite and ceremony of Religion being profaned, all the prayers and hymns of praise appointed for the worship of the Deity [were] burlesqued by a perversion to the horrid occasion'. The evening ends in a general debauch of 'loose songs and gross lewdness'.

Chrysal also recounts what was to become perhaps the most famous story about Wilkes and Sandwich. During one of the satanic rituals Wilkes releases a concealed ape dressed as the devil that leaps on Sandwich's back while the Earl is trying to summon Lucifer. Frightened out of his wits, Sandwich implores the ape to release him: 'Spare me, gracious Devil! Spare a wretch, who never was sincerely your servant! . . . spare me . . . till I have served thee better. I am as yet but half a sinner.' Once again, Wilkes is made to show up the craven and hypocritical character of Sandwich. And once again Sandwich clothes himself in righteousness, arguing successfully for Wilkes's dismissal from the society: 'he exerted all his eloquence, two [sic] shew the enormity of the crime of attempting to turn any of the rites and ceremonies established by the laws of the society into ridicule'.

Johnstone's account, playing on the expectations of the reader, creates the lushest and most luxurious scenes of aristocratic libertinism, the most degraded expressions of blasphemy. It made the Order of Medmenham every bit as bad as it might have been imagined to be. And it reinforced the contrast between Wilkes, a humorous clever outsider, and Sandwich, a privileged, morally weak figure, outwitted by Wilkes yet able to enact a spiteful revenge. The power of the anecdote of the ape – and it has remained a key story about Wilkes and Sandwich ever since its first telling – lies in its humorous encapsulation of the Wilkite view of the relationship between the two men.

Sandwich's reputation as a libertine remained with him into old age. In 1789, when he was more than seventy, a young girl, called Mary Driscall, was hectored by her teacher, thrown out of her boarding school, and given a bad character merely for talking to him. His notoriety made him an object of sexual fantasy. His surviving correspondence contains letters written by women seeking assignations with him. These were written not by prostitutes and courtesans – though these also survive – but by women seeking pleasure rather than financial reward. The author of one anonymous letter describes herself as 'of good family and looked upon by the commonality of people as a fine woman'. She tells Sandwich that 'she has seen him and loves him' and 'begs an interview, when she flatters herself he can have no objection to her person'. She adds in a postscript that 'she is a person of character – and not one that wants to be in keeping'.

Fanny Denton from Bristol wrote a number of letters to Sandwich seeking (unsuccessfully it would seem) to entice from him his views on love and marriage and to confess her own wicked thoughts. In early 1773 she told Sandwich, 'I talk of love – *you* are a master in the soft theme – is love so charming oppression as the poets say, or are its torments greater than its joys? Can true love be found only in wedlock? Is it not a higher crime to marry with indifference than to be mistress to the man one loves?' After posing her questions Denton breathlessly pours out her own views: 'They call marriage a divine institution – I look upon it as entirely human, necessary only

Sandwich, towards the end of his life, accompanied by two young women, whose identities are not known, but have sometimes been thought to be Martha Ray and his later mistress, Nelly Gordon. It has also been suggested that they are the Abrams sisters, two well-known vocalists, but the ageing libertine is the centre of attention.

in a political sense. Notions are too free perhaps, but they are sheltered in happy obscurity, the world is unacquainted with them and I pass in it for a woman of virtue.' Yet she also betrays guilt: 'I have no claim to the sacred character. I have a polluted *mind* – though I must do myself the justice to say, I would not be *easily* seduced[.] the man must be clever he must have a soul – mere sensual pleasure could not satisfy me.' She ends by calling on Sandwich, 'the most gallant man of his country', for his advice and counsel.

Sandwich did not reply to Fanny Denton's request, but he kept her letter, along with those of other admirers. The survival of this archive, with its details of sexual conquest, fantasy, procurement, seduction and hard-hearted libertinage, is intriguing. Did Sandwich, the orderly bureaucrat as well as rake, routinely file away his correspondence? Or perhaps, having been labelled the greatest libertine of the age, he wanted to keep the evidence of his own exploits. A true libertine knows no shame. The charge that Wilkes and his followers repeatedly laid against Sandwich was that he was a hypocrite, that he surrounded himself with the odour of sanctity when at heart he was a rake. Perhaps saving his private correspondence for the eyes of posterity was an act of pride.

In recording Sandwich's part as a rake in a series of scandalous stories, parts of the correspondence read like a sentimental novel. The letters surrounding his seduction of Edith Williamson are a case in point. Sandwich met Edith one evening in 1759 in Ranelagh Gardens, the fashionable pleasure garden, where she had been taken, unknown to her mother, by a group of friends. He took her to the house that he used in Berkeley Row, Mrs Price's, and spent the night with her. Having taken his pleasure, on the following morning he treated Edith with indifference. Some time later she wrote to him explaining her youthful innocence: 'I don't excuse myself. I am fallen from virtue but to none but Your Lordship[.] you were the first and

I can safely swear the only one I ever had anything to say to . . . I was ignorant of the world and undoubtedly committed many indiscretions.' Yet what especially hurt her was Sandwich's cynical attitude towards her: 'Was I not given to know the very morning after I was ruined how indifferent I was to Your Lordship when but the night before you promised . . . constancy [and] said it should be my own fault if you ever left me, in what have I been to blame . . . what I feel upon Your Lordships account almost distracts me.'

By this time Edith's mother had learned of her fate and she wrote a terse letter to Sandwich asking him to leave her daughter alone. The tenor of Mrs Williamson's letter angered Sandwich, but he agreed to abide by her wishes and to compensate her for her loss. In response her tone of anger turned to one of apology and importunate thanks: 'My sorrows and ignorance of the great world may have lead me in the course of this affair to have said and done many things inconsistent with Your Lordship's dignity and high station in life', she conceded. But she then appealed to Sandwich as a father: 'the feeling of a distracted and tender mother plead my excuse which Your Lordship as a parent can be no stranger'. 'I hope', she added, 'you will never know the affliction and anxiety that attends a circumstance like mine . . . Such a sting must surely touch a heart like yours, and make it bleed at the reflection of a deed of that sort, when the fleeting momentary joy is past, passion subsides and reason resumes her seat.' Yet, though Sandwich had ruined her daughter, she felt obliged to return him her thanks: 'far be it from me to reproach Your Lordship; indeed I have no right to do it for if Your Lordships behaviour on this occasion has won me to you, banished all resentment from my breast and placed gratitude in it instead which as I have no visible way of showing, can be only in my prayers to heaven, for your felicity here and hereafter'.

The case did not end there. Much to the distress of her mother,

Edith made clear that she was determined to continue to see Sandwich. Yet here the interests of her parent and of Sandwich, who had no further use for her, coincided. All Edith could do was write a bitter, sarcastic letter to the Earl: 'As I find Your Lordships conduct has been all along so very justifiable to be sure I can have nothing to reproach you with and think you highly to be commended for behaving so strictly honourable when it is correspondent with your inclination.' 'I have promised my mother', she conceded, 'to make no further attempts to see Your Lordship so I shall be no more troublesome to you.' But her final words were defiant, 'you have made me completely miserable but that I dare say will not give Your Lordship the least concern'. Shortly after this, she ran away from home, unable to face the shame she had brought on her family.

Some years later Edith wrote twice to Sandwich asking for his help and patronage. On the first occasion she asked him for a place as an Admiralty housekeeper. She felt obliged to apologize for her past: 'Your Lordship likewise knows but too well my personal indiscretions but as they are past and have been and still are severely repented of I hope your goodness will not remember them to my prejudice.' On the second occasion she asked for help for her new husband, a mason, asking for a job for him in the Chatham naval dockyards. But she died shortly thereafter, leaving two young children in the care of her mother, who asked Sandwich to help place one of them in a charity school, so that the boy could become a productive member of society.

This story is full of the elements of sentimental fiction: a powerful, aristocratic rake bent on taking his pleasure, who also acts on a libertine code of honour; an innocent and gullible young woman, unable to resist, or even complicit in her seduction; a distraught mother who abjectly appeals for the return of her daughter; family misfortune; and, finally, the death of the woman who has lost her innocence. And like nearly all such tales, its context was one of great inequalities of power and wealth, modulated through disparities of age and gender.

Though the archives of many eighteenth-century aristocratic men probably contained sexually compromising material, it is difficult to imagine anyone else being the recipient of the kinds of anonymous letters and personal requests that Sandwich received. Such correspondence could only have been written by those who, as they repeatedly confirmed, did not know Sandwich personally but were familiar with his public reputation.

Ironically, the only comparable figure was probably John Wilkes. Despite their differences, they had much in common: public ambition and a commitment to male conviviality and to the pleasures of the flesh. Yet, though Wilkes was privately reviled and was sometimes attacked by government newspapers, on the whole he avoided public obloquy for his dissolute life. Sandwich, on the other hand, was repeatedly execrated for his. Wilkes's licentiousness was seen as a sort of liberty, while Sandwich's smacked of aristocratic privilege. Wilkes seemed generous and convivial while Sandwich appeared mean and heedless of the rules of male friendship.

As a result Sandwich's conduct became the chief, though not the sole example of misconduct for the growing number of publishers and critics who were mostly, though not exclusively associated with reformist and radical politics, and who tried to connect private depravity with political corruption. As we have seen, Sandwich always aimed to distinguish between his public and private personae, but ended up orchestrating an attack on Wilkes's private morality. Yet to do so was to invite obloquy. Wilkes realized that both the contemporary press and prevailing sensibility made it essential for public figures to fashion their own reputation; this, despite his efforts at newspaper management, Sandwich failed to do. Neither he nor his apologists tried to shape an alternative view of himself, a task that eventually was to fall on the shoulders of twentieth-century historians. Sandwich remained aloof, stoical in the face of personal attack, but he paid a large price for his hauteur. It was part of his sense that larger opinion did not matter in politics; but he forgot that the most successful politicians are often those who tell the best stories.

CHAPTER 5

Missing Stories:
Martha Ray and
the Life of the Mistress

LORD SANDWICH made no attempt to conceal his relationship with Martha Ray, any more than he did his activities with dozens of other women. Her portrait was hung in his Admiralty apartments and survives as naval property to this day. Martha Ray lived in the First Lord's apartments when Sandwich was in town, and presided at his table, in the company of naval officers, natural philosophers and musicians who regularly included Sir Richard Bickerton, Sir George Collyer, the poet Richard Owen Cambridge, the botanist Daniel Solander, Charles Burney, the author John Hawkesworth, and the musician Joah Bates. She often appeared with Sandwich in public, enjoying concerts or accompanying him on business. In June 1775, for instance, she took a trip down the Thames in an Admiralty yacht, *The Augusta*, with Sandwich, his secretary, Joah Bates, several naval officials, the botanist and explorer Sir Joseph Banks, and the Society Islander known as Omai, who had been brought back to Britain in 1774 in *The Adventure* by Cook's second in command, Captain Furneaux. Three months later she took another trip to visit Cook's recently arrived *Resolution*, back from its second South Pacific voyage.

In London it was not difficult for Ray to mingle openly with Sandwich's naval and musical friends. In Huntingdonshire Ray enjoyed the house parties at Hinchingbrooke, but she had to be much more circumspect in the presence of local gentry. Sandwich and Ray received several anonymous complaints. 'A friend to propriety' warned her not to send Sandwich's servants on errands 'in her own name'. 'It is very disagreeable', complained this high-minded correspondent, 'to be obliged to remind those who forget themselves that their real situation precludes them from all intercourse with reputable families.' Young girls, whose marriageability depended on a spotless reputation, could not afford to be seen in the company of a gentleman's mistress, even if he were one of the county's most powerful aristocrats. Local gentry were insulted by Ray's appearance in the stands at Huntingdon races: 'I make no doubt but a moment's reflection will suggest to you the reason which made Miss Ray's appearance in the stand at the races offend him – to some others it was a high insult and as they could have done it with propriety I must confess I am surprised that they did not show more resentment.'

Sandwich seems to have been sensitive to these sensibilities. Cradock recounts an incident during one of the Christmas series of oratorios at Hinchingbrooke, when Ray was approached by 'a lady of rank'. Sandwich asked a friend to intervene: 'As you are well acquainted with that lady, I wish you would give her a hint that there is a boundary line in my family, that I do not wish to see exceeded; such a trespass might occasion the overthrow of all our musical meetings.' Sandwich's concerns did not prevent one of his guests, the courtier Lord Denbigh, from satirizing his festivities:

> When Lords turn Musicians to gather athrong,
> And keep pretty Misses to sing them a song;
> When Nobles, and Bishops, and Squires are so silly,

> To attend at the levee of Miss Ray and Billy.
> When to shew most respect for the lord of the place is,
> By listening to fiddlers, and praising his mistress.

Sandwich and Ray struggled hard to work out the protocols of a more reputable disreputability – to reconcile private desire with the public face of the family – but the effort led to conflict between them.

The couple may have acted as if they were man and wife, but they were constantly confronted by other people's knowledge of their adulterous relationship. In the spring of 1776 Omai was being taught English by Granville Sharp, the philanthropist, scholar and ardent opponent of slavery. While discussing the Ten Commandments, the two men disagreed over polygamy. Omai remarked that 'two wives – very good; three wives – very, very good', but Sharp, who had got Omai to admit that he would kill any man who made advances to one of his wives, urged on him 'the first principle of the law of nature . . . that no man must do to another person any thing that he would not like to be done to himself'. After a long silence Omai took three pens from the inkstand on the table where they were sitting. 'There lies Lord S———' , he said as he laid one of the pens on the table. He took another pen 'and laid it close by the side of the former pen, saying, "and there lies Miss W———"', a woman whom Sharp described as 'an accomplished young woman in many respects, but, unhappily for herself, she lived in a state of adultery with that Nobleman'. Omai then took a third pen and 'placing it on the table at a considerable distance from the other two pens, as far as his right arm would extend, and at the same time leaving his head upon his right hand, supported by his elbow on the table, in a pensive posture, he said, "and there lie Lady S———, and cry!"' Sharp, whose politics and morals were directly opposed to those of Sandwich, was delighted: 'Thus it is plain that he [Omai] thoroughly understood the force of the argument from the law of liberty, respecting the gross injury done to the married lady by her husband in taking another woman to his bed.'

Ray was one of those commonly called a 'demi-rep'. Though such women had long been the companions of gentlemen and aristocrats, the term only came into general use in the middle of the eighteenth century. It referred to a woman who was more than a casual mistress but less than a respectable wife. Demi-reps often had murky or disreputable pasts, were not of the highest social rank, but lived with their aristocratic or genteel keepers as if they were wives. In the 1760s Edward Thompson published a series of extremely successful poems attacking those women who covered their base depravity (as he saw it) with the fig-leaf of uxorious respectability. 'Give me rhyme', he wrote, 'to lash each vicious step,/And check the conduct of the DEMI-REP!' Thompson castigated the deceit of such relationships, 'Where Matrimony veil's th' incestuous Life/And Whore is shelter'd in the name of Wife', and portrayed the women as wicked schemers who hid their vice:

> This Town's infested by a pack of Dames,
> Burnt with the hottest meretricious flames:
> Chaste as unfired coals they seem, but sin
> Has to a cinder burnt them up within

Thompson's poems – *The Meretriciad* which went through numerous editions, *The Demi-Rep*, *The Courtesan* and *The Court of Cupid* – surveyed the heights of low morality. His commentary was both general and highly specific: he named names. He satirized such famous figures as the beauty Kitty Fisher, the lover of Augustus Keppel, Lord Anson, General Ligonier and Lord Pembroke; Fanny Murray, to whom *The Essay on Woman* was dedicated and who numbered Sandwich among her conquests; the singer and actress Ann

Catley, the consort of Sir Francis Blake Delaval, noted for her lewd performances in the bedroom and on stage; and a host of other courtesans and mistresses. A strain of deep misogyny runs through Thompson's satires. Men are the dupes of their own desires:

> The Ladies pick our pockets, and our brains,
> And we, still blinded – rest their dying Swains

But women, despite or perhaps because of their appearance, are corrupt and corrupting.

> Rotten or sound – pray did you never buy
> A golden pippin, lovely to the eye?
> And when you'd enter'd once the tempting skin,
> Found it quite rotten to the core within?
> Its thus with women, and its thus with fruit,
> Hundreds I've known, and simile might suit.

These, of course, are familiar satirical themes, but they focus, as Thompson's detailed surveys, repeated in several of his poems, make clear, on a particular sort of woman – a person who successfully uses her sexual charms and social skills for personal advancement: someone who is poor and often plebeian but flaunts her wealth and appears aristocratic; someone ostensibly respectable but actually depraved; someone who is not what she appears to be. Some of these women were clearly courtesans rather than consorts or spouses, but it was the genuine demi-rep who was most feared because she was the most successful in crossing moral boundaries and confusing categories.

It might be said that Martha Ray's position was rather different from most of these demi-reps. She did not, as far as we know, have a succession of lovers, but throughout her life on the public stage remained the companion of one man. She was as much a common-law wife as a mistress, nine times pregnant, the manager of Sandwich's household. But it was difficult for her to escape being seen as a demi-rep, and the different stories of her relationship with James Hackman only reinforced this. And because almost all the stories about mistresses of the great and powerful involved tales of youthful indiscretion and seduction, periods of abjection and prostitution, it was hard to separate a figure like Ray from the young girls in the brothels in King's Place whose ambition was to find a rich keeper, or even from the poor women who sold themselves on the streets and worked in the bagnios. They were all viewed as fallen women and, by virtue of that fact, a threat to respectable society even when they were within it. The repeated emphasis on Martha Ray's respectability – in the press reports after her death and in Cradock's memoir published years later – was designed to distance her from the worst excesses of this morally tainted world.

By the 1770s the demi-rep had become a widely recognized figure in the press, the embodiment of a moral problem. In the spring of 1775 the *St James's Chronicle* published a long essay, signed ADOLE-SCENS, pointing to the dilemma that such women posed for young men. Man's greatest enemy, it began, was not man but 'the other Sex (whom with insinuating smiles allure us to our destruction)'. 'It will readily be conceived', remarked ADOLESCENS, 'that the modest Fair-one is more capable of depriving a Man of his Reason (that tutelary faculty bestowed by pitying Heaven to guide and direct us) than she who has lost her inestimable Virgin Treasure.' But this would be an error: 'amidst the Crowd of licentious Females, I have found one species her equal, if not her superior, in artfully administering the Circean Dose'. A woman of this sort has 'insinuating Manners and Address', she is a 'Siren' fatally attractive to young men: 'Her own sense has sufficiently secured her from all low and vulgar Prejudices, and without the disgusting boldness of a Prostitute, she has acquired the easy Freedom of the Courtesan, which gains upon the young and gay ten times more than the stupid bashfulness of some modest Women.' She seems to offer everything that a man would want:

> A Man rises from her Bed with that exultation of Spirits, from having possessed so sensible and fair a Creature, that he cannot persuade himself he has been doing wrong, and wasting his Vigour in a barren Field of Pleasure. See her Abroad, her Habit is Elegance itself, without being in the least tawdry – the perfect *simplex munditiis*; nor can the least mark of infamy be traced in any of her other features.

But her duplicity leads men into error. 'Surely', the writer concludes, 'the gratification of sensual appetite with an object ever so lovely, in any but a lawful manner, renders a Man the Slave instead of the Master of his Passions.' And, as a result, it 'makes him unfit for serious Avocations, overwhelms his Reason in a Torrent of Rage and Desire, and gives rise to a perpetual Series of Painful Reflections'.

The public became conscious of demi-reps as a result of a number of famous scandals, but the figure of mistress/wife was truly institutionalized in the pages of a periodical named the *Town and Country Magazine*, which first appeared in 1769.

The *Town and Country* was the most successful of a number of magazines that mixed gossip and scandal with short stories, essays and vignettes. In Goldsmith's *She Stoops to Conquer* (1773) Mrs Hardcastle, the rural gentlewoman eager to follow metropolitan fashion, relies on its gossip: 'I take care to know every tête-a-tête from the Scandalous Magazine.' The frontispiece of 1781 captures the magazine's flavour: 'A LADY on the *Haut Ton*, enraged at her Intrigues being revealed, upbraids MERCURY AND MOMUS for exposing them to the World, who, smiling, and pointing to the TOWN and COUNTRY MAGAZINE, intimate that such Characters are fit Subjects for SATYR, who in the Back-Ground archly beholds the Interview.'

As the rival of the *Lady's Magazine* and the *Sentimental Magazine*, the *Town and Country* was best known for its monthly têtes-a-têtes which the editors proudly proclaimed 'have so peculiarly distinguished this Magazine from all others'. An engraving of two facing silhouettes, one male, the other female, led each story, in which a fashionable intrigue or affair was exposed to the public, ostensibly as a 'Mirror to Vice and Folly, that they [the lovers] might view their own scandalous or ridiculous actions through a just Medium'. Some of the pairings are of adulterous aristocratic couples like Lady Sarah Lennox and Lord William Gordon, but more often they are those of a rich, aristocratic and often old man and a young, beautiful and often poor woman. Thus Commodore John Byron was linked with 'Betsy', one of his servants; Colonel Barré, a celebrated MP, was paired with a poor Scottish girl he had rescued from suicide; several aristocrats were linked to the daughters of impoverished clergy, while the Marquis of Granby was connected to the daughter of a Windsor shopkeeper whom he had first met as a schoolboy at Eton. Other female partners included several milliners, actresses like Mrs Abingdon and opera singers like Gabrielli, a smattering of high-class courtesans, often from high-class brothels such as Charlotte Hayes's establishment in King's Place, and a number of fallen women, like Miss C, the mistress of the lawyer Alexander Wedderburn, who had been 'drugged and seduced by a peer'.

The early issues of the magazine included tête-a-têtes of some of the most important politicians and their mistresses, including John Calcraft and George Ann Bellamy, the Duke of Grafton and Nancy Parsons, and Lord Halifax and Mary Anne Faulkner. Not surprisingly, Martha Ray and Sandwich were among the first couples to be featured.

Most têtes-a-têtes told the story of how an affair began, usually by regaling the reader with the lovers' earlier indiscretions. The 1769

The typically rather crude engraving of Ray and Sandwich produced as a tête-a-tête in the *Town and Country Magazine* in 1769.

feature on Sandwich and Ray was no exception. Sandwich's libertine past was revealed in an allusion to his affairs with Fanny Murray, one of the most famous courtesans of her generation, the dedicatee of Wilkes's *Essay on Woman*, and with Lucy Cowper, known for 'her wit and sprightliness'. But Sandwich features as a minor character in the piece, for it is principally devoted to the story of how the lovely Martha Ray became the consort of one of the nation's most notorious politicians and libertines. The tale is a seduction narrative (a warning to young women) in which Ray is portrayed as a callow girl made vulnerable by novel-reading and romance, who is basely seduced by a libertine with a penchant for virgin flesh. According to this story,

Sandwich is not Ray's seducer but the person who rescues her fortunes after she loses her honour.

The *Town and Country*'s version of Ray's family history is a tale of shabby gentility. We first meet her at a boarding-school in Chelsea, one of the female academies that their critics claimed encouraged fanciful ideas and increased female vulnerability to seduction. Her education is interrupted when her father dies and she is forced to work with her mother as a mantua-maker. Accepting her misfortune, 'She calmly submitted to this stroke of fate, and chearfully went through even the drudgery of the profession.' But all her leisure hours were taken with novel-reading, which 'gave her a romantic turn; and she could not help feeling a secret desire of imitating the bold heroines who braved fortune, and every danger incident to the sex, in yielding to the amorous passion'. Predisposed to love, 'a loose idea had never entered her mind', until she is pursued by Sir Thomas F——k, a rake and 'devotee of Venus'. Her 'decency and reserve' in response to his advances only increases his determination to seduce her: 'A girl of more experience than our heroine, might have been imposed upon by such an experienced suitor, skilled in all the artifice of intrigue, all the wiles of seduction, all the deception of his sex.' Wooed at the playhouse, where Sir Thomas declares his love for her during a performance of *Romeo and Juliet*, and encouraged by her friend Miss Peggy Silver, who has been recruited in his cause by Sir Thomas, Ray is beguiled by the prospect of an advantageous marriage and lured into taking a day trip to the Star and Garter in Richmond, where she is plied with spiked champagne. Drugged into slumber, she is raped by Sir Thomas. 'When Miss Ray awoke and found herself dishonoured, she raved, she cried, she swooned! A heart of adamant would have felt at such distress – her cruel ravisher still more obdurate, coolly and insensibly left her to the care of the waiters.' Deprived of her virtue, Ray briefly becomes Sir Thomas's mistress, until he discards her for a new conquest. As the verses in the *Town and Country* story put it,

> Till at last a cruel spoiler came
> Cropt this fair rose, and rifled all its sweetness,
> Then cast it like a loathsome weed away.

Desperately Ray casts about to mend her fortunes. The *Town and Country* sententiously reminded its readers, 'A female who has once quitted the path of virtue knows no bounds to licentiousness, especially when prompted by necessity.' Soon Ray is working with Mrs Harding, a well-known bawd and procuress who, it is claimed, introduces her to Sandwich. The story ends in Ray's triumph. Such are her talents that she is able to monopolize Sandwich's affections, occupying a 'sumptuous' house in Westminster. Her boarding-school education and mellifluous voice enchant Sandwich: 'She often sings and plays to him; and she has frequent concerts at her house for his entertainment, to give her still greater opportunities of displaying her talents, and thereby increasing his satisfaction.' 'In a word', the article concluded, 'he has made her a handsome settlement, and she so completely engrosses his affections, and concentrates all his desires, that there are great hopes that she will be able to soften some of his most disagreeable *features in the portrait* of her lover.'

Like many of the short fictions and têtes-a-têtes in the *Town and Country*, Martha Ray's story mixes moral admonition with a prurient enthusiasm for its protagonist. What begins as a warning to young girls about the dangers of novel-reading and the irresistibility of an experienced male libertine, ends as a celebration of the musical, social and sexual skills that bring Ray status and fortune. The reader is asked to avoid the dangers that lead to Ray's downfall but is shown how her seduction leads to her success. Ray's experience shows that a young woman's use of her charms can bring the benefits of fortune and social advancement. The glittering prizes of an immoral life are viewed with a mixture of fascination and repugnance. In certain respects, then, this is a happy tale. Ray is not immoral but merely romantic and misguided. (Nearly all seduction stories in which women lose their virginity because of drugs, potions or spiked drinks take a relatively benign view of the victim, because their insensibility meant that they could not consent to their ruin.) In the end, she makes the best of a bad job. To succeed as a demi-rep is, after all, the very best that a fallen woman can hope for.

A second account of Sandwich and Martha Ray's relationship, which appeared in the *Town and Country* after Ray's death and was no doubt published to cash in on the notoriety of her murder, is significantly different from the story told in 1769. Gone is the earlier tale of her seduction by Sir Thomas F——k. She is no longer a fallen woman looking for a protector, but is seduced by women friends into selling her virtue for a good life. In this new version of the story, Ray, apprenticed as a mantua-maker (on this all accounts seem to agree), is introduced by her indolent and feckless father, a stay-maker, to a group of wicked women, Signora Frasi, Signora Galli, Mrs Courage and Mrs Pope: 'Every one of these ladies had at times afforded gratification to lord S——'s desires, as well in an amorous as in a harmonious manner; and some of them had borne him children, particularly Signora Fr-si.' All these former lovers of the Earl, it is claimed, are now acting as bawds, looking out for young women to satisfy him: 'It was a rule with his lordship, in the progress of his amours, as an adept in intrigue, to convert his cast-off mistresses into procuresses; and each of the ladies of this *groupe*, now figured in that predicament.' They chide Martha Ray for working as 'a drudge' and hold out the prospect of a life 'in a far more brilliant sphere'. At this stage Martha is eighteen, 'her person was uncommonly graceful, her physiognomy engaging, and her voice peculiarly harmonious'.

Sandwich falls for her precipitously, offering a settlement of £300 a year for her favours. Thanks to the blandishments of his former lovers, Ray is soon installed as his mistress. In this version both Ray and Sandwich are culpable: Ray, because she allows herself to be seduced by the prospect of power and riches, Sandwich because he does not rescue Ray after her fall but is responsible for her loss of virtue.

A similar story was published in a salacious survey of London's brothels and courtesans entitled *Nocturnal Revels; or, the History of King's-Place, and other modern nunneries . . . by a monk of the order of St Francis*, which appeared in the same year as Ray's murder. The author, as Caterina Galli complained bitterly to the Earl of Sandwich, set out to blacken the Italian woman's character and blame her for Ray's death. *Nocturnal Revels* describes Galli as 'a tall, genteel woman, with fine black eyes, jetty locks, regular white teeth and a complexion varied *selon la mode du jour*'. Less charitably she is called 'a woman of intrigue since puberty, and has had as numerous a succession of lovers as any salacious female in Europe'. She is first blamed for betraying Ray's intrigue with Hackman to Sandwich, because of her own designs on the young man. 'Signora G. had herself entertained a *penchant* for Mr HACKMAN', but when she was ignored 'her rage and resentment broke forth, and, in an ebullition of choler and revenge, she revealed all the secrets she had been entrusted with to Lord S——'. Not content with betraying his mistress, she intercepts and returns to Hackman a letter intended for Ray, which leads Hackman to believe that Ray has rejected him. His agony drives him to his bloody deed.

The accounts of Martha Ray's life after her murder are, of course, coloured by her terrible death. The happy story of 1769 becomes a tragedy in which a woman who decides on an immoral life because of its rewards, dies because of her companions in vice. She is not drugged and debauched by a male libertine, only to triumph in her misfortune, but chooses to enter a depraved world of immoral women, one of whom perfidiously leads her to her destruction. In the first tale she is an unwitting victim who recovers from early misfortune; in the later accounts she moves inexorably towards the fate of a woman of loose virtue. This latter version of the story sits well with Manasseh Dawes's account in the final editions of the *Case and Memoirs of James Hackman*.

Magazines like the *Town and Country*, pamphlets, newspapers, novels, stories and trial reports were all preoccupied with a sexual economy that, despite its blatant bias in favour of men and wealth, gave women a wide range of powers. An essay that first appeared in the *Hiberian Magazine* in April 1779, and which was reprinted a year later, put Martha Ray's career in the context of this trade in money and desire:

> Illicit love now reigns triumphant, pervading all degrees, from the peer, (we had almost said prince), to the peasant: obedient to its impulse, or the stronger dictates of interest, the fair ones of the present age submit their mercenary charms; and the men equally distinguished for dissipation and inconstancy, relinquish the happiness of a virtuous union, to violate the marriage bed; – engage in the laudable pursuits of seduction; – or revel in the arms of incontinent beauty.

The author of this version of Ray's life, Christopher Jackson, lacked details of Ray's life but did not think this an obstacle to writing her biography: 'If probable conjecture can be admitted to supply the deficiency of authentic information, it may certainly be made use of in writing the memoirs of a modern courtesan.'

The lives of such women, Jackson maintained, 'are generally uniform, however as individuals, they may differ in point of situation or personal attractions: pleasure and interest are the ultimate objects

of their views, and their occupations'. Women who lose their virtue
– 'their sex's noblest boast, and brightest ornament' – fall into two
types, the sentimental victim and the shrewd schemer. The first
'possess that degree of sentiment, sensibility, and delicacy of thinking,
which, without a portion of prudence sufficient to direct them in
their intercourse with the world, often proves subversive of the virtue,
and destructive of the happiness of their owner'. Such women, 'though
they are the most amiable, are too the most amiably weak principles
of our nature'. Like Ray in the 1769 *Town and Country* version of her
ruin, they fall prey to 'men, skilled in the arts of seduction, who,
Proteus like, can assume the semblance of vice, or virtue, at will;
find a peculiar facility in making these qualities the ready instruments
to effect the ruin of their possessor'. We should sympathize with the
fate of such amiable victims, says Jackson: 'virtue mourns, and sympathy pays the tribute of a tear, to the lamentable fate of sensibility
and beauty'. This is the often-repeated sentimental narrative of the
fallen woman.

But there is another sort of courtesan, less sympathetic, more
shrewd, more in command of her fate. In the second rank, according
to Jackson, 'may be classed those, who, perhaps, an equal share of
beauty, have hearts which are less susceptible of tender impressions:
such form an early and a just estimate of the world; as well as of
their own qualities and endowments; acquire the art of displaying
these to advantage, by attention to, and a dextrous management of
the passions, and foibles of their admirers'. Here Jackson draws on
an enduring fear, repeatedly expressed in accounts of every type of
fallen woman – demi-reps, mistresses, courtesans and prostitutes –
that male seduction, though responsible for a woman's loss of virtue,
also gives her a power and independence that enables her to exploit
men for her own ends. Freed from the obligation to conserve their
chastity, such women, neither dutiful daughters nor chaste wives, are

femmes seules, free to pursue their desires, and therefore objects of anxiety as well as fascination.

The Midnight Spy, a moralizing but prurient pamphlet published in 1766, which took its readers on a tour of London brothels and houses of ill repute, repeatedly pointed to the dangers of women who render men helpless. Thus Peggy, a tavern whore, 'can mould a man to her mind as the potter does clay, perhaps she's as fine a sized woman as the town affords, and then for a skin, eyes, and shape, she's the paragon of her sex'. In a bagnio in Covent Garden, a young girl specializes in old and impotent clients: 'That little ogling hussy is versed in all the arts of her trade, and has cunning enough to fleece the greatest miser in Christendom. As she is young and handsome, she is the flame of those dotards, whose desires outlive their ability, and who always pay for what they cannot do.' A successful whore traps a wealthy gentleman 'who stood in need of high provocatives to stimulate his depraved appetite', just as the famous courtesan Kitty Fisher gets an old noble lord to pay 'twice for what he could not do'. The aim was to control an older man 'more flexible to the Commands of a mistress than a young and vigorous lover'.

If ordinary prostitutes and courtesans were skilled manipulators, the women who were at the top of the trade, demi-reps kept by aristocratic libertines, were doubly so. Success could only be achieved by those who were hard-heartedly devoted to their own advancement, who saw their amours as a business. When the actress and singer Ann Catley was in Ireland, 'her amours offered no variety of incident; she received her lovers with ease; if they did not rise to her price she dismissed them with apathy and that price was always proportioned to the idea Nan formed of their fortune'. Edward Thompson ironically professed to admire Miss Clem-ns, 'who by her motions in the wriggling trade,/Two sterling thousands, fairly, cleanly made'. 'Of all the Nymphs that *Venus* bred', he wrote,

> None ever had the cunning, and the art,
> To thumb the guineas, and to steal the heart.
> She hums the *vet'ren*, for the youths regards,
> And plays in turns on him the harlot's cards;
> This is her maxim, – and as good, as true,
> Some men for profit, some for pleasure too.

It was a cliché that, just as prostitutes liked old, rich clients, so a woman seeking a keeper wanted to set up house with an older, wealthy man who could fund her extravagance, even while she took younger, lustier lovers to satisfy those sexual appetites that had been released with her original seduction.

In 1784 George Kearsley, the publisher and scourge of governments, singled out the actress, poet and lover of the Prince of Wales, Mary 'Perdita' Robinson, as the embodiment of the manipulative demi-rep: 'she is the Flora of the present day, and in her mercenary arms the infatuated youths of Libertusia [Britain] consume their vigour and their fortunes'. 'The manners of every woman of pleasure', the author concludes, 'are almost invariably the same. Gold is the only god they worship, and every softer feeling is absorbed in the pursuit of gain. The character [of Perdita] . . . at one glance exhibits to view the whole mercenary tribe in miniature. She is not more superior to them in personal accomplishments, than in duplicity, fraud and avarice.'

Once a woman had been seduced, she could never be trusted, even when treated with magnanimity. *The Midnight Spy* was emphatic on this point. 'If a man raises her [a fallen woman] from the ebb of poverty, to which her infamy has sunk her, and makes her the companion of his bed and board, notwithstanding her repeated protestations of fidelity,' the author stresses, 'you find her led by the ingratitude of her heart, when fixed in affluence, to forget her solemn promises, follow the directions of her loose desires, and daily abuse the generosity of her benefactor.' For the author of *The Midnight Spy* keeping a mistress is not an act of desire but an act of charity, one that will eventually make the man not the woman the victim. 'This life of a woman of this stamp', he concludes, 'is an eternal round of deception.'

Like an evanescent comet, the brilliant Mary Robinson shone brightly in the galaxy of London beauties but was soon plunged into obscurity. She was not much older than Martha Ray when she died after years of sickness and poverty. As the courtesan Ann Sheldon, the mistress of Sandwich's friend and confidant Robert Boyle Walsingham, pointed out, 'I know it well, that when women are brought by the seduction of men, to practice those arts from necessity, which they are accused of favouring from choice; when they have been taught by the arts of men, to look upon them as prey, they refine upon duplicity, it is their daily bread, and men become as they deserve, the dupes of those very *Delilah's* which they themselves created.' For Ann Sheldon, Jackson was wrong: there were not two different sorts of courtesan but only one. Her own experience taught her, she said, that a modern courtesan might begin her career as a passive victim but she would end it as a calculating, immoral actor. The seduction of a young girl and the decline and death of a fallen woman made for a sentimental narrative in which she could be portrayed as a victim, but the middle passage marked a time when a woman had power over men.

The palpable contradictions of Jackson's position, its obvious double standard, should not conceal its pervasiveness. Hugh Kelly's *Memoirs of a Magdalen; or the History of Louisa Mildmay*, first published in 1767 but reissued in 1782, tells the story of an ideal young couple, Sir Robert Harold, a 'sentimental rake', and the ravishingly beautiful Louisa Mildmay, who are betrothed to be married. In one highly eroticized scene the blissful relationship suddenly goes awry. Only days before their wedding is due to be celebrated, Louisa shows off a new set of night-clothes to her fiancé. As he writes to a friend:

> She . . . came down so irresistibly ravishing, that I was no longer my own master. Imagine to yourself . . . a woman, such as I have repeatedly described Miss Mildmay, dressed in a flowing robe of white satin, with her fine black hair hanging carelessly down her neck, and every thing in the most voluptuous disorder . . . For my part I am only flesh and blood; I snatched her to my bosom with a frenzy of the most passionate admiration, and almost stifled her with kisses. The extatick tenderness with which she received my embrace entirely destroyed my recollection; and a cursed sopha lying most conveniently ready to assist the purpose of my rashness, I proceeded from liberty to liberty till she was actually undone!

This account reads as if Louisa seduced Sir Robert, who ceased to have any control, to be 'his own master'. As a result he takes the view that Louisa's conduct disqualifies her as a wife. The passionate lover of the previous night becomes the sententious prig of the morning after. 'It is with me a fixed principle', he writes to a friend the next day, 'that the same woman who suffers even the man she doats upon to distraction to take advantage of an unguarded moment, will have her unguarded moments with other people.' Thus, he concludes, 'the same warmth of constitution which originally betrayed her into an indiscretion with him, is but too likely to make her guilty of indiscretions with every body else'. Note, not somebody else, but *everybody else*: by making love to her fiancé, Louisa has shown, at least in his eyes, that she is a whore.

Kelly's story, as it turns out, has a happy ending. After leaving home in abjection, and after resisting the sexual assaults of another admirer who seeks to abduct her (she fortifies herself by reading Richardson's *Clarissa*), Louisa eventually marries Sir Robert. Kelly's novel exposes the double standard and pleads for sympathy for female indiscretion, but the night of love and morning of disgust of Louisa's betrothed, which forms the hinge of the plot, depends on the power of a convention that meant that once seduced a woman could never be trusted. So, even as Sandwich's friends and the press claimed that they were sure of Ray's fidelity to the Earl, there was always a suspicion that she had acted in character by betraying him for a younger man.

This was certainly Jackson's view. In his eyes Ray was as manipulative and charming as Sempronia, the highly educated, politically manipulative, astonishingly vivacious wife of the soldier Scipio Aemilianus, whom she was suspected of murdering. 'The character left us by Sallust of the beautiful, the gay, and accomplished Sempronia,' he comments, 'was peculiarly applicable to Miss Ray. She was beautiful, excelled in music, singing, and dancing, with language at her command, she could suit it to any occasion; was modest, alluring, and wanton in it, by turns; and to sum up all, she had the readiest conception, and a fund of vivacity never to be exhausted.' Like other demi-reps, Ray seduced the likes of Sandwich for the money but gave her real affections to the handsome young Hackman: 'motives of mere interest induced Miss Ray to engage in amours with several, who, in rank and fortune, were superior to Mr Hackman, that he, only should boast of the united possession of her heart and person'.

Jackson was convinced that, like Sempronia, Ray used her power over her consort for political ends: 'The influence of Miss Ray over her noble keeper', he asserted, 'was extreme; and it is said that many who now possess lucrative and honourable posts, in the ecclesiastical, civil, and military departments, are indebted to her mediation for their advancement.' He even believed that Ray was privy to secrets of state.

Almost every demi-rep involved with a leading political figure in the 1760s and 1770s was accused either of encouraging corruption because their extravagance placed their lover in financial difficulties, or of using their position to take bribes and peddle influence. Writing about George Ann Bellamy and John Calcraft, the *Town and Country* remarked, 'This nation has long had just reason to complain of the state-vultures that prey upon its vitals: pensions and sinecures have been lavished upon the mistresses of men in power and their favourites.' Army agents like Calcraft had 'amassed immense riches, squeezed out of the pittance of the poor soldiers and the still poorer half-pay officers'. Nancy Parsons was accused of speculating in stocks she had bought with bribes from place-seekers soliciting her influence with the Duke of Grafton. And Mary Anne Faulkner when in Ireland with Lord Halifax, set herself up, it was said, as a broker of offices and places: 'There was no office, no employment in any one department to be disposed of, but through her means and procurement; and on these she fixed her own price. Enormous sums were raised through this channel of negotiation, and where money was not to be had, bonds, annuities, and dividends of the profit and income of each employ were daily executed and secured.' The lesson, according to the author of Miss Faulkner's memoirs, was that 'it is impossible for *ladies*, who have any hand in the administration of national affairs, to preserve their integrity; that is, they are more liable to what is vulgarly called bribery and corruption, in the selling and procuring of places, employments &c than men; or at least that they do it, *with a much better grace*'. Their cupidity and extravagance fuelled their corruption.

So Christopher Jackson's account of Ray's life paralleled those of other demi-reps who were depicted as corrupt and scheming. To portray Ray in this way after her murder was unusual, but during her lifetime many commentators thought of her as a shrewd woman taking advantage of the lovelorn Earl. This version of Martha Ray's life is not a sentimental narrative about the vulnerability and impeccable character of a female victim but the story of a demi-rep on the make.

A number of Sandwich's enemies claimed that he was totally in thrall to his mistress, dispensing patronage and cash at her behest. The most vicious attack on Ray before her death, a mock opera written by the mad dramatist Israel Pottinger and entitled *The Duenna*, published (though never performed) in 1776, portrayed her as a manipulative harridan and Sandwich as an impotent, besotted old rake. She speaks of him as 'sneaking, pimping, incapable', an 'old goat' and 'the pandar of your own vices'. Extorting money and jewels from him, she forces him into embezzlement and bribery. After giving her a bill for a hundred guineas, he comments, 'I must now to business; and try how to raise a sum, by advancing some worthless scoundrel over the head of a hundred men of merit.' Private vice is the source of public corruption.

In 1773, the *London Evening Post* published a letter claiming that an agent of Sandwich's, Henry Cort, was soliciting buyers for a place as a Commissioner of the Navy for a fee of £2,000. This offer was traced back to a Mrs Brooke, who, it was claimed, was 'an acquaintance of, and very intimate with Mrs Margaret Ray'. Sandwich took the printer of the paper, John Miller, to court, bringing the ancient and largely obsolete charge of *scandalum magnatum* against him. The evidence of Sandwich's wrong-doing was flimsy and suppositious, and the court awarded him the substantial sum of £2,000 in damages. But the favourable verdict did not dispel continuing rumours that Ray's support was one means of gaining naval promotion. In 1777 Sandwich received an anonymous letter telling him that a broker by the name of Archer was claiming to sell naval commissions through the offices of Martha Ray; and there is at least one surviving letter that shows that its author thought a bribe of £400 to Sandwich's mistress would help secure a naval promotion. According to Horace

Walpole, the Duke of Richmond, in a House of Lords debate in March 1778, 'reflected on Miss Ray, Lord Sandwich's mistress, who was supposed to sell favours in the Admiralty for money'.

Ray was also accused of other sorts of influence. George Forster, who had served with his father as a naturalist during Captain James Cook's second voyage to the Pacific (1772–1775), believed that Ray's hostility explained why his father was forbidden from publishing the official (and highly lucrative) account of the voyage. Complaining bitterly of Sandwich's 'unjust' conduct, he attributed it to Ray's petulance at not being given one of the tropical birds brought back from the Pacific on *The Resolution*: 'You were accompanied by a lady, who having seen our live birds, which we had destined for the Queen, manifested an unbounded affection towards the pretty creatures, and a violent longing to be made mistress of them. The keeper had no orders to part with them, and therefore the lady after repeatedly signifying to him that she wished to have them, went away highly dissatisfied.' 'Our misfortunes', said Forster, 'owed their origin to the lady just mentioned, as she might have found a great pleasure in revenging herself upon those who were very innocently the cause of her disappointment.'

Even after Ray's death rumours of her corrupt influence, though much rarer, did not go away. An anonymous female correspondent wrote threateningly to Sandwich: 'as to the money Miss W. [i.e. Ray] died possessed of, the publick only guess how it was got, but I will inform them particularly – that it was at the ruin of many a brave man, who had every rascal put over his head, who could muster a purse worth your favourites acceptance of which you had your share'.

Recent historians of British naval history have been at pains to exonerate Sandwich and Ray from corruption and to show that the First Lord was, by the standards of his day, an able and honest administrator. But it was widely believed, not least by Sandwich himself, that even as he grew older, he remained extremely susceptible to female charms. 'You will think me made of very combustible matter', he wrote to an admiral, 'if I own to you that even at my time of life I am capable of receiving very strong impressions from a few hours acquaintance with a very agreeable woman . . . but . . . I must own that after 55 a man in love is a ridiculous being.' Sandwich's libido may not have inhibited his attention to his duties, but in the eyes of hostile observers it did blur the line between his public responsibilities and his private libertinism.

Critics asserted that the probity of public offices was compromised by the presence of Sandwich and Ray's disreputable friends. The appointment in the 1770s of Ray's companion, Miss Berkeley, as a housekeeper in the Navy Office, outraged one of Sandwich's anonymous correspondents. After describing her as sexually promiscuous, the writer added, 'You cannot want to be informed how she came into your family; where at present she maintains a firm footing by being a most useful pander to your mistress who in return renders her mutual service and thus by their joint labours, with a little assistance from Steve-n a favourite servant or two, the Admiralty and Hinchingbrooke are converted into brothels.' This could only happen, the letter went on, because 'We all know with what an iron rod she [Martha Ray] rules you; and when you happen to offend her by plucking up too much spirit, we all see how glad you are to make it up by asking her pardon, and if it should be necessary, dropping a tear'. The letter concluded with a bold moral exhortation:

> For shame, for shame my Lord! Cast off this ignominious yolk, and be a man; let not the follies of your old age exceed those of your youth; a dupe in grey hairs is a most contemptible character indeed. Do not flatter yourself that these things are concealed from the world, or that our most gracious sovereign will suffer the admiralty of England to be governed by two common prostitutes.

Within a year of Ray's death Sandwich's new mistress, Nelly Gordon, was also accused of claiming unlimited influence over him. One correspondent complained that he had had to listen to Miss Gordon's sister regale passengers on a stage coach 'with dialogue of what past between Lord Sandwich and her sister'. The letter ends, 'a very pretty thing for a man but should have his countries welfare at heart toying with a wench that is not worthy to be picked off the dung hill and entertain the passengers with telling that Your Lordship told her sister that she soon would be in as much power as the late unfortunate ——'.

At the heart of these accusations lay the commonly held view that the relationship between an aristocrat and his mistress was an exchange of money for sexual favours. A mistress or demi-rep, even more than a wife, had to appear as an object of conspicuous consumption. 'Behold her dress, her table and her house!' wrote Edward Thompson. 'Nothing can be more grand, more rich, profuse.' Her appearance told spectators about both her success and the prowess of her lover. Neither a mistress nor her keeper wanted her to appear in anything less than the finest clothes; failure to do so signalled a failure of the relationship and then, ultimately, of a woman's power to attract and seduce men.

Many relationships began with an act of financial extravagance that showed a man's willingness and ability to keep a lover. Sophia Baddeley, the singer and beauty who was the subject of endless gossip in the 1770s, began her relationship with Lord Ancaster when he met her in a shop and bought her a single pineapple for a guinea. Sir Peter Lester won Ann Sheldon's favours with 'fine buckles, and beautiful china . . . Wine, also, was poured in upon me.' Totting up her spoils, Sheldon reckoned 'I received from his generous attachment, upwards of an hundred pounds during the first week of my acquaintance with the enamoured little knight'. To her delight, he also liked to show her off in public: 'His carriage . . . was at my service, and, with no small satisfaction, did I enter it, for the first time, to present my figure in its new and exalted state to the gazers of *Hyde Park*.'

Ray's position was somewhat different from figures like Baddeley and Sheldon, who had a succession of keepers and lovers. But like them she was concerned with the status and rewards of her position as well as with its security. She enjoyed the pleasures and perks of her situation, spending £270 on a shopping spree in Brussels in the summer of 1775 and running up large debts. Her extravagance did not sit well with Sandwich's financial difficulties and his penny-pinching ways. In 1765 one of his friends, the diplomat Sir William Gordon, twitted him about his meanness: 'Hug, embrace and caress Dear Patty [Ray] for me. This I know you would at any time rather do than give her a new gown.'

A year later Sandwich and Ray were embroiled in a major quarrel triggered by the Earl's refusal to continue to pay her debts. Ray was in a stronger position than some demi-reps – she had talents other than those of a lover that could make her a good living. She began to explore the possibility of leaving Sandwich and beginning a career as a professional singer. Herbert Lawrence, a lawyer who acted as an intermediary between the two, explained the situation to Sandwich: 'It was I think about the middle of this summer that Miss Ray asked me, in a jocular manner, whether I thought her voice would do for the stage. I answered her by asking whether whither and why she had any thoughts of that kind. Her answer was that her present situation was very precarious and that it was incumbent on her to take care of herself.' Lawrence warned her against acting without consulting Sandwich, but her friends encouraged her to approach John Beard, the former tenor, a friend of Handel and the genial manager of Covent Garden Theatre. A friend of Sandwich's, Richard Phelps, was sent to deal with Beard, who assured him that he 'would never take her upon any account unless he knew your [Sandwich's] inclination went along with it'. Asked for his candid appraisal of Ray's talents, Beard said he would pay her more than Charlotte Brent, the top London soprano of the 1760s, and that 'she would indisputably make £1,000 per annum'. He added that if Sandwich did approve of her embarking on a career, he very much hoped that the Earl would ensure that she came to Covent Garden.

Sandwich's first response was to think that she had a new lover (an accusation Ray vehemently denied), then to close off the possibility of employment for her on the stage. He contacted not only Beard at Covent Garden but also David Garrick at Drury Lane to ensure that neither would employ her. He then began to negotiate with her, promising that he would make provision for her in his will. As Phelps wrote at the end of the quarrel, 'I believe with Your Lordship that her intention was more in terrorem than from any resolution she had taken to embrace that way of life.' Her concerns, he wrote, were the fault of youthful misjudgment rather than malevolence. Ray herself sent an effusive and supplicant letter of thanks to Sandwich:

> Dear Lord Sandwich, it is impossible for words to express how happy your kind letter has made me as by that and every other action which has passed of late, between you and me, I have had fresh reason to be convinced how sincere your love is towards me in every point. I can with grate truth, say of this moment, I am most much happier than I ever was in my life, and I am quite convinced your love for me, is such that I never could have believed had I not seen so many proofs of it . . . I assure you everything which I can possibly add, towards making your life happy, I shall study and think but to my duty in return for so many proofs of sincere love.

Throughout the negotiation Phelps and Lawrence were concerned to reassure Sandwich and placate his anxieties about Ray's infidelity and plans for employment. Ray poured out her gratitude, though her letter makes clear the conditions of her affection, turning her victory in obtaining a major concession from Sandwich – it is clear that he did agree to pay off her debts – into a paean to his generosity.

Six years later Ray and Sandwich had a similar quarrel. Tensions had been high between them because Sandwich had excluded Ray from Hinchingbrooke during the festivities held in the spring of 1772 to celebrate his eldest son's coming of age. Ray was furious at this insult and wrote Sandwich a tart and sarcastic letter complaining about his willingness to put local sensitivities before her interests and dignity. 'Till now', she ended her letter, 'I flattered myself that my happiness was the first thing Lord Sandwich studied but I am mistaken in that point – no matter – I hope I am born with a proper spirit to resent and take care of myself in time.'

By the autumn Ray had had enough: 'I must beg of you to reflect and think of your treatment towards me and my family. I believe few others besides myself would submit to the many insults I have received and for no return on earth. You are very sensible, Lord Sandwich, that I have no sort of obligations to you or yours. Certain it is, that I have made myself party to your pleasures of every kind . . . I leave you to judge whether this is treatment for the person who you profess so great an affection for.'

Yet what galled Ray was not so much her mistreatment as the refusal of Sandwich to reveal what provision he had made for her and her children: 'Your reply was this. That I must trust entirely to you in that particular and more you added that I had no right to mention these sort of things to you.' Ray's response was to refuse to leave London to join him at Hinchingbrooke, to refuse to help in his musical concerts, to lay out her debts for him (they amounted to more than £1,200), and to refuse him sex.

Once again Sandwich's first thought was that Ray had a lover: 'I have not seen any symptoms of infidelity to me, tho' if I was called upon oath to that opinion I should decline taking the book.' Surely, he surmised, she would not 'set me at defiance, without she had some expectation elsewhere?' But what particularly worried him was Ray's demand for a settlement: 'she has pressed strongly for a settlement after having lived eleven years with me without such an idea'. In a long plea for help written to his friend the Earl of Loudoun, he complained bitterly of Ray's presumption: 'giving way to a woman in unreasonable points never does any good, besides I never did nor never will make a settlement, it is too foolish a proposition to tell the reasons against it'. At the same time he feared the separation that he was beginning to think was inevitable: 'I will not conceal from you', he confided, 'that nothing can be a greater calamity to me than the loss of Miss Ray, but as things stand at present unless you can interpose I see very little probability of preventing it; I am vexed to death at this event.'

Sandwich turned to Loudoun because he believed that Loudoun's mistress and housekeeper, Mrs Walker, was partly responsible for Ray's demands. The two women had been spending a good deal of time together, sometimes with their lovers but quite often alone. Ray had been struck by Loudoun's largesse. As Sandwich complained, 'She upbraided me with my want of generosity, after having told me that you had this year paid £1500 for Mrs Walker.'

Unfortunately for Sandwich Loudoun took Ray's part. It was common for aristocrats to make some provision for their long-term lovers, usually in the form of an annuity, especially if they had children. Loudoun was hard pressed to see why Sandwich would not do so: 'I am sorry you never will give Miss Ray a settlement', he replied. 'Think who she is[:] a fine woman whom you debauched very young, who you tell me has lived with you eleven years.' Besides, he added, 'I see she still professes your fondest wishes she has brought

you a . . . fine family of children whom you seem as fond of as a
father can be of children.' Nor did she appear to have been unfaithful:
'From all I have seen in her conduct or could gather from her conversation I never could observe she had the least attachment or even
thoughts of any other man and indeed from all I have ever heard and
I hear a great deal of rumour I do not believe she ever has had any
other man but Your Lordship.'

Loudoun's tacit rebuke went unheeded, and in his later letters to
his friend Sandwich made no reference to Martha Ray's demands. At
the same time she seems to have decided to make terms. Law Reynolds, who was negotiating with her on Sandwich's behalf, was working hard to achieve some sort of compromise between them. Ray,
though still angry at Sandwich and defiant at his threats, shifted her
ground, claiming that she did not want a settlement, only to see his
will so as to ensure the future of her children. In this way she could
avoid the accusation that she was behaving like a tough demi-rep
bent on getting the best deal she could, and portray herself as a
concerned mother:

> All I wrote was to see your Will. If that request is unreasonable
> tell me and in writing but supposing I had not a Settlement I
> think I had a good right indeed Lord Sandwich I must tell you
> that you treat me very ill in every particular but assure yourself I
> am not without spirit and proper resolution and depend on one
> thing that you shall never fright me into compliance that the
> consequences be ever so hard to us both if you think proper to
> come to town you may settle every point properly.

As Reynolds pointed out to Sandwich, showing Ray the will was
a small concession to make: 'the power of altering that pleasure and
the probability of the many alterations that may happen in your
circumstances, must render of very little consequence to her to see

[the will]'. Some days later the couple were reconciled, and Ray once again wrote an effusive and thankful letter to her lover.

The publicity that surrounded Ray's murder was meant to conceal these quarrels and tensions, which were certainly known to many of Sandwich's circle and which might have been extremely damaging if made public. Quarrels over money and the lack of financial provision for Ray and her children would have placed Sandwich in a poor light, enhanced his reputation for meanness, and reinforced speculation that Ray had good reasons to encourage a younger lover. When the papers reported that Ray was to be buried in the clothes she was wearing on the night she was murdered, and that her jewels would be deposited in the coffin – the whole 'said to be worth £2,000' – Sandwich appeared to advantage, a keeper so grief stricken, so generous and loyal to his lover as to ensure the brilliant extravagance of her appearance even in death. Similarly the papers emphasized the mutual determination of Ray and Sandwich to secure their children's future: 'Miss Ray made it a rule, on the birth of every child, to solicit her noble admirer for an immediate provision for it, which was invariably acquiesced in, so that the issue of this lady will have nothing to lament from her sad fate, but the circumstance of having lost a tender mother, as they were secured in pecuniary matters from any possible contingencies.' There was no mention of debts and extravagance, no sense that Ray's relations with Sandwich involved anything more than the loving obedience expected of an eighteenth-century wife.

Telling a certain sort of story usually requires suppressing others or, at least, omitting those that are inconveniently incompatible. The sentimental narratives told in newspapers that emphasized the misfortunes of the victims, and portrayed them as *acted upon* rather than as capable of exercising their powers, were able, indeed were intended, to overlook, elide or omit stories about the actors – the libertine and mistress, the gentleman and the whore – whose dealings made up another kind of episode in the titillating tale of eighteenth-century moral laxity. They were designed to tell readers that Ray's death had nothing to do with this latter sort of story, that she was not part of the sexual demi-monde. The newspaper reader was encouraged to retell the story of Ray's death one way, but to do so depended upon mis-remembering or forgetting the stories that had been told by moral reformers and Sandwich's political opponents for the previous sixteen years. These tales, which celebrated and deprecated rich men's exploitation of women, female vulnerability and manipulative power, were never entirely repressed and were to resurface again and again.

Ironically, however, Sandwich was the unwitting (and surely unwilling) beneficiary of Ray's murder. Martha Ray's life had been dominated by stories about Sandwich, about his libertine ways and corrupt politics. But after her death in 1779 these were overshadowed by Hackman's deed. The soldier turned clergyman became the chief protagonist, emerging a year after the murder as one of the first full-blown romantic heroes.

CHAPTER 6

———— ❦ ————

Love and Madness,
A Story too True

THOUGH THE STORY of James Hackman's murder of Martha Ray was not forgotten, public interest in the case had already waned by the autumn of 1779. There seems to have been something of a backlash against the repeated publication of scandals in high life. 'Nestor' wrote to the *Gazetteer* in July that 'There are many of your old readers who are more concerned with the state of the nation than with the weaknesses and indiscretions of foolish women'. Other readers complained that there was so much scandal that newspapers could no longer be read by the family. But the story of Hackman and Ray was not driven off the pages of the newspapers by irate readers. Instead it gave way to more and more coverage of the bloody conflict between Britain and its North American colonies. A newspaper reader was far more likely to encounter Lord Sandwich as a beleaguered government minister than as a grieving lover.

The American war went from bad to worse, the government stumbled from crisis to crisis, and by the spring of 1780 groups of gentlemen, merchants and traders all over England began to form associations for economic and political reform, mobilizing a nationally co-ordinated petitioning campaign against the government. Lord Sandwich was one of their main targets, widely held to bear much of the blame for the failing war effort. Even in Huntingdonshire disgruntled gentry organized a petition against the government, despite Sandwich's best efforts to thwart opposition in his own county. His adversaries called for his resignation: 'Throw yourself once more into the arms of some blooming beauty; indulge your age in the enjoyment of her youthful charms; let her smiles indemnify you for the general hatred and execration. Placed in better hands, this nation will soon regain her former glory, splendor and importance.' Politics dominated public discussion and the press, edging out even readers' letters. 'Many other favours from our correspondents are only kept back by the great quantity of parliamentary matter that occurs', explained the editor of the *St James's Chronicle* in March 1780.

But not even politics could keep out of the public eye a work that had a more profound effect on the subsequent history of the Hackman–Ray case than any other single publication. *Love and Madness, A Story too True* rewrote the events of the previous April as a mutual but doomed romance, refigured a complex story with many voices as the tale of a single tortured sensibility driven to madness and, by connecting James Hackman the murderer to Thomas Chatterton, poet, faker and suicide, ensured a place in literary history for both Martha Ray and her killer. No other version of their story resonated so powerfully in subsequent ages.

In the spring of 1780 the publisher George Kearsley launched an elaborate publicity campaign to promote *Love and Madness, A Story too True*. This collection of sixty-five letters, nearly three hundred pages long, and priced at 3s. 6d. – cheap for a work of such length – claimed to be the correspondence between Hackman and his victim. Up to this point only two letters by Hackman or Ray had appeared in print – Hackman's proposal of marriage and the note that he had left for his brother-in-law on the night of the murder. Kearsley's *The*

Case and Memoirs of James Hackman had been based on oral testimony. It claimed to be 'taken from the mouth of Mr Hackman while in confinement and reduced to writing by a person who . . . knew him, and respected his very amiable and fair character'. It had also been reported in the press that Hackman had destroyed his correspondence with Ray shortly before he killed her. The appearance in *Love and Madness* of letters allegedly by Hackman and Ray, which Kearsley claimed to have obtained from Frederick Booth, Hackman's brother-in-law, caused something of a sensation. Now the true story would be revealed in the words of its most important participants.

Stuck between notices for Mr Christie's auctions and the latest number of the *Novelists Magazine*, the first advertisements for *Love and Madness* mentioned neither Hackman and Ray nor the publisher, playfully inviting readers to identify the plot and its main characters. They read:

> This day is published price 3s 6d
> LOVE AND MADNESS. A story too true. In a series of letters between Parties, whose names would perhaps be mentioned, were they less known, or less lamented.
>   Governor. Who did the bloody deed?
>   Oroonoko. The Deed was mine.
>   Bloody I know it is; and I expect
>   Your Laws should tell me so. Thus self-condemn'd,
>   I do resign myself into your Hands,
>   The Hands of Justice.
>   Oreoonoko [sic].

The only clue to the book's protagonists lay in the quotation from the final scene of *Oroonoko*, Thomas Southerne's perennially popular theatrical adaptation of Aphra Behn's novel about love and slavery in Surinam.

But Kearsley's puzzler cannot have overtaxed its readers. The play was a standard of the London theatre repertory, remained popular long after many other Restoration plays had been forgotten and, in what was almost certainly a piece of opportunism designed to cash in on Hackman's crime, was hurriedly staged at Covent Garden less than two weeks after he had been executed.

Despite their obvious differences, there were close parallels between Hackman and the captive prince who is the hero of Southerne's play. Both were 'slaves to love', driven to kill and to die by the ardour of their attachments. Both appeared to be victims of betrayal, both loved women who were in thrall to older and more powerful men, and both faced their deaths with dignity. To compare Hackman to Oroonoko was to the advantage of the former, imbuing him with the high status, simple dignity, love of liberty and forthright morality of Southerne's hero.

Equating Hackman with Oroonoko also set up a parallel between Ray and Imoinda, their lovers, though one had to ignore the vital differences between the two women. Imoinda is Oroonoko's wife, abducted by her father-in-law and sold into slavery. Reunited with her husband, himself tricked into slavery by a perfidious Christian sea captain, she suggests their mutual suicide to escape the punishment of their captors against whom they have rebelled. Their deaths represent mutual union. When Oroonoko wavers, Imoinda comes to his aid: 'I must assist you,/And since it is the common cause of both,/'Tis just that both be employed in it./Thus, thus 'tis finished, and I bless my fate/That where I lived, I die, in these loved arms'. In the play the two lovers die by mutual desire, in order to be free. So to cast Hackman and Ray as Oroonoko and Imoinda is to rewrite their tragedy as a story of a shared passion, focusing on the power of mutual love rather than the enormity of Hackman's crime. The advertisement's epigraph made clear what sort of story *Love and Madness* would tell.

Over the next month Kearsley repeatedly placed this advertisement in most of London's papers, including the *London Evening Post*, the *Morning Post*, the *St James's Chronicle*, the *Gazetteer*, the *Morning Chronicle*, and the *Whitehall Evening Post*. The brunt of the campaign was borne by the *Morning Post* which ran the advertisements every three or four days from 3 March until the end of April.

Not until early April, immediately before a slightly amended new edition of *Love and Madness* appeared, were Hackman and Ray identified in the newspapers. Kearsley inserted three 'puffs', paragraphs that appeared to be news items, to enhance what must already have been substantial book sales. In the *Morning Post* the letters were praised as inoffensive, instructive – 'as the dreadful consequences of the passion of love, unrestrained by virtue, are painted in the strongest natural colours, which fill the mind at once both with horror and pity' – and recommended as 'beyond all doubt . . . the best collection of love letters in the English language'. A paragraph in the *Gazetteer* a few days later pointed to Lord Sandwich's 'amiable portrait, as it is drawn in Love and Madness', while an item in the *Morning Chronicle* claimed it was impossible to read the book 'without the sensations of pity, easier to be conceived than described, for the unhappy couple who are the subjects of the book'. The *Chronicle* dangled before its readers the prospect of what might have been a happy outcome of the love story: 'Had Hackman's passion kept within the usual bounds, of even the most sanguine lover, or Miss Reay sacrificed less to gratitude, they might at this time have been happy in the possession of each other.' All three items emphasized how the correspondence placed Hackman and Ray in a good light: 'Considering their respective situations, these letters do both parties great credit; they are warm, yet modest; sentimental, yet lively.'

The tone of the advertising for *Love and Madness* was reassuring: the letters reminded readers of the dangers of unrestrained love, yet offered them a fascinating read; they provoked horror and pity but did not place Hackman or Ray in a bad light. The book encouraged a proper sentimental response and also reassured the reader by claiming to solve the mystery in which the case was shrouded.

The amount of publicity devoted to *Love and Madness* was very unusual, especially for a work that was neither a magazine nor a serial publication, the two sorts of literature most heavily advertised by booksellers in the London press. But Kearsley was eager to follow up on the success of *The Case and Memoirs of James Hackman* and was prepared to spend liberally in order to promote *Love and Madness*. It is not possible to know exactly the cost of Kearsley's campaign, though in the 1780s single advertisements in a paper like the *Gazetteer* were priced at 5s. 6d.

Whatever the expense, Kearsley's investment paid off. *Love and Madness* was repeatedly reprinted during the spring of 1780; a new edition, with minor corrections, a fuller table of contents, and a few additional moralizing notes, appeared in the first week of April. The book became an instant bestseller and quickly went through six editions. Nor was it just an overnight sensation: *Love and Madness* was still in print in the 1820s. A (somewhat abbreviated) French edition appeared with the title, *Les Fureurs de l'Amour, ou hist. Et corr. Authentique de J. Hackman et de Miss Marthuroy, assassinee d'un coup de pistolet par son amant* in the early nineteenth century.

Love and Madness was in fact a compilation of letters composed by a young Essex gentleman and lawyer, Herbert Croft, a minor denizen of Grub Street who spent most of his life struggling to be a man of letters. In a letter published in 1782 Croft wrote of *Love and Madness*, which he claimed to have 'put together in a few idle hours', as containing 'every syllable which I have made Hackman relate', and in the 1786 edition of *Love and Madness*, dedicated to the recently deceased Samuel Johnson, he confessed: 'The LVIIth Letter is auth-

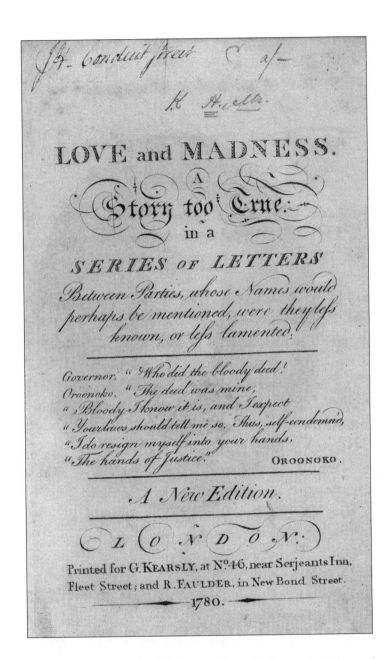

The elaborate, italicized title page of one of the many editions of Croft's *Love and Madness, A Story too True.*

entic, and the address to the Court was delivered by Hackman. Of the rest the outline only is true.' Nearly fifteen years later he again publicly acknowledged that he had written almost all of the text.

One of the most skilful aspects of *Love and Madness* is the way it repeatedly plays on the reader's anxiety about its status as fact or fiction. The challenge is issued in the very title – '*Love and Madness, A Story too True*'. On the one hand the reader is titillated with the prospect of an intimate view into the true feelings of the protagonists as expressed in a passionate private correspondence. 'These papers', Croft quotes Hackman as saying, 'which will be delivered to you after my death, my dear friend, are not letters. Nor know I what to call them. They will exhibit, however, the picture of a heart.' On the other, long discussions of literary controversies together with the repeated insertion of hints about the denouement of the story (such as the account of the execution of the clerical forger, Dr William Dodd) stretch the reader's credulity to the limit. Are these letters, or are they not a window into the soul of their creator(s)? And who is their creator? At one point, as the text cheekily remarks, 'We cannot bear to see the author only peeping over the top of every page, to observe how we like him.'

Nevertheless Croft's letters were sufficiently plausible to make contemporaries reluctant to condemn them as fakes. The *Monthly Review* tartly remarked that 'these letters are given as the correspondence of the late unfortunate Mr Hackman, with Miss Ray', adding, 'of their authenticity we can say little; for though we profess ourselves critics, we pretend not to be conjurors'. Other reviewers echoed the sentiments of the *Town and Country*: 'with regard to the authenticity of the correspondence, we shall leave it to the readers' own judgment to determine; and shall only observe, that many of the epistles are pathetic, descriptive and affecting'. Only the *Gentleman's Magazine* branded *Love and Madness* an obvious fraud: 'In this age of literary fraud we are not surprised that a tale so bloody should give rise to a supposititious correspondence. The parties, who are the late unhappy Mr Hackman and Miss Ray, it is needless to add, never penned a line of these 65 letters, except the 57th, which was printed in the Sessions-paper [i.e. the published trial record].' Yet even this reviewer conceded that the letters 'have some intrinsic merit'.

This reluctance to condemn *Love and Madness* as a fraud and the somewhat lackadaisical attitude towards its status as either fact or fiction is not primarily attributable to the credulity of its readers. *Love and Madness* fitted into a recognizable genre of works whose appeal lay in their effective crossing and re-crossing the boundaries between the genres of history and fiction. Novels had long used the term 'history' in their titles; indeed in the 1760s, the Scottish critic Hugh Blair designated novels and romances as 'fictitious histories', and novelists frequently used the techniques of authentication employed by historians – the quotation of documents and records, the recording of the testimony of eyewitnesses, an account of how and where they had obtained their source materials. Daniel Defoe was, of course, the master of this genre – his *Memoirs of a Cavalier* (1720) and *A Journal of the Plague Year* (1722) are both presented as historical documents and reflect on the ways in which we determine what is 'authentic'. Many writers of fiction wanted their work to be treated as if it were history – hence Samuel Richardson's protestations when William Warburton proposed that he preface his novel *Clarissa* with a declaration that the work was entirely imaginary. Richardson wanted 'to avoid hurting that kind of Historical Faith which Fiction itself is generally read with, tho' we know it to be Fiction'. Such faith was important to those who wanted to legitimate fiction by claiming that, like history, it embodied an instructive truth, even if it did recount actual events. Its moral effectiveness depended upon its plausibility.

It was a short move from fiction written and read as if it were history to fictions based on contemporary characters and circumstances. The spread of biography and the growth of the newspaper press – the vehicle by which the world was first acquainted with Hackman's murder of Ray – made the move possible. In the 1770s a succession of widely reported, high-profile aristocratic scandals spawned a number of novels whose success depended on readers recognizing the figures on which they were based: *The Unhappy Wife: a series of letters* (1770) about Lady Sarah Bunbury's break-up with her horse-loving but emotionally tepid husband; *Harriet, or the Innocent Adulteress* (1771), which used materials from the scandal of the Duke of Cumberland's affair with Lady Grosvenor; and *The Correspondents: an original novel, in a series of letters* (1775), which purported to be letters between Lord Lyttelton and his mistress, Mrs Peach. The pleasure in reading these lay in the possibility that they might be true, a prospect that could be enjoyed only if they were known to be works of fiction. (If they were works of history they had to be treated as if they were true.) At the same time they played with the idea that, even if the facts were not correct, they expressed a moral truth about the characters they depicted and the stories they told. The genre affirmed the boundary between history and fiction by asking the reader to move back and forth across it.

The plausibility of *Love and Madness* was sustained by its scrupulous adherence to the known facts about Hackman's murder of Martha Ray and because it remained faithful to a story-line that was already well known. It confirmed and elaborated the link that the earlier *Case and Memoirs of James Hackman* had made between the Hackman–Ray story and sentimental narrative. Croft merely made it into an epistolary novel.

Love and Madness was Croft's most notorious literary success in a career that was, by and large, a failure. Genteel poverty and spendthrift habits made him a regular inmate of debtors' gaols – he was even seized by bailiffs on the day of his second marriage – and he was forced to avoid his creditors by living in Hamburg, Lille and Paris. A graduate of Oxford and a student at Lincoln's Inn, successively lawyer and clergyman, and eventually a baronet (though no wealth or estate came with the title), Croft doggedly devoted his life to literary pursuits, most notably his project to revise and improve Dr Johnson's dictionary. In 1787 he claimed to have two hundred quarto volumes of manuscripts for a new dictionary, but his proposals for publication failed to find enough subscribers. Like most hacks he tried his hand at many literary projects. He wrote an advice manual and edited a short-lived literary magazine. Like many a hack, too, he was a seasoned drinker. One of his companions at the bar was Frederick Young, the dissolute and estranged son of Edward Young, whose 'The Complaint: or, Night-Thoughts on Life, Death and Immortality' (1742–5) was one of the century's most popular poems. Croft's claim to fame was to have had his life of his friend's father incorporated into Samuel Johnson's 'Lives of the English Poets'.

Croft was certainly a learned man, well read in Latin, Greek, Hebrew and Anglo-Saxon literature and a good speaker of French, German and Italian. He was a political conservative, paid to defend Lord North's administration against the strictures of Edmund Burke, and took time off in the weeks after the publication of *Love and Madness* to attend a county meeting at Chelmsford, speaking against political reform and warning of the tyranny of democracy. In his politics, biography, periodical writing and ambitions as a lexicographer he aspired to emulate his hero, Dr Johnson. But, though Croft dedicated the 1785 edition to the 'great Cham' of English literature, Johnson did not much approve of *Love and Madness*, telling Boswell that he disliked its mixture of fact and fiction.

At its most superficial level, *Love and Madness* takes the conven-

Published by J.B.Nichols & Son. March 1,1828.

Sir Herbert Croft as he wished to be remembered: 'a dictionary maker' and
upright man of letters, like his hero, Dr Johnson.

tional form of a romantic tragedy. Beginning during the winter of
1775–6 in the rooms of snow-bound Hinchingbrooke, Sandwich's
country house, the plot charts the lovers' first tentative steps towards
mutual passion, their difficulties in meeting without detection and
their fears of discovery, particularly by Omai. Vowing not to violate
Sandwich's hospitality by making love under his roof, they meet in
an inn at Hockerill, while Ray is travelling back to London, and
spend the night together.

The story of how Hackman and Ray consummated their affair
would have been familiar to readers because it closely followed the
plot of another notorious love story, the adulterous romance between
Lady Grosvenor and George III's errant and womanizing brother, the
Duke of Cumberland. Like Grosvenor and Cumberland, Ray and
Hackman use the journey between town and country to spend the
night together; and both couples chalk marks on the doors of their
inn rooms to let their lovers know where they are sleeping. But,
while Croft's account of Ray and Hackman's rendezvous ends in bliss,
Cumberland and Lady Grosvenor, in a scene that resembled nothing
more than a traditional British bedroom farce, were caught when
servants of Lord Grosvenor, having watched the couple through a hole
bored in the door, broke in and caught them in their night-clothes.

Lord Grosvenor's subsequent prosecution of Cumberland for 'criminal conversation' with his wife was a tremendous scandal because of
its prurient detail – a prince heavily disguised with a false wig and
turned-up coat, assignations in the back rooms of shops, semen on
the floor – and because of the huge damages Lord Grosvenor was
awarded – no less than £10,000. But the case was firmly etched on
the public conscience by printers and booksellers who were friends
of Kearsley and who used the case to attack the libertine ways and
moral bankruptcy of the aristocracy. Many accounts of the trial
appeared in newspapers and pamphlets, and in the year of Ray's

murder booksellers published a nine-volume compendium of aristocratic adultery trials in which the Grosvenor case filled nearly two
volumes.

Unlike the royal duke, however, Croft's Hackman is no libertine.
As he makes clear in a letter to Ray the day after he first makes love
to her: 'You once said that a nearer acquaintance would make me
change my opinion of you. It has, I *have* changed my opinion. The
more I know you, the more chastely I think of you. Notwithstanding
last night (what a night!), and our first too, I protest to God, I think
of you with as much purity, as if we were going to be married.' His
lovemaking is not a sign of moral depravity but of that uxoriousness
that ironically will lead to his demise.

Soon, with Ray back in London, her suitor is pressing her for her
hand in marriage. Much of the correspondence of the spring of 1776
is taken up with the crisis provoked by Ray's steadfast refusal to wed
Hackman. Writing repeatedly from the Cannon Coffee House, round
the corner from the Admiralty where she was staying, Hackman
swears a vow of chastity until she changes her mind: 'notwithstanding
the dear night at Hockerill, and the other which your ingenuity
procured me last week in D. street, I swear by the bliss of blisses, I
will never taste it again, till you are my wife'. But Ray remains
adamant – '"Torture shall not force you to marry me" Did you not
say so?' – and urges Hackman to rejoin his regiment in Ireland.
Hackman's passion contrasts with Ray's prudence and pragmatism,
her concern for financial security and for the future security of her
children.

Once in Ireland Hackman is plagued by jealousy – 'I wish you
happy, *most* happy; but I cannot bear the thoughts of your receiving
happiness from any hands (man, woman, or child) but mine' – and
is horrified by Ray's suggestion that the couple's financial problems
could be solved if she became a professional singer: 'persist in your

idea of going on the stage; and, as I live, I'll come over and make a
party to damn you the first night of your appearance. Since you will
not share my fortunes, I will not share your earnings.' But when in
the summer Hackman falls ill, Ray's stern determination gives way
to frantic inquiries about his fate – 'for God's sake! Where are you?
. . . It's more than a month since I have heard from you. A month
used to bring eight or ten letters' – which are placated only with
the news of his recovery.

In the following spring it is Ray's turn to be afflicted with a
serious illness. Hackman hurries back to London, but cannot see his
lover, and is reduced to pacing up and down outside the Admiralty
windows, hoping for a sign from her servant. A deathbed note arrives
for Hackman at the Cannon Coffee House – 'My mistress bids me
write this from her mouth – "these are the last words I speak. My
last thoughts will be on you, my dearest dear H. . . Be a friend to my
children. My little girl".' But only two hours later Ray is miraculously
saved: 'at the hazard of my life I write this to tell you Heaven has
spared my life to your prayers'.

Ray's suffering and weakness excites Hackman. When he finally
sees her some days after her crisis, he finds it hard to keep his vow
of chastity:

> What a struggle! The time of year, the time of day, the situation,
> the danger from which you were hardly recovered, the number of
> months since we had met, the languor of your mind and body, the
> bed, the everything . . . yet, when your strength failed you, and
> grief and tenderness dissolved you in my arms; when you reclined
> your cheek upon my shoulder, and your warm tears dropt into my
> bosom; then . . .

But, holding back from this scene of erotic vulnerability, he only
steals a kiss.

The plot moves swiftly from these crises to the arrival of Hackman in London in January 1779, when he renews his request to Ray to marry him. The final letters between the couple are confused and ambiguous, but clearly indict Caterina Galli of the charge of convincing Hackman that Martha Ray has a new lover. The deception is all the more dramatic as one of Hackman's last letters to Ray implies that he is busy making arrangements for their marriage with her approval. It is as if the couple are snatched at the very last moment from the joys of connubial bliss only to be plunged into gory tragedy.

Thus far *Love and Madness* is a typical tale of romantic passion in which the purity and vivacity of the love between Hackman and Ray is contrasted with Ray's need to make a living, fulfil family obligations and remain faithful to a man who does not excite deep affection but who has acted fairly by her. As Hackman puts it in one of his earliest letters, 'To my little fortunes you are no stranger. Will you share them with me? And you shall honestly tell his Lordship that gratitude taught you to pay duty to him, till love taught you there were other duties which you owed to H[ackman] . . . M[artha]. weigh us in the scales.' The piquancy of their affair is seasoned by the dangers of illicit love: the assignations in parks and inns, the furtive notes and stolen kisses that heighten the romance and that can be found in almost any of the romantic novels that weighed down the shelves of circulating libraries.

Croft may portray the relationship between Ray and Hackman as one of mutual love, but *Love and Madness* is a very one-sided account of the lovers' affections. Hackman writes the overwhelming majority of the letters, and his missives run the full gamut of sentimental cliché. From the outset his writing is excessive: filled with palpitations of the heart, that key organ of sensibility, brimming with tears and weeping, and replete with literary reference and allusion. Describing his response to Martha's musical talents Hackman writes: 'Observe – when I write to you I never pretend to write sense. I have no head;

you have made me all heart, from top to bottom. Sense – why, I am out of my senses, and have been these six weeks. Were it possible my scrawls to you could ever be read by any one but you I should be called a madman.' 'I certainly am either curst or blest (I know not which)', he goes on, 'with passions wild as the torrent's roar. Notwithstanding I take this simile from water, the element out of which I am formed is fire . . . I have a burning coal of fire: your hand can light it up to rapture, rage, or madness.' As he proceeds he writes himself into a virtual frenzy: 'Men, real men, have never been wild enough for my admiration; Othello (but he should have put *himself* to death in his wife's sight, *not* his wife), Zanga, are *my* heroes. Milk and water passions are like sentimental comedy. Give me (you see how, like your friend Montaigne, I strip myself of my skin, and shew you all my veins and arteries, even the playing of my heart) – give *me*, I say, tragedy, affecting tragedy, in the world, as well as in the theatre. I would massacre all mankind sooner than lose you.' Yet as he reaches his climax, Hackman becomes conscious of his weakness and vulnerability: 'Inconsistent being! While I am ranting thus about tragedy and blood and murder, behold, I am as weak as a woman. My tears flow at the idea of losing you; yes, they do not drop only, they pour. I sob like a child.'

While the language attributed to Hackman is all of the heart, of its palpitations and passion, the letters purportedly written by Ray are generally cautious and caring. Though she comes across as loving Hackman almost to the last, she consistently chooses prudence over passion. When she explains the value of her relationship to Sandwich, and tells Hackman to go to Ireland and rejoin his regiment, she writes: 'Be a man, I say you *are* an angel. Join your regiment.'

But we get little sense of Ray as an individual; she is the object of Hackman's desire, and her own feelings are an obstacle to its fulfilment. *Love and Madness* elaborates a theory of male romantic desire and possession. As his second letter exclaims: 'Suppose *he* [Sandwich] has bred you up – Suppose you *do* owe your numerous accomplishments, under genius, to him – are you therefore his property? Is it as if a horse that he has bred up should refuse to carry him? Suppose you *are* his property – Will the fidelity of so many years weigh nothing in the scale of gratitude?' What Hackman seeks is another form of possession, not the physical or bodily possession sought by the rake or libertine, nor the proprietorship of the gentleman for his mistress, but a romantic union of the spirit. Hackman wants to dissolve the distinction between the lover and the loved one, to achieve a degree of interpersonal transparency that dissolves the self in the other, or, perhaps, to put it more accurately, of the other in the self. When he is awaiting execution in prison, he claims to be plagued by the idea that Ray is possessed by another in heaven, and his dying wish is to be buried at her side. Pleasure and desire are here linked to the pain of their unattainability, their constant delay, the impossibility of their fulfilment except in fleeting moments, through the imagination or, ultimately, through death.

This is the dark side of Hackman's vision. Croft's epistolary narrative is littered with corpses, the sad victims of romantic passion. Hackman repeatedly tells Ray stories about the tragic consequences of love, tales that foreshadow the fate that awaits the lovers but also express Hackman's changing mood. In the first months of his affair with Ray he describes the deaths of a young Italian and a Frenchwoman in Lyon who overcame the obstacles to their love in a ritual suicide that mimicked a marriage ceremony. Decorating an altar in a chapel, the bride dressed in white with rose-coloured ribbons. 'The same coloured ribbons were tied to the pistols. Each held the ribband that was fastened to the other's trigger, which they drew at a certain signal.' Hackman tries to distance himself from this eroticized fulfilment of thwarted love celebrated in Edward Jerningham's poem

Faldoni and Theresa – 'As on one stem two opening flowers respire,/ So grow our lives (entwin'd) in one desire' – but confesses himself drawn to the lovers' fate.

From Ireland Hackman regales Ray with the story of a Yorkshireman murdered by his wife and her lover and, though condemning the crime, fantasizes about the feelings of the couple as they stand on the gallows: 'I protest, I would willingly embrace with M. the cruelest death which torture could invent (provided she were on a bed of roses[)], than lead the happiest life without her.' Soon after he is begging Ray to send him a copy of the French translation of Goethe's *The Sorrows of Young Werther*, while vehemently denying the book will have any effect on his conduct: 'Nonsense, to say that it will make me unhappy, or that I shan't be able to read it! Must I pistol myself, because a thick-blooded German has been fool enough to set the example, or because a German novelist has feigned such a story.' But she is terrified by his request: 'The book you mentioned is just the only book you should never read. On my knees I beg that you will never, never read it! Perhaps you *have* read it. Perhaps! I am distracted.'

Hackman cannot leave the theme of romantic suicide alone. Soon he is comparing the dilemma of Martha Ray with that of Jane Watson, a nineteen-year-old from Enniskillen married to a good man but enamoured of another. Torn between love and duty, the young girl poisons herself, leaving an admonitory note: 'with *an advice to all people never to suffer a passion of any sort to command them as mine did in spite of me*'. As the story reaches its climax, so the sense that love can become a sort of possession or madness, leading its victims to act against their best interests, becomes more pronounced. Writing about a footman who shot and wounded a servant who refused to marry him, Hackman declaims, 'Oh love, love, canst thou not be content to make fools of thy slaves, to make them miserable, to make them what thou pleasest! Must thou also goad them on to crimes! Must thou convert them into devils, hell-hounds!' And in the final letters before he shoots Ray, Hackman struggles with the temptations he feels to end his own life. Discussing the notorious suicides of the Smith family, who killed their child and then themselves because of a crushing burden of debt, and the case of two young French soldiers who shot themselves at St Denis, apparently because they were disgusted with everyday life, Hackman forces himself to the conclusion that every suicide, no matter what its justification, is an act of madness.

He is consumed by the news from Caterina Galli that Ray no longer cares for him and has a new admirer. Suicide may be a crime but it 'can paint no punishment equal to what I suffer here'. Writing to a male friend, Charles, the recipient of his final letters, he pours out his agony:

> If you will not let me fly from my misery, will you not let me fly from my passions? They are a pack of bloodhounds which will inevitably tear me to pieces. My carelessness has suffered them to overtake me, and now there is no possibility, but this, of escaping them. – The hand of Nature heaped up every species of combustible in my bosom. The torch of Love has set the heap on fire. I must perish in the flames. At first I might have extinguished them – now they rage too fiercely.

Hackman's last letter before his suicide note contains yet another account of a love triangle in which an Italian murders his best friend's bride and then attempts suicide. But Hackman claims to have no designs on Ray's life: 'As yet the Devil has not tempted me to plunge my *Eloise* along with me into the unfathomable depths of destruction.' The letter accords with Hackman's assertion at his actual trial that he did not plan to kill Ray but was prompted to murder her by a momentary impulse. Like the *Case and Memoirs of James Hackman*,

Love and Madness argues the case for 'irresistible impulse'. As the text puts it, 'The stream of my passions, which had been stopped, now overwhelmed me with redoubled violence. It hurried me after them. Jealousy suggested a new crime; and nerved anew the arm of despair.' Both texts acknowledge and reject the notion that male romantic love is a form of madness, a contradiction that the legal notion of 'irresistible impulse' so neatly elided.

Croft's novel defends Hackman from the charge of premeditated murder and also makes the case against suicide. Hackman condemns suicide right up to the moment when he decides to take his own life. In case the reader has missed this message, Croft reiterates it in the very last letter in *Love and Madness*, in which Charles passes on a few of Hackman's literary fragments to a friend. Charles condemns *The Case and Memoirs of James Hackman* as 'a miserable business' for suggesting that Hackman's attempted suicide may have been justified, 'because that life is made wretched by a capricious and ungrateful woman'. On the contrary, he points out, Hackman was always troubled by the effect his actions might have on others, a view proven by one of his last letters which reiterates his abhorrence of self-murder. 'The torture of my situation is this,' Hackman writes, 'that not one word can be said in my favour, unless you will say I am mad. But God knows I possess all my senses and feelings much too exquisitely.' Yet this is not what he most regrets. 'Often, very often, I consider my crime with respect to the influence it may have upon the world. An example represented in life by view, has more effect than a precept preached by virtue. No one will imitate me by murdering the object of his love, but I may be considered by despair, or by folly, as another precedent in favour of the propriety of suicide.' He longs to make clear his condemnation of such a crime. 'Could my countrymen know how I abhor this part of my crime, how thoroughly I was ever convinced (except during my phrenzy), and how perfectly I am now persuaded, that *our own lives are no more at our disposals, than the lives of our fellow creatures,* I should expire in something less of mental torture.'

Though Croft obviously wished to exploit the sensationalism and prurience about the Hackman–Ray case that guaranteed a bestseller, he took pains to underscore the moral tenor of *Love and Madness*. The first time he distinguishes his own views from those of Hackman is in a note added to the corrected edition of 1780, attributed to the editor of the Hackman–Ray correspondence, which claimed, 'Werther was clearly a bad man. Had he not died by his own hand, he did not deserve to live. The writer who either relates or feigns his dangerous story, is not a much better man.' In a letter of 1782 Croft wrote of 'blunting the edge of Hackman's shocking example'. Similarly in the appendix to the 1786 edition, in which Croft admitted the letters to be a fiction, he stressed their didactic content. (He even sent a copy to the Earl of Sandwich, claiming that 'Nothing in this will offend I hope; which is very far from its intentions', and offering to alter anything that gave offence.) When Charles Moore published his *A Full Enquiry into the Subject of Suicide* in 1790 (Croft was one of the book's subscribers), he launched a full-scale attack on the pernicious work of Goethe by contrasting its amoral sympathy for suicide with Croft's 'effort of genius and imagination in behalf of such serious and religious principles, as might serve to counteract all defenses of suicide from this purposed and atrocious example'.

But Croft had other ends in view. To be sure, *Love and Madness* was both tragic romance and moral tale, but it was also an original reflection on the power of literary genius. Croft not only defended the genre of factually based fiction, thus placing *Love and Madness* in a literary tradition whose most distinguished practitioner had been Daniel Defoe, but also propounded a view of literary genius as an ability to convince readers of the truth in fiction.

This can be seen most clearly in what, at first sight, seems the oddest feature of Croft's text: the curious interruption of the story of Hackman and Ray at the very moment when their relationship reaches crisis point in the spring of 1779. The growing tension and pace of the narrative is suddenly punctuated by an extended – 120-page – letter discussing the career, talents and fate of Thomas Chatterton, the young Bristol poet who had apparently committed suicide in 1770 in a London garret after an undistinguished career as a Grub Street hack.

Chatterton's fame rested not on his occasional journalism – much of it written for the *Town and Country Magazine* which had published the tête-a-têtes of Sandwich and Ray – but on his alleged 'discovery' of fifteenth-century verses, letters, heraldries, biographies, sketches, genealogies and chronicles about Bristol. These verses and prose manuscripts, supposedly written by a priest, antiquarian, poet and scholar called Thomas Rowley but actually the work of the young Chatterton, painted a vivid picture of a thriving literary culture in the medieval city. They seemed to give the lie to the idea of an unlettered Dark Ages and to link the work of Chaucer to the English Renaissance; in short, to rewrite the history of English poetry. Like many great fakes, Chatterton's materials fascinated historians, critics and scholars because they provided a missing link in a story that was of far greater importance than the manuscripts themselves. As Thomas Warton, the first historian of English poetry, put it: 'If it should at last be decided, that these poems were really written so early as the reign of king Edward the fourth, the entire system that has hitherto been framed concerning the progression of poetical composition, and every theory that has been established on the gradual improvements of taste, style, and language, will be disarranged.'

During his lifetime Chatterton had tried unsuccessfully to get the patronage and support of the aristocratic antiquary Horace Walpole and the bookseller James Dodsley. But within a year of his death the antiquarian and literary world was buzzing with rumours about the works of Rowley; soon famous antiquaries, aristocratic dilettanti and literary giants like Samuel Johnson and Oliver Goldsmith were visiting Bristol to seek the true identity of the documents' author, to find the chest in which the manuscripts had been discovered, and to negotiate with Chatterton's friend, George Symes Catcott, a pewterer who was engaged in a lively trade in Rowleiana. Chatterton and Rowley were the chatter of high tables in Oxford and Cambridge and the gossip of the Pump Room in Bath. In 1777 a Bristol book-seller published a full edition of Rowley's works. A year later a new edition appeared that included an essay arguing that the ancient verses were in fact the work of Chatterton.

These were the first salvoes in a controversy that dominated literary debate for the next five years and rumbled on into the nineteenth century. On the one hand there were those who condemned Rowley's language and writing as a fraud perpetrated by a modern sensibility, an artefact of Chatterton's febrile imagination. On the other were the Rowleians who repeatedly asserted that a jejune and poorly edu-cated youth like Chatterton could not possibly have composed such exquisite works of literature. Both sides viewed the verses as works of the highest order, as great literature whether of the eighteenth or fifteenth century. Paradoxically, those who condemned Chatterton as a forger recognized his genius, while those who absolved him denied his talent.

On 23 July 1778 Croft had gone to Bristol in pursuit of Rowley. He visited Chatterton's family in Bristol, talked to his mother and sister, and borrowed two drawings, three poems and eight letters that Chatterton had written to them from London shortly before his death. He returned most of the letters but kept the two drawings and Chatterton's final missive, apparently gifts from Chatterton's mother. He also persuaded Chatterton's sister to write a short memoir of her brother. Obviously Croft was preparing to intervene in what was fast becoming the most fashionable literary controversy of the day.

Just as *Love and Madness* purported to solve the mystery of Hackman and Ray's affair, so the correspondence between the young poet and his family was to reveal the true facts behind the Chatterton controversy. Kearsley certainly thought the Chatterton material was important in promoting Croft's book. From the first his advertisements for *Love and Madness* highlighted it as well as vouching for its authenticity. Sceptics were invited to examine the letters and memoir at Kearsley's shop: 'The original of the last Letter from CHATTER-TON (the supposed author of Rowley's Poems) and the original letter from CHATTERTON'S sister, communicated in the Course of this Correspondence, are deposited in the Hands of the Publisher.' (It is worth noting, incidentally, that the public was never offered any such scrutiny of the letters purportedly written by Hackman and Ray.)

Obtaining Chatterton's letters was a coup for Croft, though his success came to haunt him in later years, when Robert Southey and William Wordsworth criticized his publication of the material without the knowledge or consent – and therefore not to the profit – of the poet's family. The letters were immensely valuable: they provided a detailed account of Chatterton's travails as a Grub Street hack, and they have remained vital to Chatterton scholarship ever since, not least because they made possible the attribution of many of his minor works.

Croft's use of the letters was motivated not simply by a desire for publicity and commercial success, for he took what at the time was an unusual position in the debate about Chatterton and the poems of Rowley. Like a number of other critics, he argued against the view that one so young and ill educated could have produced such accomplished verse, but he was one of the very few commentators who not only refused to condemn Chatterton for his forgery, but praised his fakery as genius. Indeed he was rebuked by Thomas Warton, the historian of English poetry, on the grounds that 'it is but a dangerous apology in favour of a forger, to say, that he was *disposed to exercise his inventive genius*'.

For Croft Chatterton's skill in passing off his work as medieval verse was a sure sign of his greatness. The ability of an author, through the skilled use of his imagination, to convince readers that what they were reading was authentic and true was a sign of creative genius. To equate such a talent with forging a bank note or a bill, as Horace Walpole did in criticizing Chatterton, was a misapprehension:

> For Chatterton's sake, the English language should add another word to its Dictionary; and should not suffer the same term to signify a crime for which a man suffers the most ignominious punishment, and the deception of ascribing a false antiquity of two or three centuries to compositions for which the author's name deserves to live for ever.

'Most readily I admit', wrote Croft, 'that, if Chatterton be an impostor (i.e. the wonderful human being I firmly believe him), he imposed on every soul who knew him. This with me, is the trait of greatness.'

The test of a great work, in Croft's view, is not its adherence to factual accuracy but its ability to move the reader, to convince and persuade through aesthetic and moral power. Elsewhere in *Love and Madness* he makes the same point when discussing the other great fake of the period, James Macpherson's 'reconstruction' and translation of the supposedly ancient Gaelic poems of Ossian. When Hackman discusses the verses with Ray, he subordinates the issue of their authenticity and authorship to the quality of their effects: 'They who do not refuse their admiration of the compositions, still think themselves justified to abuse Macpherson, for pretending *not* to be the author of what they still admire. Is not this strange?'

Chatterton, like Macpherson, takes up some literary materials – fragments and rudiments of a lost tale – and creatively transforms them into a work that moves and instructs the reader. This, as Croft makes clear at the beginning of *Love and Madness*, is not only Chatterton's (and Macpherson's) achievement but his own ambition. Talking about Daniel Defoe's use of Alexander Selkirk's memoir, Croft has Hackman remark:

> That fertile genius improved upon his materials, and composed the celebrated story of Robinson Crusoe. The consequence was that Selkirk, who soon after made his appearance in print, was considered a bastard of Crusoe, with which spurious offspring the press too often teems. In De Foe, undoubtedly, this was not honest. Had Selkirk given him his papers, there could have been no harm in working them up in his own way. I can easily conceive a writer making his own use of a known fact, and filling up the outlines which have been sketched by the bold and hasty hand of fate. A moral may be added, by such means, to a particular incident; characters may be placed in their just and proper lights; mankind may be amused (and amusements sometimes prevent crimes) or, if the story be criminal, mankind may be bettered, through the channel of their curiosity. But, I would not be dishonest, like De Foe; nor would I pain the breast of a single individual connected with the story.

This could hardly be a more accurate account of *Love and Madness* – a romance with a moral message against suicide – based, as Croft conceded in the fifth edition, on only two surviving documents and a broadly factual outline.

Love and Madness, the text implies, should be seen in the same light as *Robinson Crusoe*, *The Works of Ossian* and *Poems, supposed to have been written by Thomas Rowley*. (The point was not lost on the reviewer of *Love and Madness* in the *Gentleman's Magazine* who tartly remarked, 'We are not surprized that the forger of these letters should endeavour to extenuate the forgeries of Chatterton.') For Croft these works are all fictions but they are not forgeries – 'Is Macpherson's name mentioned in the same sentence with this unfeeling word *forgery*, even by those who believe Macpherson and Ossian to be the same?' They borrow not to copy nor imitate but to create works whose value lies in the imaginative scope and literary merit that transcend their originals. Partly concealed but by no means completely buried in *Love and Madness* is evidence of Croft's burning literary ambition.

The figure of Chatterton both links Croft to and distinguishes him from James Hackman. The young man's life is portrayed both as an instance of the terrible vicissitudes faced by hack writers like Croft and as an example of the sort of sensibility that can lead to violence and suicide. In *Love and Madness* Chatterton is portrayed as creatively self-sufficient, a natural untutored genius – 'he knew no tutor, no friend, no parent – at least no parent who could correct or assist him' – forced to face the bleak realities of the literary market-place. He struggles, as Croft also struggled, to retain his integrity and pursue his dreams while earning his daily bread, 'steeped to the lips in poverty'. He becomes 'one of the starved children of genius' bent on 'living to all eternity in the memory of Fame'. He compromises by churning out articles and paragraphs for the newspapers and periodicals, but writes his verses for posterity: 'in his own character, he painted for booksellers and bread; in Rowley's, for fame and eternity'.

Thus, on the one hand, *Love and Madness* compares Chatterton's extraordinarily sensitive literary character to Richard Savage, the poet whose irregular life and difficult genius was immortalized by his friend Samuel Johnson. On the other, he is compared to the temperamentally intense James Hackman. Chatterton's sister describes his sharply changing and extreme moods: 'His spirits was [sic] rather uneven, some times so gloom'd that for many days together he would say very little and that by constraint. At other times exceeding chearfull.' And the relatives with whom he lodged in Holborn when he came to London view Chatterton as 'a mad boy more than anything else, he would have such flights and *vagaries*', and as someone who 'appeared to have something wonderful about him'.

In *Love and Madness* Chatterton's creativity, moods and melancholy have everything to do with the fact that he was a writer. In one of his last letters to Martha Ray, the fictional Hackman compares the discussion he has had with her about the reasons for Chatterton's death to the famous medical treatise by Samuel Auguste Tissot, the English translation of which was published in 1768 as *An Essay on Diseases incidental to Literary and Sedentary Persons.* Here Croft draws on the well-established idea that authors and literary men were often victims of excessive sensibility. As a reader had once sycophantically commented to Samuel Richardson, 'Misfortune is, those who are fit to write delicately, must think so; those who can form a distress must be able to feel it; and as the mind and body are so united as to influence one another, the delicacy is communicated, and one too often finds softness and tenderness of mind in a body equally remarkable for those qualities.' Robert James's *Medical Dictionary* of 1743–5 singled out '*Literati* . . . who indulge themselves too much in Study, continual Meditations, and Lucrubrations' as especially prone to 'HYPERCHONDRIACUS MORBUS'. Tissot, a theorist of 'nerves', maintained that authors who combined a sedentary life with an active imagination were especially liable to melancholy, delusions and madness.

While this obviously applies to Chatterton, it is also an apt account of Hackman's condition. In *Love and Madness* Hackman is an author – not of books, but of letters – who, like Croft and Chatterton, repeatedly takes up fragments and stories and uses them to explain his feelings and the nature of the relationship he wishes to have with Martha Ray. Telling her a story about a woman who voluntarily joins her aristocratic lover condemned to work in the quicksilver mines of Idra – a tale designed to illustrate the virtues of standing by your man – he writes, 'I take it from some Italian letters a brother officer lent to me, written by Mr Everard, and I give it to you almost in his own words – except in one or two passages where I think he has lost the opportunity of surprising the reader.'

Hackman constantly describes the act of writing – 'what visions have I conjured up! – my pen drops from my hand' – and even fantasizes about the prospect of appearing in print: 'Well, my M——how do you like my pen to-day? Don't you think I am improved? In time I shall come to write such letters as may appear in print.' His pen progressively writes him into madness.

Love and Madness is more literary than political, its point of reference less the social forces that produce a sentimental tragedy than a reflection on the delicate sensibility that accompanies and is a sign of literary skill or even genius. Hackman is portrayed as a thwarted lover, but one whose sensitivity and sentiments derive from his literary sensibility. His condition, though the consequence of his relationship with Ray, is not attributable to love's madness (a possible title for his book that Croft eschewed for love *and* madness) but to a larger sensibility. He is the kinsman of 'the marvellous boy' Chatterton and of the sensitive hero of Goethe's *Die Leiden des jungen Werthers* which had appeared in 1774 and was first published in English in 1779 as *The Sorrows of Young Werther*.

One of the most important effects of *Love and Madness* was to make Hackman into a proto-Romantic hero whose memory would survive into the nineteenth century, and to highlight the issue of his madness, which many of the earlier accounts had downplayed or tried to evade.

Love and Madness recast a story that had previously had many actors and intertwined plots into a single, inexorable story-line with a sole protagonist, the progressively maddened James Hackman. It made the case into an exploration of individual pathology rather than a complex social drama.

Perhaps even more important, *Love and Madness*, recognizable to eighteenth-century readers as exemplifying the kind of fiction that played with the idea of being real, came to be viewed in the nineteenth and twentieth centuries as an actual collection of real letters written by the historical figures of Martha Ray and James Hackman. George Borrow, for instance, in his six-volume compilation *Celebrated Trials, and Remarkable Cases of Criminal Jurisprudence* (1825) treated Croft's work as a genuine correspondence,

> which continued for several years, displaying great warmth of mutual affection, with much coquettish dalliance on the part of the lady. It was collected and published by Dr HERBERT CROFT, in a volume called *Love and Madness*, now become scarce; and the interesting, affecting, and romantic character of the whole leads us to reprint it.

Borrow omitted the material on Chatterton as irrelevant to the romance that lay behind the murder. He even argued that an ostensible error in the text revealed the correspondence's authenticity. 'The editor cannot but observe', he wrote, 'that if Mr H. had not, in this subsequent letter, by the merest accident in the world, explained those lines, they would have thrown an unjust suspicion of suppositiousness on this whole volume, and few people would have believed those letters to have been genuine.' Comparing a fictitious account of love's madness unfavourably to Croft's book, Borrow cited the letters in *Love and Madness* as a instance in which nature outstripped art. Though, as we shall see, others in the nineteenth century were more sceptical, this view persisted. Gilbert Burgess, the nineteenth-century editor of a reissue of *Love and Madness – The Love Letters of Mr H. & Miss R., 1775–1779* (1895) – asserted that the letters were genuine, brushing aside Croft's acknowledgment in the sixth edition that he had written them himself. Sandwich's most distinguished modern biographer gingerly follows Burgess in depriving Croft of his authorial role, and a recent history of capital punishment treats the novel as a window on to the world of eighteenth-century punishment. In almost every subsequent account of Ray's murder Croft's ideas and language creep in. His fiction, unrecognized by those unfamiliar with an eighteenth-century genre, has become history. His history-as-romance was a source of inspiration for at least two twentieth-century novelists, Constance Hagberg Wright and Elizabeth Jenkins. Croft always depicted the affection between Hackman and Ray as mutual and all-embracing; the version of the affair propagated on the title page of the novel and reproduced in Kearsley's advertisements with its quote from Southerne's Oroonoko. It never contemplated the possibility that Ray had rejected Hackman in 1775, had no intention of marrying him, and was distraught in 1779 when he returned to haunt her. Croft's book is a novel of sensibility, not a gothic tale, in which Hackman is a man of feeling, not a bloody spectre.

Love and Madness kept the story of Martha Ray and Hackman alive into the next century. Though the material on Chatterton made Croft and his novel unpopular with Southey, Wordsworth and Coleridge – they regarded it as literary theft – the book's importance as a source for poets and scholars interested in Chatterton also helped keep it in print and largely explains the survival of copies in research libraries today. The British Library copy I used to write this chapter was owned by Joseph Haslewood, an antiquary and collector who helped Wordsworth and Coleridge's publisher, Joseph Cottle, to prepare his Bristol edition of Chatterton's works, which appeared in 1802.

Haslewood's copy includes cuttings of the advertisement for the first edition and a series of newspaper clippings of crimes of passion which end with the trial in 1804 of a clergyman 'who said he would be another Hackman'. But the most telling clipping is a poem of 1794 which attests to the reception of *Love and Madness* as a mutual romance gone wrong:

> On Reading 'Love and Madness'
> O love! Thou powerful guider of the soul;
> Why mix with anguish thy endearing bow;
> Why wound alike two fond, two tender hearts;
> Or why with poison taint thy barbed darts?
> Reason replies: 'Tis Heav'n's supreme decree,
> That pleasures unalloyed can never be;
> Lest we forget our hopes of bliss above,
> And should from crime to crime with rashness rove.

CHAPTER 7

Wordsworth and the Doctors

LOVE AND MADNESS painted a much bolder picture of Hackman's madness than any earlier work, and, even while it claimed that he had succumbed to a sudden irresistible impulse when he killed Martha Ray, it interpreted his affliction as a specific form of mental illness, love's madness. At the time of the murder, this had not been a usual response. Hackman's prosecutors had downplayed his supposed madness in order to secure his conviction, and his supporters and apologists, as we have seen, wanted to dissociate the mad act of killing from Hackman's otherwise normal mental state. Much of the commentary on Hackman's fate evaded the issue of madness, sharing Boswell's view that the case showed men how important it was to struggle to keep their passions in control. In his letter published in the *St James's Chronicle* of 15 April 1779, Boswell quoted an essay he had written on the passions associated with sexual love. 'The natural effect of disappointed love, however shocking it may appear, is to excite the most horrid resentment against its object.' This he described as a masculine impulse, making 'us prefer the destruction of our mistress, to seeing her possessed by a rival'. Such conduct is natural and normal, Boswell claimed, an impulse of 'unrestrained nature', but he conceded that 'wherever passion is stronger than principle, it bursts forth into horrid deeds'. The moral was clear:

'The use to be made of so striking an instance as that of Mr Hackman is to make us watch the dawning of violent passion and pray to God to enable us by His Grace to restrain it.' Hackman's general character appeared no better and no worse than any other man's and, as such, he was to be pitied, not treated as an object of 'abhorrence' or 'contempt'. Love's madness did not fit into the prevailing narratives about Hackman's crime; male passion did. Hardly any of the newspapers took the view that Hackman was mad, though an occasional correspondent suggested that he would be better off in Bedlam than Newgate. But this view, expressed in the first day or so after the murder, receded as the public came to know more about the attractive and personable young man who was Martha Ray's killer. Only one pamphlet, *The Genuine Life, Trial, and Dying Words of the Reverend James Hackman*, published by Sandwich's old enemy the radical publisher John Miller, claimed that Hackman was truly insane. 'The unfortunate Mr Hackman', its author wrote, 'continued for some days under the influence of the same insanity, which probably operated with him at the time of the perpetration of the dreadful deed.' Hackman 'talked about Miss Reay, with all the extravagance that the maddest love ever suggested, and declared he cared nothing for life, since he was deprived for ever of her'. The tract concluded, 'A line in Pope's *Eloisa* might with great propriety be pronounced over his bier: "O may we never love as HE has lov'd".' As the invocation of Pope implies, love's madness was far more likely to appear in the poetry column of the newspapers than in the debate about Hackman's conduct. Such verses were designed to evoke a mood rather than tell a story. On 5 May 1779 the *Public Advertiser* printed a long poem 'supposed to have been written by Hackman on the morning of his execution'. After describing Hackman's feelings in the face of death, it then explores the powerful emotions that lay behind his brutal crime:

Driven by Love extreme, and black Despair,
I murder'd in my Heart, an Angel there.
O! wretched Sense of Feeling exquisite,
Expos'd to keenest Misery, or Delight.
Nerves that vibrate in Agony of Pain,
Then stretch to Joy each Ligament again.
When Reason left the Vessel in full Sail,
How was I wreck'd in Passions maddest Gale.

The verses expose the same nerves and ligaments – the same physiology of love's madness – that Croft's novel so vividly describes. Verses such as those published in the *Public Advertiser* enabled their author and the paper's readers sympathetically to explore the emotions of romantic infatuation and obsession, feelings that were at once fine and noble and full of murderous desire. Such verses but, above all, the success of Croft's account of Hackman's progressive deterioration help explain how Hackman's case passed into contemporary medical literature on insanity. It was cited by Erasmus Darwin in his *Zoonomia: or, The laws of Organic Life* (1794–6) as the example of 'the third stage of "erotomania" or sentimental love', and by Joseph Mason Cox in the second edition of his influential *Practical Observations on Insanity* (1806) where he discusses 'Love, its Modifications, and Effects'.

The medical literature on insanity in the late eighteenth century placed great store on the narration of case histories, the explication of the precise individual circumstances of an afflicted patient in order to understand the nature of the complaint. Hackman's well-publicized crime provided the sort of circumstantial evidence that doctors liked to include in their published case histories.

Erasmus Darwin, who singled out Hackman's case, was one of the most influential physicians of the late eighteenth century. The grandfather of Charles Darwin, he was educated at Cambridge and Edinburgh, practised in Lichfield, and was a prominent and much-published member of a number of scientific and medical circles in London and the provinces. He was offered the post of royal physician by George III, but preferred to remain in the provinces. His epic poem, *The Botanic Garden* (1798), with its survey of modern life and of the Linnaean classification of nature, was one of the most successful (and controversial) poems of the eighteenth century.

Zoonomia, the culmination of Darwin's life's work, on which he laboured for more than twenty years, painted a sweeping, evolutionary picture of man and his relations to nature. Darwin's study of the 'laws of organic life' is an analysis of the different stimuli – irritation, sensations of pleasure and pain, volition and association – that animate organic life. Its first volume lays out human physiology, anatomy and psychology, the second discusses all the diseases to which humans are prone. Love's madness appears in a long section on the diseases of volition in which most of the known forms of madness are examined.

Diseases of volition, Darwin explains, are a peculiarly human complaint, the distortion of the faculty that 'distinguishes mankind from brute animals; which has affected all that is great in the world, and superimposed the works of art on the situations of nature'. Erotomania or sentimental love, 'described in its excess by romance-writers and poets', is found only in persons of the most exquisite sensibility, and not in those 'who have not had leisure to cultivate their taste for visible objects, and who have not read the works of poets and romance writers'. It is at once the complaint of a refined person, and fuelled, as Croft described, by works of the imagination and literature. Erotomania seizes the patient, possesses him so powerfully, because sentimental love 'is supposed to supply the purest source of human felicity'. It is enhanced through absence from the loved one and by memory and imagination.

Darwin divides erotomania into three phases. In the first, the passion of love 'produces reverie', which 'alleviates the pain of it, and by the assistance of hope converts it into pleasure'. The lover then seeks peace and solitude so that his dreaming will not be interrupted. Stage two begins when reverie fails to assuage the pangs of love 'as when it is misplaced on an object, of which the lover cannot possess himself'. At this point the disease is not irremediable, but can be 'counteracted or conquered by the stoic philosophy'. But if this fails, there is little hope. 'When a lover has previously been much encouraged, and at length meets with neglect or disdain, the maniacal idea is so painful as not to be for a moment relievable by the exertions of reverie, but is instantly followed by furious or melancholy insanity; and suicide, or revenge, have frequently been the consequence, as was lately exemplified in Mr Hackman, who shot Miss Ray in the lobby of the playhouse.' Though, as we shall see, Darwin was well aware that most patients being treated for love's madness were women, his discussion is entirely from the male point of view.

The idea of love's madness dated back to Plato's Phaedrus and received its most eloquent and mordant expression in English in Robert Burton's *Anatomy of Melancholy* (1621). But Darwin, like many of his contemporaries, saw love's madness as a modern condition, a consequence of the leisure, refinement and taste that were made possible by modern society. Modern abundance led to a proliferation of desire, the elevation of feeling and heightening of sensibility in ways that were unheard of in less developed societies. Thus the physician and moralist, Thomas Trotter, wrote,

> as the ambition or ingenuity of man finds out for him new employments; these, while they draw forth latent talents, call forth new passions and desires: so that however much he may be styled a creature of habit, he is in many respects the creator of his own temperament . . . A large city or town may be truly called a hot-bed for the passions . . . Where the savage feels one want, the civilized man has a thousand. Devoted either to love or ambition, these

impress all his actions with extraordinary vehemence, perseverance, and enterprise ... Everything within his view is calculated to prompt his desires and provoke his passions; no antidote is opposed to suppress the one or to moderate the other.

This is the root of those modern disorders that manifest themselves as diseases of nervousness or sensibility. Love's madness is no longer viewed as a consequence of a particular mixture of the body's humours, but is seen as a complaint brought on by the effect of modern life on the body's nerves and fibres.

Trotter's and Darwin's analyses – as in non-medical works that were concerned to examine modern man and his place in society – contain a theory of the mind and body that incorporates both a physiological view derived from Enlightenment associationalist psychology (a theory of the human nervous system and the place of the human heart) and a social theory, most brilliantly expounded by the Scottish philosophers and political economists like David Hume and Adam Smith, about the contemporary condition – about European modernity – and its effect on people's feelings. Romantic love and its discontents is seen as a peculiarly modern phenomenon, found most acutely in those who were most sensitive to poetry, fiction, music and nature. The condition is at once desirable and pathological. Greater refinement, greater sensibility, a greater capacity for love, are all signs of higher civilization and associated with persons of nervous, even hysterical disposition. Though this theory was originally a view about mankind, it quickly became gendered, and came to be associated with women. As David Hume put it in his essay on Delicacy of Taste and Passion: 'How far delicacy of taste, and that of passion, are connected together in the original frame of mind, it is hard to determine. To me there always appears very considerable connection between them. For we may observe that women, who have more delicate passions than men, have also a more delicate taste of the ornaments of life . . . and the ordinary decencies of behaviour.' The civilizing process was at once pathological or might have pathological consequences, and was associated with women.

This meant that Hackman's case posed something of a problem for the medical men. Although Hackman appears in such works as Darwin's as a test-case for love's madness, he was also an anomaly: a case of male erotomania at a time when such a condition, both in imaginative and medical literature, was increasingly linked with women. (Female patients confined because of love's madness in mental hospitals outnumbered men in this period by a ratio of approximately four to one.) This anomaly is revealed in the examples that Darwin uses to round out his account of Hackman, all of which refer to women. Thus he first compares Hackman to Dido, who killed herself when deserted by her lover, an experience that seems to fit with many of the cases of eighteenth-century women who suffered love's madness brought on by male betrayal or desertion. And, though the female killing of male lovers was rare, he also compared Hackman to Medea, who murdered her rival lover and her own children to avenge the loss of Jason's love. Darwin concludes his remarks with a quotation from Dryden:

> Earth has no rage like love to hatred turn'd,
> Nor hell a fury like a woman scorn'd.

He knew that there was a male as well as a female clinical pathology, as his example of Hackman makes clear, but nonetheless considered love's madness a predominantly female complaint or the result of a feminine sensibility. His perspective explains why Hackman was portrayed as being 'unmanned' when he killed Ray, and as returning to manhood when he contemplated his fate with such stoicism before his execution.

* * *

In March 1798 a young Cambridge graduate living in Alfoxden, a large secluded house with a view of the sea on the edge of the Quantock hills in Somerset, sent off an urgent letter to the Bristol bookseller and publisher Joseph Cottle. William Wordsworth wanted a copy of Darwin's work and wanted it immediately: 'I write merely to request (which I have a very particular reason for doing) that you would contrive to send me Dr Darwin's Zoonomia by the first carrier.' He suggested where Cottle could obtain a copy if he did not have one himself. The volumes arrived at Alfoxden a week later and were not returned until 9 May.

The winter and spring of 1798 was one of Wordsworth's most prolific and creative periods as he strove to finish the collection that Cottle was to publish, anonymously, as *Lyrical Ballads, with a few other Poems* in September of that year. In these months Wordsworth composed 'Goody Blake and Harry Gill', 'The Complaint of a Forsaken Indian Woman', 'The Idiot Boy', 'The Last of the Flock', 'We are Seven', 'Simon Lee, the Old Huntsman', 'Anecdote for Fathers', and 'The Thorn', and worked on 'The Ruined Cottage' and 'The Old Cumberland Beggar'.

Two of these poems had direct connections with Darwin's work. 'Goody Blake and Harry Gill' was based on an actual case that Darwin discussed under the heading *mania mutabilis* in the section of *Zoonomia* on 'Diseases of Increased Volition', the same section that examined love's madness. Darwin described the 'insane' response of a young Warwickshire farmer to being cursed by an old woman he had caught stealing sticks from his hedge: 'Heaven grant, that thou mayest never know again the blessing to be warm.' The farmer's imagination sends him shivering to his bed, loaded with blankets, where he remains until his death twenty years later. The case fascinated Wordsworth as it had Darwin because it revealed the astonishing psychosomatic power of the imagination; it engaged the poet and the scientist in both of them.

At the same time that he was writing 'Goody Blake and Harry Gill' Wordsworth began work on 'The Thorn', a poem that tells the story of a woman who repeatedly returns to a small mound on a hilltop by a thorn tree. She has been deserted and left pregnant by her lover, a classic victim of love's madness. In Wordsworth's terse phrase: 'She was with child and she was mad'.

No more I know, I wish I did,
And I would tell it all to you;
For what became of this poor child
There's none that ever knew;
And if a child was born or no,
There's no one that could ever tell;
And if 'twas born alive or dead,
There's no one knows as I have said;
But some remembers well,
That Martha Ray about this time
Would up the mountain often climb . . .

I did not speak – I saw her face;
Her face it was enough for me;
I turned about and heard her cry,
'Oh misery! Oh misery!'

So Martha Ray, at least for the narrator of 'The Thorn', ceases to be a victim of a man suffering from love's madness and becomes the apparent perpetrator of an act of madness, the infanticide of her illegitimate child. She becomes a familiar literary and medical figure, a woman suffering love's madness as a result of her desertion by the man she loves. She, rather than James Hackman, is the figure to compare with Dido and Medea.

Wordsworth's use of Martha Ray's name in this verse has puzzled and worried many critics, some of whom have dismissed it as a lapse of good taste. Why should Wordsworth have chosen to insert this real-life character into what was obviously a work of the imagination? And why does Martha Ray appear in a part so different from the one she played on the stage of London life? Wordsworth may have been reminded of her as he scanned the pages of the second volume of *Zoonomia*, and read the entry on erotomania, but his knowledge of the case had a more intimate source than the pages of Darwin's treatise, which he read with great care in those spring months.

One of Wordsworth's best friends was Basil Montagu, the third surviving child of Martha Ray and the Earl of Sandwich. Basil had been born in 1770, as had Wordsworth. The two men had much in common when they were introduced in London by William Godwin, the radical philosopher, novelist and husband of Mary Wollstonecraft. They moved in the same radical literary and political circles, shared many friends from their days as Cambridge undergraduates, and both, despite their very different backgrounds, one aristocratic the other middle class, were plagued by financial difficulties. (Indeed, because of a loan from Wordsworth to Montagu in 1795 in return for an annuity on the former's life, the two men's financial affairs remained messily entangled for many years and were not finally resolved until 1817, when Montagu eventually acquitted himself of his debt.)

Their acquaintance was intimate. For a while the two men may even have lived together. Through Montagu, Wordsworth met John Frederick and Azariah Pinney, the sons of a rich West India Bristol merchant, who helped him escape from London by lending him a family house at Racedown Lodge in north Dorset. Wordsworth, sometimes visited by Montagu, remained in this remote spot before moving in July 1797 to Alfoxden House, to be close to his new friend, Samuel Taylor Coleridge. Throughout his time in these two West Country retreats, Wordsworth lived together with his sister Dorothy and with the lugubrious little boy they were both educating,

Basil Montagu's young son, called Basil Caroline Montagu in joint honour of his father and mother.

Caroline-Matilda Want, whom Basil had married in 1790, had died in childbirth in 1793. Lord Sandwich had cut off relations with Basil, when he had married this local Huntingdonshire girl of low social standing. Now he was struggling to cope with his grief, look after the boy and make a living as an aspiring barrister in Lincoln's Inn. As he wrote in his account of his relationship with his son:

> My child was with me: he was entrusted to my protection when I was little able to protect myself. By an accident I became acquainted with Wm Wordsworth. We spent some months together. He saw me, with great industry, perplexed and misled by passions wild and strong. In the wreck of my happiness he saw the probable ruin of my infant. He unremittingly . . . endeavoured to eradicate my faults, and to encourage my good dispositions . . . After some time he proposed to take my child from my Chambers in London in[to] Dorsetshire, where he was about to settle with his sister.

In fact the boy Basil remained with the Wordsworths from September 1795 until August 1798, shortly before they left for Germany. Throughout his life Basil senior remained profoundly grateful to Wordsworth for what he had done. 'I consider having met William Wordsworth the most fortunate event of my life', he wrote in his memoir. As late as his seventieth year he was still thanking the poet: 'God bless you and thank you for your lessons to me at a time when they were most valuable.'

Dorothy grew extremely fond of young Basil. 'He is my perpetual pleasure', she wrote to her childhood friend and closest confidante, Jane Marshall. When Basil arrived at Racedown he was, she said, 'extremely petted from indulgence and weakness of body; and perpetually disposed to cry', but he soon recovered in the bracing, country air. 'He is quite metamorphosed', she wrote with obvious pleasure, 'from a shivering half starved plant, to a lusty, blooming, fearless boy.' The boy was isolated, his only company 'the flowers, the grass, the cattle, the sheep that scamper away from him when he makes a vain unexpecting chase after them, the pebbles on the road etc'. She proudly regaled her friend with tales of his Spartan imperviousness as he played in the pouring rain and of his curiosity about the secrets of nature. William was less impressed: Basil, he told Francis Wrangham, a close friend of the boy's father, 'is quite well' but 'he lies like a little devil'. (One of the *Lyrical Ballads* – 'Anecdote for Fathers', subtitled 'Shewing how the art of lying may be taught' – was prompted by an example of Basil's mendacity.)

Together the Wordsworths adopted a system, loosely based on Rousseau's ideas of education, for the young boy: 'We teach him nothing at present but what he learns from the evidence of his senses. He has an insatiable curiosity which we are always careful to satisfy to the best of our ability. It is directed to everything he sees, the sky, the fields, trees, shrubs, corn, the making of tool, carts etc etc. He knows his letters, but we have not attempted any further step in the path of book learning. Our grand study has been to make him happy.' At Alfoxden they even let him play with another little boy, though he was, according to Dorothy, 'a very naughty spoiled child'.

This picture of youthful rural bliss was not shared by the young Basil when he looked back on those years. In 1812, according to his father, he 'day after day, vilified Wordsworth: he had stated, that when living with his sister they had treated him with such cruelty that he was constantly employed in the most menial occupations: and, but for the pity of the poor Villagers, who privately supplied him with such pittance as they could ill share, he should have been starved'. He treated the Wordsworths' poverty as a personal slight. But Basil junior was plagued with mental illness (as were other of

Basil Montagu's children), and repeatedly believed that those who were kind to him were bent on doing him harm. His surviving letters are those of a misanthropic young man who is painfully conscious of his own maladies and of what he described in a letter to his step-mother as 'my repugnance to saying civil things'. He died a young man after a lifetime of illness, depression and bad feeling, his face marked by what William Wordsworth called a 'hectic flush'.

The five-year-old boy whom Dorothy loved so dearly and who was later to pour scorn on her kindness sometimes accompanied the Wordsworths on the long rural walks they took almost every day. On 19 March, a few days after William had written to Cottle thanking him for the copy of Darwin's *Zoonomia*, the three of them climbed up to the Quantock hills. Dorothy's Alfoxden journal records, 'Wm and Basil and I walked to the hill-tops, a very cold bleak day. We were met on our return by a severe hailstorm. William wrote some lines describing a stunted thorn.' Martha Ray's grandchild was thus present at the birth of the poem in which she was reincarnated as a child murderer.

The intimate connection between Wordsworth and Martha Ray's family may, at first sight, make his use of her name all the more remarkable. But the invocation of Martha Ray – unquestionably jarring to those who then knew and now still know the historical figure – fits well with the professed purpose of Wordsworth's poem. In the advertisement to the first edition of the *Lyrical Ballads* of 1798, Wordsworth described the poems as 'experiments', a view he elaborated in the preface to the 1800 edition. They were an attempt 'to ascertain, how far, by fitting to metrical arrangement a selection of the real language of men in a state of vivid sensation, that sort of pleasure and that quantity of pleasure may be imparted, which a Poet may rationally endeavour to impart'. Wordsworth wanted his experimental technique, his use of ordinary language, to capture –

in a way that he felt the flowery and affected verse of his contemporaries could not – the 'infinite complexity of pain and pleasure', 'the fluxes and refluxes of the mind when agitated by the great and simple affections of our nature'. He was painfully conscious of how difficult it was for the poet, though always concerned with 'the spontaneous overflow of powerful feelings', to capture the psychological and moral complexity of human sentiments buried deep in the silent depths of the human heart. While the poet 'describes and imitates passions', he wrote, 'his situation is altogether slavish and mechanical, compared with the freedom and power of real and substantial action and suffering'.

The *Lyrical Ballads* were experiments, certainly, and none more so than 'The Thorn', but they were also case histories, instances of ordinary people subject to intense feeling, examples of the moral intensity of everyday life. Like the carefully observed accounts written by Erasmus Darwin and Joseph Mason Cox of the emotional turmoil of their patients, Wordsworth's poems were anatomies of human feelings, but they were written 'in the real language of men' rather than the language of medical science.

Wordsworth's concern for imagination and feeling might sound like an affirmation of the sort of sensibility that shaped the earlier stories of Martha Ray, James Hackman and the Earl of Sandwich; but it is not. Wordsworth shared the sentimental desire to evoke and understand intense human feeling but he had no truck with 'the degrading thirst after outrageous stimulation', nor with the florid, repetitious and ultimately vacuous language that formed its expression, the 'eternal talking of love, woe, and delicious tears' that made a travesty of human suffering. We can well imagine him being repelled by the overblown sentiments that Croft attributed to Hackman.

In his published notes on 'The Thorn', Wordsworth explained that he used his narrator 'to exhibit some of the general laws by which superstition acts on the mind'. As he commented in the advertisement to the first edition, 'The poem of the Thorn, as the reader will soon discover, is not supposed to be spoken in the author's own person: the character of the loquacious narrator will sufficiently shew itself in the course of the story.' In a note to the 1800 edition Wordsworth was less coy about his storyteller: 'The Reader will perhaps have a general notion of it, if he has ever known a man, a Captain of a small trading vessel for example, who being past the middle age of life, had retired upon an annuity or small independent income to some village or country town of which he was not a native, or in which he had not been accustomed to live. Such men having little to do become credulous and talkative from indolence; and from the same cause, and other predisposing causes by which it is probable that such men may have been affected, they are prone to superstition.'

The old sea captain's narrative is a singular mixture of garrulous meanderings, moving description, tentative conjecture, precise description – as in the famous line on the muddy pond near the thorn tree – ''Tis three feet long and two feet wide' – and village gossip. The first seven stanzas which vividly describe the thorn, with its attributes of human misery – 'a wretched thing forlorn' – the pond, the beautiful hill of moss that resembles a child's grave and 'the wretched woman' in a scarlet cloak – suffuse exact, meticulous detail with a deep sense of foreboding which focuses on the thorn itself. As many critics have noted, the most common literary (and folkloric) association with a thorn tree was illegitimate birth and infanticide. And the narrator's return to the thorn is a repeated invocation of a murky story whose details may be obscure but whose resonance is palpably dark and sinister. This feeling is heightened by a third voice – not the captain's, nor the miserable woman's – which repeatedly demands an explanation for the woman's strange conduct:

> But wherefore to the mountain-top
> Can this unhappy woman go,
> Whatever star is in the skies,
> Whatever wind may blow?

At this point in the poem the sea captain's relation mixes deep uncertainty with his obsessive ('adhesive' is Wordsworth's term) but futile desire to understand the nature of the misery of the cloaked woman.

> I cannot tell; I wish I could;
> For the true reason no one knows . . .

The poem fragments into a frenzy of supposition and speculation. Facts dissolve into rumour. We are told for the first time that Martha Ray is the woman's name, that she was left by her lover for another and driven into madness, but beyond this nothing is certain or sure. 'They say' . . . ''Tis said' . . . 'Old Farmer Simpson did maintain' . . . 'I've heard many swear' . . . 'some will say'. A miasma of rural gossip envelops the story. Unidentified voices tell of Ray's madness, her pregnancy, of her hanging or drowning her child, and burying it on the hill. The sea captain does not know what to believe.

> No more I know, I wish I did,
> And I would tell it all to you;
> For what became of this poor child
> There's none that ever knew:

He resists the story he hears even as he becomes complicit in its repeated telling. 'But kill a new-born infant thus!/I do not think she could'. When 'many swear' they have heard the voices of the dead on the mountain, he comments, 'I cannot think, whate'er they say,/ They had to do with Martha Ray'. For all his doubts the narrator keeps coming back to the story triggered by the associations of the thorn. In Wordsworth's words, 'It was my wish in this poem to follow the manner in which such men cleave to the same ideas; and to follow the turns of passion, always different, yet not palpably different, by which their conversation is swayed.'

But what the reader and perhaps the narrator (despite his reluctance to accept such a conclusion) come to learn in 'The Thorn' is that nothing is quite what it seems or is said to be. On the top of the mountain

> I looked around, I thought I saw
> A jutting crag, and off I ran,
> Head-foremost, through the driving rain,
> The shelter of the crag to gain,
> And, as I am a man,
> Instead of jutting crag, I found
> A woman seated on the ground.

The poem's radical indeterminacy makes it difficult to pin down both the narrator and the story. Wordsworth did not originally give the story-teller a character – as he did for example in 'The Ruined Cottage' – and suggested someone like the sea captain only in the 1800 edition. The person whose urgent questioning helps the main narrator unfold the story is not identified and, apart from 'Old Farmer Simpson' we have little sense of the source of the rumours and suppositions that make up the tale. Martha Ray is named, of course, but here naming furthers rather than undercuts the confusion and ambiguity. Both historically and in the poem she is the victim of love's madness, but in the former case she is murdered, in the latter she is a murderer herself. To readers who knew about the young woman shot by James Hackman (and this certainly means almost everyone in Wordsworth's circle) using 'Martha Ray' as an embodiment of misery and suffering is both apposite and jarring.

Perhaps, as some critics have suggested, 'The Thorn' is so radically indeterminate that it can be seen entirely as an artefact of the narrator's imagination. Yet it also seems to explore the question that Wordsworth formulated with such clarity in the 1802 preface to *Lyrical Ballads*, namely how do we grasp and represent human suffering? The views of the narrator of 'The Thorn' oscillate between a rather leaden empiricism and credulous superstition. He sees Martha Ray's suffering:

> I did not speak – I saw her face,
> Her face it was enough for me;
> I turned about and heard her cry,
> 'Oh misery! Oh misery!'

But he can neither understand nor properly explain it. It is both palpable (even if imagined) and mysterious. Wordsworth's poem, then, is an account, both critical and sympathetic, of the difficulties and failures of the narrator. There is both a parallel with and a difference between the poet, seeking to understand and depict suffering, and the sea captain who intuitively or imaginatively grasps the depths of human misery, yet cannot really account for it.

One of the most marked features of 'The Thorn' is the narrator's simultaneous preoccupation with but desire to avoid the person of Martha Ray. He looks, but he turns away. He encourages his questioner to view the thorn, pond and hill of moss, but only when Ray is absent: 'I never heard of such as dare/Approach the spot when she is there'. The answer, he suggests, lies in the place itself: 'Perhaps when you are at the place/You something of her tale may trace'. The one account or explanation of Ray's suffering that is absent is Ray's own. It is as if the narrator's inability to grasp her anguish is explained by her absence as a storyteller. He fails to engage directly with her suffering because her voice is drowned out and goes unheard by the gossipy and superstitious villagers who crowd the poem.

In the final stanza we are left with the poem's two key elements

– the thorn and Martha Ray's suffering – but they are juxtaposed
rather than connected:

> I cannot tell how this may be,
> But plain it is, the thorn is bound
> With heavy tufts of moss, that strive
> To drag it to the ground.
> And this I know, full many a time,
> When she was on the mountain high
> By day, and in the silent night,
> When all the stars shone clear and bright,
> That I have heard her cry,
> 'Oh misery! Oh misery!
> 'O woe is me! Oh misery!'

The narrator is left with a thorn covered in moss whose import he
does not really know, and with a disembodied voice, the essence of
pain, which he hears but which no longer has an identity.

'The Thorn' has long remained one of the most difficult and controversial of Wordsworth's contributions to the *Lyrical Ballads*. It
immediately attracted the criticism of Southey: the 'author should
have recollected that he who personates tiresome loquacity, becomes
tiresome himself', a comment echoed by Coleridge in his *Biographia
Literaria*, where, despite his general enthusiasm for the poem, he
tartly observed that 'it is not possible to imitate a dull and garrulous
discourser, without repeating the effects of dulness and garrulity'.
But the poem also had many admirers, including Wordsworth's and
Basil Montagu's friend, the journalist Henry Crabb Robinson, who
wrote to his brother that 'I wd rather have written the Thorn than
all the tinsel gawdy Lines of Darwin's botanic garden'.

The presence of Martha Ray – the historical personage – in one
of Wordsworth's *Lyrical Ballads* is consistent with the exploration in
'The Thorn' of the difficulties of representing human suffering and

of the ambiguous territory occupied when the poet tries to evoke imaginatively 'real and substantial action and suffering'. Basil Montagu's rackety life – the murder of his mother when he was nine, his breach with his father at twenty, the death of his wife at twenty-three, and the failure to secure any of the Sandwich inheritance – was well known to Wordsworth. Perhaps – and this is pure speculation – the vicissitudes of his friend and Basil junior's presence as a constant reminder of the family's domestic misfortunes, led him to choose the name of Martha Ray.

However this may be, the presence of Martha Ray in 'The Thorn', like the success of Croft's *Love and Madness* with its discussion of forgery, fact and fiction, shows how the case of Hackman and Ray was gradually stripped of its historical context and its characters removed into the realms of fiction, medical pathology and poetry. James Hackman and Martha Ray became two different archetypes of love's madness, one apparently based on fact and posing awkward problems for medical science; the other a strange fiction, but one much more in accord both with clinical analysis and a prevailing literary sensibility.

CHAPTER 8

The Nineteenth Century

THE MEMORY OF MARTHA RAY and her murderer lived on into the nineteenth century, but not surprisingly, as time passed and the events of 1779 receded into the distance, details of the murder became hazy and the incident less prominent. Less often singled out as a special case, the story of Hackman and Ray became one tale among many of tragic misfortune and violent crime. There was a flattening of affect, a decline in the depiction of the psychological and emotional intensity that surrounded the murder; a complex narrative was reduced to a formulaic story. Nevertheless the affair lived on into the new century, kept alive in the person of Basil Montagu, who was prominent in literary and legal circles, and by a growing fascination with high and low life in the era before the French Revolution. The story came to be regarded not as a singular event – except in the life of Basil – but as a symptom or example of the manners and morals of an earlier age.

This was possible because critics, journalists and historians interpreted the cataclysmic events of the Revolutionary Wars and the struggle with Napoleonic France as marking a radical break with the past. Though Hackman and Ray were not forgotten, the events of 7 April 1779 seemed, rather like the charming figure of Basil Montagu himself, to be both of another age and yet curiously insistent, a presence in the modern world but perhaps not of it. Rewritten and retold in the reviews and magazines that dominated late Georgian and Victorian journalism, re-moralized in compendia of crimes and deathbed confessions, Sandwich's libertinism, Ray's misfortune and Hackman's obsession were stripped of their psychological complexity and refashioned as parts of an exemplary anecdote, designed to reveal both the depravity of an earlier age and the distance from it.

Basil Montagu's life – begun as the illegitimate offspring of an aristocratic libertine and his mistress and ending as a pillar of Victorian society whose name was a byword for reform – mirrored this transition. Yet throughout his life Montagu acted like a figure out of an eighteenth-century sentimental novel. He combined the unworldliness, optimism and naivety of Goldsmith's *Vicar of Wakefield*, the sensibility of Henry Mackenzie's *Harley, the Man of Feeling*, the eccentricity of Sterne's *Tristram Shandy*, and the tragic figure of the orphaned child, struggling to make his way in a world that he only slowly understands and that he wishes to flee by finding shelter in domestic felicity. No wonder his friends repeatedly commented on his old-fashioned sensibility.

Orphaned at nine, an unhappy school child who wanted to run away to sea, Montagu was prone to passionate enthusiasms and sharp swings of mood. Throughout his life he was haunted by his mother's death. It is a shock when reading an otherwise elegant and erudite essay of his on pleasure in the fine arts, published in the 1830s, to be confronted by the sudden question, 'Who would be pleased with a picture of his murdered mother?' in a discussion of the power of aesthetic effect.

Montagu struggled against the incubus of his youth, repeatedly reminding his friends of the tragic experiences he had had to overcome. In 1799 he wrote to his friend, Josiah Wedgwood the younger:

I have for some months enjoyed a portion of tranquility and happiness which I am not conscious of ever having before experienced during the course of my existence. I have had what are called troubles, too. I have, however, satisfied my mind upon moral subjects. I have passed through Hell. I shall not look back. I am not deceived if my investigations will not tend to my permanent comfort through life.

As he passed through the ages of man Montagu sought out relationships to replace the stable family life he never had. He spoke of his friend William Godwin, whose utopian philosophy he fervently embraced in his youth, as if he were a parent, and he told the son of Sir James Mackintosh, his second mentor, 'I attached myself as a son to your father.' When he became successful and prosperous he himself attempted the role of mentor and paterfamilias. He was, said his friend the journalist Henry Crabb Robinson, 'fond of playing the patron'. His house was often the refuge for an aspiring writer or unsuccessful poet, and he was famously promiscuous in his offers of shelter and pecuniary aid.

In his youth, as he later ruefully admitted, Montagu was carried away by revolutionary fervour that probably grew out of his upbringing and eventual rejection by the aristocratic family of which he formed a part. (He was bitterly disappointed by the protracted case brought by the creditors of his late father in the Court of Chancery that he quite erroneously thought would have given him a share of the Montagu inheritance.) He railed against the courts and hereditary privilege, refusing to practise law on the grounds that it was corrupting. Such was his anti-aristocratic zeal that Godwin, bent on enjoying the gothicism of a bygone age, was shocked by his vehement denunciation of the evils of privilege when they both visited Kenilworth Castle in 1797: 'He expressed nothing but indignation at the aristocracy displayed, and joy that it was destroyed [in France].'

Like many members of his generation, Montagu later moderated his views and abandoned the republican utopianism of his youth, chiefly because the lawyer and politician Sir James Mackintosh persuaded him of the importance of working within existing institutions instead of rejecting them or hoping for their overthrow. Ceasing to be a radical, he nevertheless remained throughout his life a passionate adherent to liberal and improving causes. Together with Sir Samuel Romilly, he was an ardent proponent of legal reform and a founding member of the 'Society for Diffusing Information on the Subject of Capital Punishment and Prison Discipline' established in 1808. Montagu's testimony against the death penalty to the Commons Select Committee on Criminal Laws, whose report was published in 1819, eloquently put the case for legal reform and was the template for the revisions of the penal code undertaken by Robert Peel and the Whigs in the 1820s and 1830s. As William Hazlitt, writing in his support, commented, 'It makes almost a pamphlet, or what Mr Cobbett would call "a nice little book" on the subject.' Montagu worked tirelessly on behalf of offenders, telling Thomas Holcroft – a fellow opponent of capital punishment – that he attended the bar of the Old Bailey 'from a desire to save the lives of culprits'. He proudly regaled his friends with stories of those he had rescued from the gallows. Whether because of his mother's murder or not, he was convinced that 'crime proceeds not from *reason*, but from *passion*', believing that only public abhorrence of crime could secure its prevention.

As he grew more successful, Montagu became a pillar of the liberal establishment and a Victorian patriarch: the host, with his third wife, of a literary salon at 25 Bedford Square graced by the likes of Charles Lamb, Henry Crabb Robinson, Coleridge, Hazlitt and Thomas Carlyle, the advocate of teetotalism and vegetarianism, and the mentor and guardian of such aspiring literary figures as Hartley Coleridge, Frances Kemble and Harriet Martineau.

Montagu was a minor, though much-loved, literary figure. His legal work and publications left him, as he often complained, with little time for other writing. But he wrote essays and short books on laughter and human understanding, and edited a well-received and much-reprinted collection of the works of seventeenth-century thinkers and divines like Richard Hooker, Jeremy Taylor and Sir Thomas Browne. His pamphlet on 'Some Enquiries into the Effects of Fermented Liquors, by a Water Drinker', complete with an essay by Charles Lamb entitled 'Confessions of a Drunkard', was translated into French and German. (Hazlitt satirized his obsession in his essay 'People with One Idea'.) The author of more than forty works, Montagu made the seventeenth-century lawyer and philosopher Francis Bacon his lifelong study. He edited his works and wrote the biography that prompted Macaulay's famous essay on Bacon.

But Montagu the friend, companion and patron was better regarded than the author. As Frances Kemble remarked, 'I have a general impression that his personal intercourse gave a far better impression of his intellectual ability than anything he achieved in his profession or in letters. His conversation was extremely vivid and sparkling, and the quaint eccentricity of his manner added to the impression of originality which he produced upon one.' Like Boswell before him, Montagu had a great knack for being in the right place at the right time. He consoled Godwin at the deathbed of Mary Wollstonecraft in 1797 and wrote letters for him in the first hours of his grief, frequented the Wednesday evening meetings hosted by Charles Lamb, and attended Coleridge's lectures. His candid remarks concerning Wordsworth's anxieties about the moral conduct of Coleridge were responsible for the famous breach between the two poets in 1812. Montagu was also a good friend of Leigh Hunt, the liberal journalist and editor of the *Examiner*. He dined at Hunt's house in February 1817 when his host first showed Keats's verses to Godwin and Hazlitt.

A year later he tried, unsuccessfully, to prevent the suicide of his friend Sir Samuel Romilly, who was so mortified at the death of his wife that he took his own life. Montagu specialized in misfortune. On a long walk in 1821 Hazlitt, heartbroken about his latest fruitless love affair, poured out his woes to him about Nancy Walker, later enshrined in *Liber Amoris*.

His friends and acquaintances have left a picture of Basil Montagu as an exceptionally lovable and loving man, though one who was also annoying and exasperating. 'I love him very much', said Godwin, while complaining of his views. Coleridge blew hot and cold about him, but felt affection for his oddity: 'As for the state of his mind it is that which it is and will be – God love him! He has a most incurable forehead . . . A kind, gentlemanly affectionate-hearted man, possessed of an absolute *Talent* for industry; would to God! He has never heard of Philosophy.' But at the end of Coleridge's life Montagu was still one of his closest friends. Basil was one of only six recipients of a mourning ring distributed at Coleridge's wishes after the poet's death.

Henry Crabb Robinson gave with the one hand but took away with the other: 'he was a man of generous impulses, but wanting consistency and full of ostentation and pretence'. Thomas Carlyle, no lover of London's literati, called him 'an honest-hearted-goose'. Harriet Martineau commented on his 'curious strain of sentimentality', while his son-in-law Bryan Waller Procter (the poet 'Barry Cornwall') saw Montagu and his wife as figures from another age: 'The manners, at once stately and genial, of Mr Basil Montagu and his wife, have few or no counterparts in modern society.'

Montagu was notoriously absent-minded, habitually displaying, as Wordsworth put it, 'his usual fidelity to the art of forgetting'. He left Wordsworth's shirts with Coleridge rather than taking them to London, wrote letters that he never posted and left a manuscript at the house of an acquaintance. His cavalier attitude towards debts and money also infuriated several of his closest friends. He was always soliciting in a good cause: asking Lamb for a contribution to a pillar for Thomas Clarkson, the anti-slavery advocate; offering patronage and help, much to the irritation of Carlyle, or bending the ear of a guest about 'some tale of legalized injustice'. But his good-heartedness, his optimistic faith in improvement and a happier world, suffused his friends with warmth, even when they mocked his absurdities.

No man could have been less like his father. Sandwich's friends were libertines and conservative politicians wedded to the status quo; Montagu consorted with poor poets, radical philosophers, and political reformers. Sandwich was a pillar of the old order, his son a crusading advocate keen to alleviate human woes. Basil was impulsive, giving and financially generous where his father had been parsimonious to the point of meanness. Sandwich was a man of system and order; confusion and chaos – though he was always industrious – marked Basil's life. If Sandwich loved women and the pleasures of the flesh, Basil was inordinately uxorious, faithful to his three wives and luxuriating in domesticity, writing in 1801 to his friend the younger Josiah Wedgwood: 'My boy's asleep, my wife playing up-stairs, and I am as happy as I wish.' Unlike his father he devoted his life to 'the Preservation of Health, the Regulation of the Passions, and the Conduct of the Understanding'. He claimed to want the words 'He was a lover of all quiet things' inscribed on his tombstone. It is difficult to imagine Sandwich writing, as his son did in an essay on 'The Patriot and the Demagogue' that *The foundation of patriotism is virtue in private life.* – The patriot is reared amidst the charities of home; he learns to love his country, from his mother's song: from his father's prayer: from his wife's respect and tenderness: from his children's love and duty.' Sandwich always drew a distinction between

The young and pensive Basil Montagu, bearing more than a passing resemblance to his father.

his private pleasures and his public duties. Basil regarded public and private morality as one and the same, indistinguishable and mutually reinforcing.

Yet in one respect Basil was unmistakably his father's son. Thomas

Carlyle commented on the remarkable resemblance between the two. He describes him as of

> Good middle stature; face rather fine under its grizzled hair (brow very prominent); wore oftenest a kind of smile, not false or consciously so, but insignificant, and as if feebly defensive against the intrusions of a rude world. On going to Hinchingbrooke long after, I found he was strikingly like the dissolute, questionable earl of Sandwich . . . who indeed had been father of him in a highly tragic way!

Carlyle was not the only friend of Montagu's to be struck by the family resemblance. Leigh Hunt, accompanying Hazlitt to an exhibition of paintings at the British Institution, was struck by a 'portrait of an officer in the dress of the time of Charles the Second'. 'What a likeness to Basil Montagu' he exclaimed. It turned out to be a painting of an earlier Lord Sandwich.

More to the point, most of Montagu's large circle of acquaintance were aware of his tragic childhood; they were complicit in his account of his life. When Carlyle first met Montagu in the winter of 1824–5 he was not yet the tyro of his later years, only a minor and peripheral figure on the edge of London's literary circles, but he picked up the gossip about Montagu's tragic early life: '[His mother] pretty Miss Ray, carefully educated for that function; Rev. Ex-dragoon Hackman taking this so dreadfully to heart that (being if not an ex-lover, *a lover*, Bless the mark!) he shot her as she came out of Drury Lane [sic] Theatre one night, and got well hanged for it.' For the acerbic and cantankerous Carlyle the tale was 'musty' and Herbert Croft's *Love and Madness*, which he also knew, 'a loose foolish old book . . . not worth reading'. But he also felt that Montagu's quiddities stemmed from his early misfortunes: 'Poor Basil! No wonder he had his peculiarities, coming from such a genesis, and with a life of his own which had been brimful of difficulties and confusions!'

Leigh Hunt was equally curious about the fate of Montagu's mother. In his collection of topographical and historical anecdotes published as *The Town, its memorable characters and events* (1848, but written fifteen years earlier), he devoted a long section in his discussion of Covent Garden to Hackman and Ray and their 'tragical scene'. Hunt began by speculating about the nature of Hackman and Ray's relationship and the question of Ray's feelings for the young man. Like many nineteenth-century commentators, he turned to Croft's *Love and Madness* for help: 'According to his [Croft's] statement, Hackman urged her to marry him, and Miss Ray was desirous of doing so, but fearful of hurting the feelings of the man who had educated her.' But, for all his reliance on *Love and Madness* he knew that Croft's version of what happened, though plausible, was not entirely reliable: 'Sir Herbert's book, though founded on fact, and probably containing more truth than can now be ascertained, is considered apocryphal.' Eventually Hunt plumped for a highly moralized explanation of the story, accepting Croft's assertions on the grounds of Sandwich's failings. 'Upon the whole', he concludes, 'we have no doubt that he was a cold and superficial person, and that Miss Ray would not have been sorry had Hackman succeeded in retaining her heart.' As for Hackman, 'the great cause of his mischance . . . appears to have been the violence of his temper, – the common secret of these outrageous love stories'. Hunt saw him 'not as a bad-hearted man, merely selfish and passionate', but condemned him as 'weak, willful, and by his readiness to become a clergyman from a Captain, perhaps not very principled'. He concluded his account by seeing the case as a moral exemplum: 'The truest love is the truest benevolence; it acquires an infinite patience out of the very excess of its suffering, and is content to merge its egotism in the idea of the beloved object. He that does not know this, does not know what love is, whatever he may know of passion.' We cannot know how much Hunt's view of the affair was informed by his friendship with Montagu, though the characterization of Sandwich as 'cold and superficial' may be that of his son. Hunt, however, drew his account not only from Croft's fiction and his knowledge of Basil, but also from the memoirs and letters of the later eighteenth century that appeared in growing numbers between the Regency and the high Victorian age. He particularly relied on the 1826 memoirs of Joseph Cradock, Sandwich's close friend. Cradock was a Leicester country gentleman, a minor literary figure, a keen promoter of concerts, especially those for charitable causes, an avid landscape gardener, and an amateur actor and playwright. (He had a theatre at his house in the village of Gumley.) He wrote odes, poems, plays, advice literature, a novel, and accounts of his travels, as well as his memoir. He met Sandwich through their mutual musical interests and soon became part of the Earl's inner circle of friends. He frequently attended the oratorios performed at Hinchingbrooke and was a regular guest at Sandwich's dinners at the Admiralty. No one so close to Sandwich and Ray had written publicly about them since Ray's murder.

Cradock's *Literary and Miscellaneous Memoirs* painted a fragmentary but nonetheless detailed account of Sandwich's household. What they did not do, as Leigh Hunt pointed out, was cast any light on the motives and circumstances of the murder. In fact, Cradock had remarkably little to say about Hackman. He claimed to have been present when Sandwich first asked Hackman and his superior officer, Major Reynolds, to dinner and cards at Hinchingbrooke. He described the card-playing after supper while Hackman looked on, and Sandwich's early retirement with a headache. After cards Cradock and the other guests, including Hackman, unpacked a lunar telescope sent to Sandwich from Dollonds and, with the aid of the Earl's black servant James, assembled it on the lawn to examine the heavens. But this cameo is Hackman's only role in the memoirs. As Cradock honestly admitted, 'This was the only time I ever saw Captain Hackman.' And he was equally convinced that no one, with the exception of Ray's chaperone (whom he identifies as a Miss Berkeley, not Caterina Galli), knew the true nature of the affair. To the obvious disappointment of some of his readers – reviewers complained that his stories of Hackman and Ray 'had been printed fifty times before' – and despite his intimate acquaintance with Sandwich's household, Cradock cast no new light on the mystery behind Hackman's actions.

But Cradock was much less concerned with the murder than with portraying Sandwich and Ray in a favourable light. He depicts Sandwich as a faithful friend, energetic man of business, and genial host, painting a picture of a small circle of naval officers and musicians who relished one another's company and the Earl's generous patronage. He was especially concerned to defend Sandwich against the charge of licentiousness: 'I can attest, and call any contemporary to ratify who might have been present, that we never heard an oath, or the least profligate conversation at his Lordship's table in our lives . . . No man . . . was more careful than Lord Sandwich not to trespass on public decorum.' The reader is never left in any doubt about Sandwich's deep attachment to Martha Ray. Most of the anecdotes about Sandwich's trauma after her murder come from Cradock's pen: his awkward conversation with the Earl before the portrait of Ray over the chimney-piece; the house party at Walsingham's from which Sandwich fled when one of Ray's favourite airs, 'Shepherds, I have lost my Love', was sung after supper.

Cradock was equally sympathetic to Ray. He repeatedly emphasized her skills not only as a singer, but as a member of 'good company'. At Hinchingbrooke, he says, Miss Ray was 'the first attraction'. During the concerts 'Her voice was powerful and pleasing, and she has never been excelled in that fine air of [Handel's] Jephtha, "Brighter scenes I seek above"; nor was she less admired, when she executed an Italian bravura of the most difficult description'. He emphasized that, despite her difficult position – as a kept woman who could not be noticed by respectable members of society – Ray conducted herself as a 'pattern of discretion'. In a telling anecdote, he explained both the difficulties she faced and the admiration she excited. The wife of the Bishop of Lincoln told him that 'She had never seen Miss Ray before', and that she 'really [was] hurt to sit directly opposite to her, and mark her discrete conduct, and yet find it improper to notice her'. Ray 'was so assiduous to please, was so very excellent, yet so unassuming. I was quite charmed with her, yet a seeming cruelty to her took off the pleasure of the evening.'

Cradock did not flinch from speaking about Ray's financial circumstances. He reported a conversation with her shortly before her death in which she complained that she had no settlement from Lord Sandwich and asked him to speak to the Earl on her behalf. Cradock's response showed that he already knew that this was a sore point: 'I need not express my surprise; but I instantly assured her, "that no one but herself could make such a proposal, as I knew Lord Sandwich never gave any one an opportunity of interfering with him on so delicate a subject".' She replied by telling him that she was thinking of becoming a professional singer. She didn't want to be a burden to Sandwich, she said, and 'as her voice was then at the best, and Italian musick was particularly her forte, she was given to understand that she might succeed at the Opera-house'. Perhaps Cradock, who had friends in the opera, would help her get 'a most advantageous engagement'. But Cradock was not to be led, and he put Ray's request down to her nervousness about the crowds and ballad singers who milled around under the Admiralty windows, shouting out threats and insults.

Martha Ray emerges from Cradock's account as a credible person and not just as a series of clichés and stereotypes. She fears for

Sandwich and her children and charms the guests at Hinchingbrooke. David Garrick is bewitched by her attentions. She takes trips down the Thames with Sandwich and his Admiralty retinue, and joins in a lively party in Vauxhall Gardens that ended with catches and glees 'in which Miss Ray principally partook with great spirit, and to the no small surprise of a large audience, who greatly admired, but could not make out whom it was that sung so enchantingly'.

Of course Cradock painted an idealized portrait whose general outlines were not so very different from those in the press coverage after Ray's murder in the spring of 1779. But his picture of the Sandwich circle and of her place within it, his recognition of Ray's fears and apprehensions, and his unstinting admiration for her – 'I sincerely esteemed' her, whose 'melancholy fate I afterwards deeply lamented' – made it possible to see her as an important protagonist in her own story.

A few of Cradock's readers recognized this. His friend William Gardiner wrote thanking him for a copy of the *Memoirs*, commenting that 'the affair of Miss Ray, though nearly forgotten by many, will interest the public like a new circumstance, and in my circle already has created many enquiries'. One reviewer recognized that Cradock, by depicting Ray as the virtuous partner of Sandwich, challenged Croft's story of the two young lovers in *Love and Madness*: 'The account of the unfortunate Miss Ray [is] . . . very affecting. Her history has been much mistaken, owing to the reliance placed on Mr (afterwards Sir Herbert) Croft's memoirs of her in a book called "Love and Madness" which is a fiction from beginning to end, and very discreditable to the author.'

But these were unusual responses. Most reviewers regarded Cradock's *Literary and Miscellaneous Memoirs* – the title betrays their character – as a rather tedious, long-winded, bonhomous collection that promiscuously mingled anecdotes about local friends, minor gentry, and leading (if somewhat unsavoury) politicians with stories of such literary giants as Samuel Johnson, Oliver Goldsmith and David Garrick. Prolix and piecemeal, warm-hearted to almost everyone, Cradock's *Memoirs* told some revealing (and often to be repeated) tales – 'the ordinary gossip of the tea-table and the drawing room' – but they did not paint the portrait of an age. And, despite Cradock's affecting portrayal of Sandwich and his mistress, there was little sympathy for the couple. He was a libertine and she a fallen woman; her death an entirely appropriate end for a woman who had lost her virtue. Cradock, liberal and sympathetic in private life if conservative in politics, gave his readers insight into the morals of an earlier time, but they had little or no interest in Sandwich's relations with Ray, which they regarded as sordid and commonplace. They were not even redeemed through their connection with the more intriguing story of Hackman and Ray.

Cradock, for all his intimacy with Sandwich and Ray, was less influential in shaping their story than two other figures, Horace Walpole and George Selwyn, whose letters and memoirs appeared between 1822 and 1845. Both were far more interested in the sensational story of James Hackman and his crime than in the hum-drum story of an earl and his mistress.

Walpole had written many detailed letters to his out-of-town correspondents while events were unfolding, and he puzzled over Hackman's motives. As soon as the murder was reported he passed on the gossip to his friends in his usual, facetious manner. 'Now Madam,' he wrote to Lady Ossory, 'can you believe such a tale? How could poor Miss Wray have offended a divine? She was no enemy to the church militant or naval, to the Church of England or the church of Paphos. I do not doubt that it will be found that the assassin is a dissenter, and instigated by the Americans to give such a blow to the state.' On the very next day he was asking how Hackman could have been so foolish: 'Is not the story full as strange as ever it was? . . . To bear a hopeless passion for five years, and then murder one's mistress – I don't understand it.' As he later wrote to Horace Mann in Florence, 'I do not love tragic events *en pure perte*. If they do happen I would have them historic. This is only kin to history, and tends to nothing.' 'It is very impertinent', he complained, 'in one Hackman to rival Herod, and shoot Mariamne – and *that* Mariamne, a kept mistress!' Yet he still wonders why the young man did it. 'It just sets curiosity agog, because she belongs to Lord Sandwich at a critical moment.' But then he cannot resist a dig at Ray's dubious reputation. Hackman, Walpole concludes, 'might as well have killed any other inhabitant of Covent Garden'.

This same tone was kept up in accounts of the murder and execution published in the four volumes of letters and anecdotes entitled *George Selwyn and his Contemporaries* (1843–4) edited by the raffish literary Old Etonian John Heneage Jesse. Selwyn was notorious for his predilection for death and the gallows – no man loved a corpse or a hanging more – but he happened to be in France at the time of the murder. (This did not prevent the papers from publishing an apocryphal story that he had hastened to the Shakespeare Tavern to sit with Martha Ray's body.) Though the black-coated spectre in the tavern was a myth, Selwyn soon knew a good deal about the crime, largely thanks to his chaplain, the Revd Dr Warner, who sent him detailed accounts by letter. Warner's potted version of the story was a masterpiece of compression:

> The history of Hackman, Miss Ray's murderer, is this. He was recruiting at Huntingdon appeared at the ball; was asked by Lord Sandwich to Hinchingbrooke; was introduced to Miss Ray; became violently enamoured of her; made proposals, and was sent to Ireland, where his regiment was. He sold out; came back on purpose to be near the object of his affection; took orders, but could not

bend the inflexible fair in a black coat more than a red. He could not live without her. He meant only to kill himself, and that in her presence; but seeing her coquet it at the play with a young Irish Templar, Macnamara, he determined suddenly to despatch her too.

Another of Selwyn's friends, the Countess of Ossory, teased him – 'How much you have missed!' – and regaled him with a series of stories about mad young men stalking women in London. The Earl of Carlisle told Selwyn that he attended Hackman's execution 'in order to give you an account of his behaviour, and from no curiosity of my own'. 'Everyone', he added, 'enquired after you – you have friends everywhere.' Warner traipsed off to Surgeon's Hall to send a report on the dissected body of the killer – 'a genteel, well-made young fellow of four and twenty'. John Heneage Jesse, who knew a good story when he saw one, padded out these letters with clippings and cuttings from the newspapers of 1779.

Yet the context and sense of period that Walpole and Selwyn conveyed were far more important to the nineteenth-century reader than any details of the crime, exciting and shocking though they were. For Victorians the style and content of these two memorialists gave them a sense of the last quarter of the eighteenth century as aristocratic, indolent, dissipated and corrupt, an interpretation that dominated literary and political commentary on the first part of George III's reign. The gossipy, witty memoirs and letters, mixing great events with private scandal and the trivial obsessions of a rich elite, were seen to embody the moral failings they portrayed. Martha Ray's murder, which exposed the disreputable private life of a prominent public figure and which Walpole and Selwyn's friends treated with fascinated prurience and cynical amusement rather than outright moral condemnation, was considered as one of the most telling examples of the spirit of the former age.

Of course Walpole and Selwyn's angle of vision was rather unusual. Walpole, the son of the first prime minister, Sir Robert Walpole, and Selwyn, the son of two officials at the court of Queen Caroline, were sinecurists, gentlemen of leisure living at the public expense. 'You get up at nine,' wrote Lord Carlisle to Selwyn, 'play with Raton [his lapdog] until twelve in your night gown; then creep down to White's to abuse Fanshawe; are five hours at table; sleep till you can escape your supper reckoning; then make two wretches carry you, with three pints of claret in you, three miles for a shilling.' Such indolence did not sit well with the Victorian reviewers.

Though both Walpole and Selwyn were Members of Parliament and state employees, their views of politics and the public political stage were insouciant and cynical; sometimes personally malicious. They devoted their lives to backbiting gossip (Hazlitt called Walpole 'the very prince of gossips') and to their private obsessions – in Selwyn's case morbid ones, in Walpole's a love of the gothic and of antiquities. Both were lifelong bachelors, rather epicene and androgynous figures – jokes about Selwyn's sexlessness were common among his friends, while Walpole liked to dress for masquerades as a nun – surrounded by women friends and admirers and by effete male companions in social circles known for their exquisite exclusiveness and snobbery.

Nineteenth-century Whigs like Thomas Babington Macaulay and Tories like John Wilson Croker, though parliamentary foes, bitter personal enemies and literary combatants in the pages of the *Edinburgh* and *Quarterly Reviews*, were united in their contempt for the world that Walpole and Selwyn depicted and inhabited. Tories condemned the old Whig politics, and Whigs, though they may have supported the views of the likes of Charles James Fox, thought the early part of George III's reign had been corrupt and immoral, devoid of industry, private probity and any sense of public duty.

Nineteenth-century male commentators were uneasy about what they considered Walpole and Selwyn's effeminate manners and ephemeral tastes, which they took to be symptomatic of an indolent, politically and morally corrupt age. They treated the two men as representatives of a class interested more in pleasure than duty and heedless of its responsibility to set the moral tone for the nation. (There was no sense of the devotion that kept Sandwich for long hours at his office.) High-minded Victorians were shocked and appalled by the eagerness with which the two men regaled their friends with scandal and gossip, publicly circulating what any nineteenth-century gentleman would have felt obliged to suppress. As Macaulay put it, in a famous attack on Walpole in the *Edinburgh Review* in 1833 (and he might just as well have been talking about George Selwyn): 'The conformation of his mind was such, that whatever was little, seemed to him great, and whatever was great seemed to him little. Serious business was a trifle for him, and trifles were his serious business.'

By the mid-nineteenth century the picture painted by Walpole and Selwyn had become something of a cliché. It can be found, with high-colouring and pointillist detail, in the novelist William Makepeace Thackeray's enormously popular *The Four Georges*. These four essays, first delivered as lectures on a tour of the United States in 1855 and eventually published in 1860 in the *Cornhill Magazine*, depicted society at the time of George III as brim full of 'awful debauchery and extravagance' and 'dissoluteness'.

Like many of his contemporaries, Thackeray seems to have been both fascinated and repelled by manners and morals before the French Revolution. He was a close friend of Mary Berry, who as a young woman had been Horace Walpole's favourite. She had been bequeathed Walpole's memoirs, edited his works and letters and boldly defended him from Macaulay's brilliant strictures. Just as Basil Montagu's friends, especially his younger protégés, looked on him as a

link to an earlier and different age, so Thackeray saw Miss Berry as
a personal connection between the present and a now distant past
which she herself described as 'so different from the business, the
movement [and the] important struggles' of the modern age. As
Thackeray wrote in the *Cornhill Magazine*:

> A very few years since, I knew familiarly a lady who had been
> asked in marriage by Horace Walpole; who had been patted on
> the head by George III. This lady had knocked at Doctor Johnson's
> door; had been intimate with Fox, the beautiful Georgiana of
> Devonshire, and the brilliant Whig society of the reign of George
> III; had known the Duchess of Queensberry, the patroness of Gay
> and Prior, the admired young beauty of the Court of Queen Anne.
> I often thought, as I took my kind old friend's hand, how with it
> I held on to the old society of wits and men of the world.

Just as he cherished the frail Miss Berry as the personification of
what he called 'the old society, with its courtly splendours', Thackeray
revelled in the description of its characters, vices and peccadilloes.
He wrote of Jesse's *Memoirs of George Selwyn*, '[here] we have the real
original men and women of fashion . . . wits and prodigals; some
persevering in their bad ways; some repentant, but relapsing; beautiful ladies, parasites, humble chaplains, led captains . . . we make
acquaintance with a hundred of these fine folks, hear their talk and
laughter, read of their loves, quarrels, intrigues, debts, duels, divorces:
can fancy them alive if we read the book long enough.' Nor could
he take his eyes off the demi-monde from which Martha Ray came,
that 'great unacknowledged world, extravagant beyond measure, tearing about in the pursuit of pleasure: dancing, gambling, drinking,
singing . . . outvying the real leaders of fashion, in luxury, and splendour and beauty'. According to Thackeray, the patricians and the
demi-monde were connected by a mutual vice, in which music, so
loved by both the Earl of Sandwich and Martha Ray, played a vital

part: 'it has brought over singing-women, and dancing-women from all the operas of Europe, on whom lords have lavished their thousands, whilst they left their honest wives and honest children languishing in the lonely, deserted splendours of the castle and the park at home'. As the pace of Thackeray's account quickens, so he piles detail on top of detail:

> We can have high life or low, the struggle at the Opera to behold the Violetta or the Zamperini – the Macaronis and fine ladies in their chairs trooping to the masquerade or to Madame Cornelys's – the crowd at Drury Lane [sic] to look at the body of Miss Ray, whom parson Hackman has just pistolled – or we can peep into Newgate, where poor Mr Rice the forger is waiting his fate and his supper.

What begins as an account of aristocratic elegance ends with the annals of crime. Thackeray's view of the period is that of John Gay's *Beggar's Opera* in which high and low life mirror one another in their depravity.

For Thackeray the Georgian age is distant and exotic, a world of oriental luxury and corruption. He compares Carlton House, the home of the Prince Regent, to the 'palace of Nebuchadnezzar' and Pall Mall to the ruins of Palmyra. (What would he have made of Liotard's portrait of the young Sandwich dressed as a Turkish pasha?) He thinks of it as a world gone for ever, and, with it, its 'principal character', men like the Earl of Sandwich: 'I fancy that peculiar product of the past, the fine gentleman, has almost vanished off the face of the earth, and is disappearing like the beaver or the Red Indian.' Values have changed – gone is an obsequiousness and defer-ence to kings and lords – and so has the system that encouraged profligacy: 'It was the good time for Patricians. Small blame to them if they took and enjoyed, and over-enjoyed, the prizes of politics, the pleasures of social life.'

At the centre of Thackeray's picture is a detailed portrait of a libertine. It might have been Sandwich but turns out to be his friend the Earl of March, afterwards Lord Queensberry, an admirer of Martha Ray who was often a visitor at Hinchingbrooke and was an enthusiast, like Sandwich, for music and young women. 'The legends about old Q.', writes Thackeray, 'are awful. In *Selwyn*, in *Wraxall,* and contemporary chronicles, the observer of human nature may follow him, drinking, gambling, intriguing to the end of his career; when the wrinkled, palsied, toothless old Don Juan died, as wicked and unrepentant as he had been in the hottest season of youth and passion. There is a house in Piccadilly, where they used to show a certain low window at which old Q. sat to his very last days, ogling through his senile glasses the women as they passed by.'

The Victorians, like Thackeray, took both a high moral tone, condemning the debaucheries of the age, and a historical perspective on the age of George III as one that created the social and political conditions in which vice could flourish. Lord Carlisle, according to Thackeray, 'was forced into luxury, and obliged to be a great lord and idler' – positively required to be dissolute – until his wife and children saved him. Stupendous wealth, craven deference, a demi-monde bent on satisfying the jaded appetites of the rich and a system of political corruption in which men 'slipped Lord North's bribes so elegantly under their ruffles' suborned all but the most morally upright. Sandwich's administration of the navy seemed to epitomize this all-embracing and almost unavoidable corruption. An age of vice made immorality inescapable. 'The only palliation or apology, and that a poor one' for George Selwyn, wrote one critic, 'is to be found in the bad taste and loose habits of his contemporaries'.

Sandwich's place as a minister in Lord North's government and his reputation as a libertine, Martha Ray's status as an adulterer, a kept woman and demi-rep, and James Hackman's obsessive and

Jean-Etienne Liotard's portrait of the young Sandwich in exotic Turkish costume, painted after the Earl's return from the Middle East in 1739. Sandwich supposedly liked the Turkish practice of polygamy.

This illustration to Thackeray's *The Four Georges* contrasts George
III and Queen Caroline's concern for the welfare of their subjects
with the vicious ways of the Georgian aristocracy.

violent conduct towards her made the events of 1779 an exemplum of the depravity that Thackeray and his contemporaries saw as characteristic of the Georgian era. As the editor of the novelist M. G. Lewis's *Life and Correspondence* remarked in 1839, the murder of Ray 'was an event, which not only created a great sensation at the time, but strikingly illustrates – although by no means in a favourable light – the moral state of English society at that period'. The whole saga, wrote another commentator in the 1840s, 'was vulgar, mean, and vicious, after all; and, divested of that colouring which imagination might throw on any event, was degrading and criminal in all its circumstances'. All three protagonists were morally tainted:

> The shame of the wretched woman herself, living in a state of open criminality from year to year; the grossness of Hackman in his proposal to make this abandoned woman his wife; the strong probability that his object might have been the not uncommon, though infinitely vile one, of obtaining Lord Sandwich's patronage, by relieving him of a connexion, of which that notorious profligate, after nine years, might be weary – all characterise the earlier portion of their intercourse as destitute of all pretense to honourable feelings.

As for the murder itself, it was 'merely the work of an assassin'. Raising himself to his full moral height, the author concluded, 'The clear case is, that he [Hackman] was neither more nor less than a furious villain, resolved to have the life of a profligate milliner's apprentice, who preferred Lord Sandwich's house and carriage, to Mr Hackman's hovel and going on foot.' The moral of this story was rooted in universal depravity, but one that especially flourished in a wicked age.

Victorian commentators complimented themselves on how much progress had been made since the bad old days of George III. The reviewer of *George Selwyn and his Contemporaries* in the *Edinburgh Review* smugly contrasted Georgian and Victorian morals: 'We are happy to say that the comparison, suggested by these volumes, between the manners and morals of the last century and our own, is highly satisfactory.' The 'unoccupied classes' no longer pursue 'coarse indulgences or strong excitements' but prefer 'Intellectual tastes'. The debauched and vicious now have sufficient 'respect for public opinion' that they 'conceal their transgressions from the world'. The few men of 'noble birth or high connexion' who are 'professed votaries of (what they call) pleasure' no longer consort with nor look to 'men distinguished in the senate, the cabinet or the court' to join in their pleasures. Alluding directly to the scandals around the Duke of Grafton, Lord Sandwich and Lord March, the author triumphantly concluded

> No prime minister escorts a woman of the town through the Crush-room of the Opera; no first Lord of the Admiralty permits his mistress to do the honours of his house, or weeps over her in the columns of the *Morning Post*; no Lord of the Bedchamber starts for Newmarket with a *danseuse* in his carriage, and her whole family in his train; our parliamentary leaders do not dissipate their best energies at the gaming-table; our privy councillors do not attend cock-fights.

So the Hackman–Ray affair, which during the eighteenth century was treated as an extraordinary, psychologically and morally complex event – an aberration that prompted self-examination and analysis – became in this new interpretation not just an instance of the Biblical dictum that the wages of sin are death (a point made by some commentators) but an incident typical of the moral depravity of its time. The moral distance between the events of 1779 and the mid-Victorian age became part of a story of progress and civilization: 'Morality, taste, knowledge, general freedom of intercourse, and liberality of opinion have been advancing', commented the *Edinburgh Review*. The circumstances surrounding the murder now seemed exotic

– because so remote, so unimaginable in the present. Of course, this does not mean that Victorian cabinet ministers never had mistresses or that violent crimes of passion were at an end; rather it speaks to a deep-seated desire to assert a rigorous public morality.

One cannot but be impressed by how often in the mid-nineteenth century the tale of Hackman and Ray was connected to a burning desire to establish that the modern leaders of society were (or perhaps more accurately should be) conducting themselves according to the high moral standards of the Christian faith. Public and private conduct, according to this interpretation, should be judged by the same criteria, before the all-seeing eye of the divinity. Misconduct in either sphere was reprehensible. At the same time (and here a note of realism creeps in) commentators recognized the frailty of human nature, the capacity of even the great and the good to err, but insisted on the obligation of concealment. The crime of the likes of Sandwich was to flaunt his mistress in public, to defy opinion and ignore censure, to appear to have no guilt or remorse about his sexual depravity. Some writers thought of Martha Ray's murder as a consequence of the Earl's openness, of the public visibility of her relationship with her keeper.

Nineteenth-century critics portrayed British leaders as having learned the lessons of revolutionary and democratic politics, of accepting the need to set a moral example and not to flout conventional morality – at least publicly. Hence the almost obsessive desire to keep private matter out of public life, the hostility to Walpole and Selwyn's chatter and gossip, Macaulay's disgust at Boswell's revelations about Johnson, the sense (not of course shared by the likes of Thomas Carlyle) that personal biography and accounts of everyday life should be excluded from history proper, which should concern itself with politics and statecraft.

There is, of course, a contradiction here: on the one hand the

Victorian critics considered domestic and public probity to be closely linked (it was said that Horace Walpole was unsuitable as a public memorialist because he was not a married man); on the other they strove mightily to keep the conduct of public affairs and private life clearly apart. The story of Sandwich, Ray and Hackman was a particularly suitable admonitory anecdote because it illustrated so well the fatal consequences of mixing public and private life, of ignoring public opinion and Christian morality. This attitude explains the repugnance that a nineteenth-century visitor to the Admiralty offices felt when he saw Martha Ray's portrait still hanging on the wall.

The story of Hackman's murder of Martha Ray was not confined to the politicians, critics and journalists who scrutinized eighteenth-century memoirs. It enjoyed much wider circulation among a large readership for the burgeoning literature about crime that became popular in the 1820s and 1830s. Fuelled in part by fears of political insurrection by the dangerous classes, this growing body of cheap illustrated literature was eager to exploit every sensational crime. Many of these so-called penny-dreadfuls concentrated on gruesome contemporary crimes. These included the Gill's Hill murder of 1823 when John Thurtell (the model for Tom Turtle in his friend Hazlitt's essay 'The Fight') killed a gambling friend and carted his body round the suburbs of London (several commentators remarked on the fact that the victim was buried at Elstree in the same graveyard that contained Martha Ray's remains); the Red Barn murder, a crime of passion complete with a festering corpse; the Burke and Hare murders in Edinburgh where victims were killed to provide bodies for doctors and anatomists; and the murder of Hannah Brown by James Green-acre, who dismembered and dispersed parts of her corpse.

In common with Hackman's crime, these murders were gruesome and sometimes the result of sexual passion, but they were publicized in a different register and intended for a different audience than *The Case and Memoirs of James Hackman*. While Dawes's sentimental and psychologically complex tract did not dwell on the act of murder itself, the nineteenth-century killings were told (and depicted in woodcut prints) in all their gory detail – decapitations, stabbings, throat-cuttings, axe murders, the flogging of bare-breasted women. The complex feelings of the killer and his victim were, more often than not, reduced to a tabloid tale of wickedness and virtue, good and evil, condemned by a morality just as rigid as that of the more high-flown critics of Walpole and Selwyn. Such copy sold astonishingly well. Kearsley may have made a handsome profit on Dawes's *Case and Memoirs*, but he never reached the sort of audience commanded by James Catnach, the best-known publisher of cheap accounts of murders, whose dying speech of William Corder, the Red Barn murderer, sold a reputed 1,166,000 copies.

For the purveyors of literary murder in the 1820s and 1830s there was simply not enough contemporary crime. Eager to arouse and retain the prurient curiosity of their readers, they adopted two strategies, manufacturing 'cocks', or fictitious crime stories, while at the same time plundering the records of the previous two centuries, rooting out the more sensational crimes and resurrecting the most famous corpses, including that of Martha Ray. To feed the growing appetite they had nurtured, they turned to the collected volumes of trials that had first appeared in the 1770s, shortly before Ray's death. These, usually called Newgate Calendars, were chronological compilations of the most remarkable, strange and violent crimes; they contained a brief account of the crimes, trials and execution of the malefactors and were often illustrated with the sort of engraving that fascinated and haunted the dreams of the legal reformer George Romilly when he read them as a child. Hackman's crime appeared repeatedly in the different versions of the Calendar published in the nineteenth century: the edition of 1809–10, enlarged in 1826–8; William Jackson's *New and Complete Newgate Calendar; or, Malefactors Universal Register*, published in eight volumes between 1812 and 1818; George Borrow's six-volume compilation *Celebrated Trials, and Remarkable Cases of Criminal Jurisprudence*; and *The Chronicles of Crime; or the New Newgate Calendar*, edited by Camden Pelham, which appeared in 1841.

Though the various versions of Hackman's crime in these volumes were in their details largely the same, the Newgate Calendars gradually shifted the interpretation of the murder. William Jackson's edition, produced while George III was still on the throne, was an exceptionally didactic collection in which the editor repeatedly warned his readers against the temptations of youth – but for his 'unhappy passion', he said of Hackman, he 'might have been an ornament to his country' – but nevertheless treated the murder as exceptional: 'There are some events of so sudden, so striking a nature, that when they happen in our own time, and within the compass of our observation, they affect us more than when we read of them in the antient authors . . . such is the case before us.' For Jackson it was inconceivable that Hackman could ever have thought that 'Miss Reay would have left the family of a noble lord at the head of one of the highest departments of state, in order to live in a humble station'. (Almost all nineteenth-century commentators agreed.) Only an 'unhappy, irregular, and ungovernable passion' could have led him in an 'unhappy moment' to commit such a crime. Only the strange power of love could have produced such foolish expectations and such a terrible outcome.

Jackson's account, then, resembled eighteenth-century versions of the murder as a strange aberration, but in later versions of the New-gate Calendar Hackman's crime was deemed typical of an age when both crimes and punishments were particularly brutal. Camden

THE

NEWGATE CALENDAR;

COMPRISING

INTERESTING MEMOIRS

OF

THE MOST NOTORIOUS CHARACTERS

WHO HAVE BEEN CONVICTED OF OUTRAGES ON

𝕿𝖍𝖊 𝕷𝖆𝖜𝖘 𝖔𝖋 𝕰𝖓𝖌𝖑𝖆𝖓𝖉

SINCE THE COMMENCEMENT OF THE EIGHTEENTH CENTURY;

WITH

OCCASIONAL ANECDOTES AND OBSERVATIONS,

SPEECHES, CONFESSIONS, AND LAST EXCLAMATIONS OF SUFFERERS.

BY

ANDREW KNAPP AND WILLIAM BALDWIN,

ATTORNEYS AT LAW.

The Tower of London.

VOL. IV.

𝕷𝖔𝖓𝖉𝖔𝖓:

J. ROBINS AND CO. IVY LANE, PATERNOSTER ROW.

1826.

Title page of one of the more expensive of the many nineteenth-century editions of *The Newgate Calendar* with tales of 'notorious characters', 'outrages' and the 'last exclamations of sufferers'.

Pelham, in the 1841 *Chronicles of Crime*, explained, 'The comparison of the offences, and of the punishments of the last century, with those of more recent date, will exhibit a marked distinction between the two periods, both as to the atrocity of the one, and the severity of the other.' Ignoring the predilection of penny-dreadfuls for recent brutal and gory murders, he explicitly linked a decline in savage crime with the legal reforms of the 1820s and 1830s, so vigorously supported by Martha Ray's son Basil Montagu, that had ended capital punishment for crimes against property. 'Those dreadful and frequent crimes, which would disgrace the more savage tribes, and which characterised the lives of the early objects of our criminal proceedings,' he confidently asserted, 'are now no longer heard of; and those characters of blood, in which the pages of our statute book were formerly written, have been wiped away by improved civilisation and the milder feelings of the people.'

As the memory faded of the circumstantial evidence of Ray's murder, Hackman's crime became just another instance in a catalogue of depravity and wickedness, historical filler in works that were prurient and titillating. The penny-dreadfuls and the cheapest versions of the Newgate Calendar, like the serial version that cost a penny an issue and first appeared in 1864, ignored overt moralizing and sermons about progress in favour of sensational detail. But even when they avoided the high-minded tone of some of the more expensive collected volumes of notorious crimes, they endorsed the view of the eighteenth century as a much more barbarous age. *The New Newgate Calendar*, for instance, depicted mid-Georgian London as exceptionally dangerous for the honest citizen: 'In the year 1768 London after dark was a perilous place for those who had to visit the outskirts of the metropolis: footpads abounded, and highway robberies were of frequent occurrence ... if the country roads were insecure, the streets of London were little safer.' The absence of police, of any attempt at criminal detection, bad street lighting – in short the lack of the amenities of Victorian life – made the eighteenth century a dark age, if a fascinating one. Popular literature and critics like Thackeray shared a progressive vision, in which the eighteenth century was a now distant because less civilized era.

This picture of the eighteenth century was reinforced in the numerous historical novels of the 1830s and 1840s that took Georgian criminals and low life as their subject. Edward Bulwer Lytton's *Paul Clifford* (1830) and *Eugene Aram* (1832), William Harrison Ainsworth's *Rookwood* (1834) and *Jack Sheppard* (1839) – all so-called Newgate novels – were hugely successful, spawning theatrical spinoffs (no fewer than eight in the case of *Jack Sheppard*) that depicted Georgian criminals in a sympathetic light. Like Croft's *Love and Madness* most of these novels were based on historical cases. Bulwer's wife read aloud to him the entire Newgate Calendar in preparation for writing *Paul Clifford*, while the story of *Eugene Aram* was taken from a strange case of 1759 in which an erudite scholar and schoolmaster was party to a cruel murder. *Rookwood* made famous the highwayman Dick Turpin, a minor criminal hung in 1739, transforming a brief if hectic escape into the epic long ride to and from York. *Jack Sheppard*, the most successful of the Newgate novels, was based on the life of a young footpad and thief, betrayed by the notorious eighteenth-century thief-taker, Jonathan Wild, whose chief claim to fame was his remarkable ability to escape from the most secure of gaols. Sheppard died at twenty-two on the gallows at Tyburn in 1724 but, thanks to Ainsworth, his memory lived on well into the nineteenth century. (Many of the children questioned by the 1852 House of Commons Inquiry into the situation of Criminal and Destitute Juveniles frequently spoke of the exploits of Sheppard and Dick Turpin.)

With the exception of Thackeray's Newgate novel, *Catherine*

George Cruickshank's dramatic rendition of Jonathan Wild's arrest of Jack
Sheppard at his mother's graveside as told in Ainsworth's novel of 1839.

(serialized 1839–40), that was deliberately designed to subvert the
conventions of the genre, these historical crime fictions were sympathetic to their real-life subjects. In part this was possible because the
criminals portrayed did not seem to belong to modern life. Few

authors were as bold as Charles Dickens in setting their Newgate novels in the near present. Turpin and Sheppard, neither of them murderers, were easily treated as swashbuckling characters in picaresque stories. Though Ainsworth, drawing on Hogarth, depicted Sheppard as an idle apprentice to contrast him with another industrious young man, he emerges as a sympathetic character, the victim of a brutal, unreformed legal system, who has the domestic virtue of a deep attachment to his mother, but who is reckless and daring. The emphasis is not on his crimes but on his spectacular escapes, which were repeatedly re-enacted to loud applause on the London stage.

Ainsworth was an entertainer not a reformer, but he gave his readers a strong sense of how terrible prison conditions and the penal code had once been. Edward Bulwer Lytton, on the other hand, was quite explicit in using the Newgate novel to further legal reform, acknowledging in the 1840 preface to *Paul Clifford* that one of his aims had been to attack the sanguinary penal code.

Hackman's crime was never, to my knowledge, used in a Newgate novel. The genre's leading figures were usually picaresque characters and not, like Hackman, respectable members of society. Fiction focused on low life and the culture of the apprentice, not high society and gentlefolk, and it looked primarily to the early part of the eighteenth century, before the apogee of aristocratic luxury in George III's reign. The Newgate novel's version of eighteenth-century crime came from William Hogarth rather than Horace Walpole – above all from Hogarth's series of prints about the Industrious and Idle Apprentice, often reproduced in penny magazines and cheap publications for the common reader. Hackman, Ray and Sandwich had no place in this world.

During the early nineteenth century critics treated Hackman's crime as an anecdote, fragment, vignette or tableau. This meant that even if they had wished to do so, they would have found it difficult to write a morally and psychologically full account of the killing, which would have required a longer, more elaborate narrative. The murder of Ray turned into a case study that conformed to a nineteenth-century historicist view that every discrete event somehow embodies the spirit of the age, and that pandered to an attitude that contrasted earlier barbarism and inequality with contemporary civilization based on fair justice and private moral probity for all ranks of society. After the mid-nineteenth century the story of Martha Ray's murder was largely forgotten. Basil Montagu, a constant reminder of his mother's tragic end, died in 1851. Readers fascinated with crime became preoccupied with the enormities of the present and less optimistic about its vision of historical progress. Though the story was still of considerable interest at Hinchingbrooke and in the surrounding villages, it was not resurrected by the Montagu family, which, unlike many other aristocratic families, did not publish the papers of predecessors such as the fourth earl. The story was only revived when fin-de-siècle aesthetes rediscovered the aristocratic and morally uninhibited eighteenth century.

CHAPTER 9

The Twentieth Century

LIKE A MODERN mobile phone conversation, the story of James Hackman, Martha Ray and the Earl of Sandwich began to break up in the second half of the nineteenth century. The story almost never appeared at any length and when it did, as in the Revd John Doran's *Saints and Sinners; or, In church and about it* (1868), it lacked detail or accuracy. (At least one account of the period supposed that Ray shot Hackman.) Contributors to the pages of *Notes and Queries*, an antiquarian journal in which pedants, antiquarians, eccentric obsessives and scholars squabbled over picayune points of historical detail, were chiefly interested in Boswell's part in Hackman's story – was he in the coach with Hackman? was he the author of letters in the newspapers? – rather than in the circumstances of the murder itself. They quarrelled over particulars but did not reconstruct the whole story, repeatedly falling back on the snippets of information contained in the Newgate Calendars.

But in the 1890s interest in the case revived with Gilbert Burgess's publication of *The Love Letters of Mr H. and Miss R., 1775–1779.* Burgess had found no new evidence. He was a recycler. He took Croft's *Love and Madness* and stripped out the Chatterton material, which he relegated to an appendix. (He did not even use the full text of the letter about Chatterton, printing instead an abbreviated version that had appeared in a reprint of *Love and Madness* published in Ipswich in 1810.) He also cut and embroidered the remaining letters. Like the publisher of the Ipswich edition, he bowdlerized the letters about Hackman and Ray's sexual relations – 'I have been obliged to suppress certain passages, by reason of their having been written at a time when there was a greater license of expression than is permissible nowadays.' Burgess also inserted a commentary designed 'to weave the letters into a coherent narrative' because he felt that 'several of the connecting links in the narrative' were missing. Above all, he abandoned Croft's rather sensational title – so much like an epistolary novel of the 1770s – replacing it with the matter-of-fact *The Love Letters of Mr H. and Miss R., 1775–1779*. The change was not accidental: Burgess wanted to claim these as genuine letters – historical documents – that revealed a true story.

In order to make his view of *The Love Letters* more credible, Burgess tried to redress the disproportionate attention that Croft had paid to Hackman. (He remained puzzled why so few of Ray's letters survived.) He set out to refashion the book as a tale of mutual, if ill-fated love. This led him to play down Hackman's madness, which had shaped Croft's narrative, and to dismiss his crime as only 'the result of a momentary impulse'. His interest was in the love affair, not in Hackman's mental state or motives. Accordingly, he gave equal billing to Mr H. and Miss R. in his title, and the publisher designed a cover that displayed two hearts with intertwined ribbons, marked 'H' and 'R'. But Burgess, of course, had no new Ray letters to complement the fictional Hackman ones, and though he made some minor excisions to the text, he could not make greater cuts without losing the shape of the story. Instead he tried to make Ray more prominent by using long passages from Cradock's *Literary and Miscellaneous Memoirs* to flesh out the character of Martha Ray.

Cradock was not Burgess's only source. He also unearthed a new

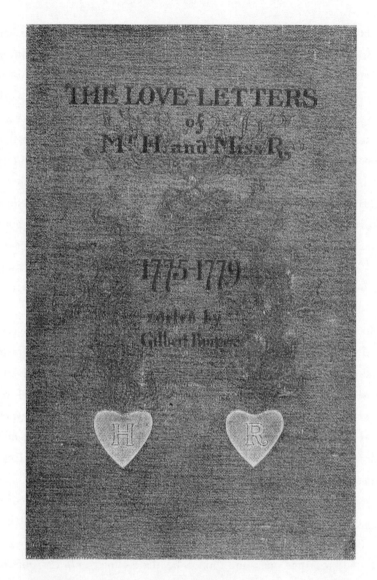

The cover of *The Love Letters of Mr H. and Miss R.* combines the symbolism of romance with the spare details of a historical document.

anecdote about Martha Ray that had first appeared in the *Life and Correspondence* of M. G. ('Monk') Lewis (1839), and that was to be repeated in almost all subsequent versions of her life. Lewis – slave-owner, playwright, friend of Goethe, Byron and Sir Walter Scott and the author of the sensational gothic novel, *The Monk: a Romance* (1796), published when he was only twenty – recalled a story told to him by his mother about Martha Ray. Anne-Marie Lewis had been a well-known beauty, courtier and accomplished musician, who had moved in the circle of amateur musicians and enthusiasts patronized by Sandwich. She told her son that she had dined with Ray on the day of the murder. Mrs Lewis noticed that 'Miss Ray seemed unusually depressed in spirits', though she rallied during the course of the afternoon, promising her friends as she left for the theatre that she would 'return as soon as the principal performance was over'. As she got ready to leave, 'Mrs Lewis happened to make some remark on a beautiful rose which Miss Ray wore in her bosom'. No sooner had she spoken than 'the flower fell to the ground'. As Ray picked it up 'the red leaves [sic] scattered themselves on the carpet, and the stalk alone remained in her hands'. Ray was visibly upset: 'the poor girl, who had been depressed in spirits before, was evidently affected by this incident, and said in a slightly faltering voice, "I trust I am not to consider this an evil omen!"' (As the editor of the *Life and Correspondence* explains in a note, in parts of Italy 'the red rose is considered an emblem of early death; and it is an evil omen to scatter its leaves on the ground'.)

This story, a sinister portent such as those that appeared in many gothic novels of the early nineteenth century, is the only new element in Lewis's version of Ray's story. The rest of his account, like Burgess's, draws extensively on Cradock's *Memoirs* to describe the social slights and personal rebuffs that Martha Ray faced with such elegance and fortitude, and to emphasize the concern of both Sandwich and

Ray to comport themselves with propriety. Even more than in Cradock's work, Lewis's *Life and Correspondence* stressed the power-lessness of Ray's position: it repeated the embarrassing stories of her being ignored at parties at Hinchingbrooke and emphasized her financial dependence on Lord Sandwich. Sandwich himself comes across as haughty, 'rigidly punctilious', 'cold, selfish, and formal', and Ray, painfully conscious of her obligations to the Earl, as fearful of him. She would never have mentioned the prospect of working in the opera, wrote Lewis, 'fearing probably that he might look on her wish to be independent as a proof of ingratitude, and afterwards become her enemy'. Her dependence, in this account, was an 'almost negative bounty'.

In Lewis's hands the story takes a form akin to the sort of gothic novel that made him famous. He foregrounds the themes of male power and money and of female dependence and weakness. We are offered a description of extremes. Ray's murder is no longer the act of a love-lorn youth but the crazed, impulsive act of a victim of possession. 'Mastered by a demoniacal impulse – the excitement of liquor having roused his before-exasperated feelings to absolute frenzy', the madman shoots his victim and then turns another pistol on himself. Lewis cannot resist turning the sentimental story of the 1770s and 1780s into a gothic melodrama.

When he recounts the story as told by his mother, Lewis ends with her sentimental response to Ray's killing: 'The effect which the dreadful intelligence [of the murder] had upon Mrs Lewis, was . . . severe.' She identified with the victim: 'Naturally of a warm heart, and alive to suffering, the peculiar manner in which she herself seemed, in some degree, connected with the event, from the incident with the rose – together with her regard for Miss Ray, and the willing sympathy she had always paid her on account of her peculiar situation – brought the matter more immediately under her notice, and her regret for the victim nearer to her heart.' Nor did Lewis's mother forget Martha Ray: 'Even to the day of her death, any mention of this unfortunate young person never failed to change her gayest mood into one of pensiveness and melancholy.'

Burgess's inclusion of Lewis's anecdotes about Martha Ray helped him present a more vivid as well as more balanced account of the love triangle between the mistress and her two lovers. But anyone alerted by Burgess to Lewis's *Life and Correspondence* who chose to go back to Lewis's text – a group that, as we shall see, included two women authors who were to write their own versions of Ray's life – would have discovered one of the first accounts in which Martha Ray was the principal figure. And, though Lewis's narrative was shaped by his gothic sensibilities, it was still a story of a woman who had deep sympathy and some personal identification with Martha Ray. The chief relationship in Lewis's account is the affinity between Martha Ray and a woman who kept an enduring memory of a tragedy in which she played a supporting part. Lewis feminizes the story: it becomes a tale of female solidarity and sympathy with the victim.

Burgess's concerns lay elsewhere. In his preface to *The Love Letters of Mr H. and Miss R.* he strenuously asserted the correspondence's authenticity. He did not believe that a learned lexicographer like Croft could write passionate love letters. 'No record of Croft's own work', he argued, 'tallies at all with the idea that he created such a romance.' Burgess claimed that after what he described as 'exhaustive investigation', he was completely 'convinced that such a document is only explainable on the grounds of a real living correspondence and that these letters are, without doubt, those that passed between Hackman and Miss Reay'. After years of neglect, they deserved to be republished and properly edited because 'The story and the letters seem to me to be a veritable "human document" of strong interest'. Burgess's choice of words is revealing. Not only the letters but even the story they tell are more than a mere narrative. In becoming a document they have moved into history.

To reinforce his view of their authenticity and explain why they had sometimes been condemned as fakes, Burgess had to write his own history of the letters. Hackman's brother-in-law, Frederick Booth, he claimed, willingly gave Kearsley the originals, or copies of the originals, because he was so unhappy about the inaccuracies and errors in *The Case and Memoirs of James Hackman*. 'It is not quite clear whether Booth was approached by Kearsly [sic] or by Croft; but that he [Booth] was satisfied with the latter's work is evident from the fact that it elicited no further protests from him.' Croft, eager for literary fame, then married the material he had obtained in Bristol about Thomas Chatterton with the letters between Ray and Hackman, which had the unfortunate effect of casting doubt on the whole correspondence: 'He clumsily put his papers into the form of a letter from Hackman, which was marked no. 49 in the original book, and is included in an appendix to the present volume. The difference in the style of this letter from that of all the others was so apparent that suspicion fell upon the authenticity of other parts of the volume.'

Burgess still had to clear a further obstacle to his claim that the letters were actually written by Hackman and Ray. What was he to do with Croft's public avowal that he was their author? Burgess put it down to Croft's vaingloriousness: 'The enormous success of "Love and Madness" tempted Croft to declare himself the author of the Chatterton excerpt, and also to hint that of the entire work only the outline was true. The word outline is easily expansible, and, considering that the letter about Chatterton, and two or three other obvious additions, formed half the volume, he was perhaps justified in claiming this portion.'

Burgess generally refrained from moral commentary about the content of the letters. His only intervention reinforced his claim that they tell a tragic tale of thwarted true love. He could not resist the temptation to underline Caterina Galli's culpability in destroying the couple's prospect of joint bliss. Commenting on a letter in which Hackman apparently praises Galli, Burgess remarked: 'Full of hope and happiness he looks forward to the new life that is before them, and he expresses his thankfulness for Signora Galli's kindness. But there is no doubt that this woman, whose conduct throughout was sinister, is morally reprehensible for the events that followed.' Galli's betrayal is a guarantee that all was well before her intervention.

Burgess repeatedly implied that the intensity of expressions of love in the correspondence demonstrated their authenticity. The real story was the love story. He was to receive support for this view from an unusual quarter. When *The Love Letters of Mr H. and Miss R.* was published in the United States, a scholar at the University of Chicago, E. H. Lewis, put Burgess's claims under the microscope in a learned article in *Modern Languages Notes.* Lewis was rigorously sceptical of Burgess's arguments. He pointed out that if Booth did not disapprove of *Love and Madness* then 'he must have seen and permitted the Chatterton letters; and a relative who, to lend false credit to Hackman as a *litterateur*, would connive at a Chatterton letter, would connive at more tampering with the dead man's *billets-doux*'. Nor was Lewis persuaded that the Chatterton material was written in a different style from many other letters in the correspondence. He also pointed to the odd absence of letters written by Martha Ray, which had also troubled Burgess. Surely Hackman would have preserved them and Croft 'would have withheld none of those then in his possession'. So far, so scholarly and tough-minded.

Lewis detected two very different styles – and therefore two different hands – in the letters, and he concluded that there must have been a set of original letters that Croft doctored. 'The letters that contain ... leisurely erudition', he argued, 'contrast strongly with the passionate single-heartedness of the true Hackman style.' The 'real' letters expressed Hackman's heart-felt 'protestations of love and eager hopes for a speedy marriage', and Croft, according to Lewis, padded these with his literary reflections and detailed discussion of other cases of love's madness. Hackman's obsessions with death and suicide were, in Lewis's view, the contrivance of Croft. The story of progressive derangement told in *Love and Madness* is a fiction; Hackman and Ray – and here Lewis follows the views of Burgess – are mutually happy lovers betrayed by Galli.

The real letters are those that come from Hackman's broken heart: 'nobody ever gave the world the story of a more genuine, a more passionately sustained devotion than that of Hackman'. They reveal the eighteenth-century man of feeling: 'From first to last he was swept on a tide of love as unusual in our modern days as it was destructive to him in those.' Lewis found these letters 'natural and credible', and wrote of 'the awful eloquence which bursts out of supreme human anguish when the victim tries to temper his pain by expressing it'.

Lewis was a scholar of rhetoric and philology who wrote a learned work on the English paragraph, but his analysis of *The Love Letters of Mr H. and Miss R.* adopts an eighteenth-century sensibility in which what comes from the heart is genuine and real, and what emerges from the head is artificial or fake. Lewis criticized Burgess's edition on these grounds. The editor of *The Love Letters*, he wrote, might have been more ruthless with his red pencil and excised many more passages to get at the 'true document'. But Lewis's critique left intact – indeed reinforced – Burgess's assertion that the letters, or parts of them, were a genuine correspondence, whose human value lay in the authentic depiction of the trials of love.

By drawing attention to Martha Ray and to the memoirs in which she was depicted sympathetically, Burgess's edition of *The Love Letters*

of Mr H. and Miss R. made possible a modern version of the murder
from the victim's point of view, while the new status of the letters
as historical documents meant that there was a rich body of material
to work with. Two writers, both women – Constance Hagberg
Wright and Elizabeth Jenkins – used them to present Martha Ray's
murder from her point of view. Wright, whose book *The Chaste
Mistress* was published in 1930, was a neophyte author whose only
other publication was a collection of oriental fairy-tales; but Elizabeth
Jenkins, who took Martha Ray as her first biographical case study in
her *Ten Fascinating Women* (1955, repr. 1968), was an experienced
writer, the author of a number of historical novels, and of successful
biographies of Queen Elizabeth and the Earl of Leicester, Henry
Fielding and Jane Austen.

Both authors were acutely conscious of the difficulties in telling
Ray's story and the obstacles that lay in the way of recovering her
character. For Wright, whose book had all the contrivance of a romantic novel but which also claimed veracity, the problem was twofold:
the figure of Ray was obscured by the historical prominence of Sandwich, and the historical record itself was patchy. Surviving portraits
of Ray failed to capture 'her inner self', recording 'her features without
capturing her charm'. Only painstaking reconstruction could bring
her to life: 'By piecing together fragments from memoirs, from journals and private letters, the real woman may be divined.' But, while
establishing her credentials as an assiduous researcher, Wright had
to concede that in telling Ray's story a certain amount of supposition
and imaginative reconstruction was needed. 'Sometimes fancy itself
must lend colour to the faded shape,' she admitted, 'or a challenged
authority be called upon to bridge a baffling hiatus.' This makes
clear that she was aware of the disputed authenticity of the letters
in *Love and Madness*, but this did not stop her from incorporating
them, without further comment, into her narrative. And, like Burgess

before her, she ended her foreword by strongly asserting the veracity of her story. 'We believe that, in the main,' she wrote, 'this picture of Martha Ray is essentially true. Such was she, and such her life-story, which the passing of one hundred and fifty years has not robbed of its pathetic interest.'

Elizabeth Jenkins was also aware of doubts about the authenticity of the letters in *Love and Madness*, but she seems to have read or, at least, to have concurred in Burgess's analysis of them. She complained that Croft's 'vexatious tampering' had given 'the whole collection of letters the reputation of being forgeries', but that their similarity to the suicide note, 'as well as other indications', meant that 'it is now considered the bulk of them as genuine'. Like others before her, she was convinced that 'it would have required much greater ability than any that Croft ever showed, to have invented them'.

Jenkins was conscious of how the memoirs and letters revealed Martha Ray through the eyes of her male admirers. 'It is not easy', she wrote, 'to gain a clear picture of Martha Ray, except obliquely, from the effect she had on two men as different from each other as Lord Sandwich and James Hackman.' She wanted to tell the story from Ray's point of view, to give a voice to someone who had previously been silent about her fate, but virtually no material written by Ray survived. Jenkins's task was to re-create her character and explain her actions using the views of others. Thus she inferred that Ray, 'quiet as she was', must have had some special attraction to excite the ardour of two such different men: 'Her attraction for . . . [Sandwich] was easily understandable, but that she should have aroused an engrossing, a besotted passion in a youth thirteen years younger than herself' was quite remarkable.

Wright's *The Chaste Mistress* was published at a time when there had been a revival of interest in the eighteenth century. The picaresque version of the era with its highwaymen, whores and tales of derring-do epitomized in the Newgate novel had never entirely vanished, and with works like Jeffery Farnol's *The Broad Highway* (1910) and the enormously successful production of *The Beggar's Opera* first staged by the Lyric Theatre Hammersmith in 1920, it achieved renewed popularity. What was novel, however, was an interest in the eighteenth century as an age of aristocracy, not in the negative register of the Victorians, with their moral repugnance at the Georgian elite's immorality and irresponsibility, but more positively as the embodiment of social refinement and good taste. A heterogeneous constituency of social and political conservatives pining for a world of order and deference, and of fashionable aesthetes and pleasure-seekers critical of Victorian taste and morality – and many were in both camps – helped to shape a new version of the eighteenth century as a time of hierarchy and public stability, private pleasure, and good taste.

Behind the new interest lay a disillusionment with parliamentary democracy, mass society and middle-brow culture. The First World War, when English gentlemen perished in unprecedented numbers while bankers, arms dealers and plutocrats filled their purses; progressive taxation and death duties (how could parliament punish the very classes it had so long deferred to?); socialism, strikes, social strife, ideological conflict and the emergence of the Labour Party as a major political force – these all seemed to herald the demise of landed aristocratic power and of traditional conservative values. The eighteenth century, and especially its landed society, seemed to epitomize the old order before the forces of vulgar modernity took control. The political and social world so brilliantly depicted by Lewis Namier in his two classic works *The Structure of Politics at the Accession of George III* and *England in the Age of the American Revolution* – both of which were published within a year of the appearance of *The Chaste Mistress* – was the very antithesis of mass politics or democratic society. Here was a world in which social distinction, influence and connection mattered and where a pragmatic commitment to sustaining the status quo and excluding all but a tiny elite shaped both politics and society. Namier set out to dispel the long-held belief that power in eighteenth-century England was sustained by bribery and corruption. Rather, he argued, the landed elite, themselves governed by paternalism and a sense of duty, elicited a natural, almost unthinking deference – a Burkean understanding of how the world was made and should be – that was one of the best qualities of the common-sensical British character.

This view of the eighteenth-century political arena sat in an occasionally uneasy relationship to a more familiar version of Georgian private life as a realm of pleasure. As early as the 1890s – the decade in which Burgess's *The Love Letters of Mr H. and Miss R.* had appeared – aesthetes and collectors were publishing small-press collections of eighteenth-century memoirs and letters, producing beautifully illustrated editions of such works as Alexander Pope's *The Rape of the Lock*, and reprinting works of eighteenth-century pornography and erotica such as John Wilkes's *Essay on Woman*. Arthur Machen's unexpurgated translation of Casanova's *Memoirs* appeared in 1894, E. Beresford Chancellor's *Lives of the Rakes* in several volumes during the 1920s. Under John Lane The Bodley Head, which published *The Chaste Mistress*, printed many eighteenth-century biographies and memoirs, as well as works of history. These included *Memoirs of Lady Fanshawe* (1905), *The Diary of a Lady-in-Waiting* (1908), the memoirs of *The Beautiful Lady Craven* (1914), John Fyvie's *Wits, Beaux and Beauties of the Georgian Era* (1909), an edition of Horace Walpole's *Last Journals* (1909), and Horace Bleakeley's study of the eighteenth century's most famous courtesans, *Ladies Fair and Frail* (1909), his biography of John Wilkes (1917) and his *Casanova in England* (1923).

Lane actively solicited such work, especially old memoirs and letters, publishing an advertisement calling on 'Those who possess letters, documents, correspondence, Mss., scraps of autobiography and also miniatures and portraits relating to persons and matters historical, political, literary and social' to contact him so that he could 'give his advice and assistance either on their preservation or publication'.

This revival was in part a recovery and celebration of the libertine eighteenth century, an apt project for the publisher of Oscar Wilde, *The Yellow Book*, and Arthur Symons, and it fitted neatly with the more lax morals and candid discussion of sexuality often associated with the fast set and bright young things – Evelyn Waugh's vile bodies – of the 1920s and 1930s. For all its hallowed traditionalism, when it came to sex the eighteenth century looked remarkably modern.

But the rehabilitation of a palpably undemocratic, somewhat raffish eighteenth century was much more than this. It was one symptom of a remarkable backlash against a mass culture that its critics thought at best standardized and middle-brow, at worst, debased and tawdry. This assault was launched by sober, high-minded academics and intellectuals (including socialists and radicals) as well as conservative traditionalists and fashion-conscious, gilded youth. In 1930, the same year that Constance Hagberg Wright's book appeared, F. R. Leavis published his jeremiad, *Mass Civilisation and Minority Culture*, Ortega y Gasset's *Revolt of the Masses* appeared in an English translation and D. H. Lawrence, in a posthumous essay printed in the *Architectural Review,* castigated Victorian industry and progress as the font of modern ugliness. 'The great crime which the moneyed classes and promoters of industry committed in the palmy Victorian days', Lawrence wrote, 'was the condemning the workers to ugliness, ugliness, ugliness: meanness and formless and ugly surroundings, ugly ideals, ugly religion, ugly hope, ugly love, ugly clothes, ugly furniture, ugly houses, ugly relationships between workers and employers.' 'The human soul', cried Lawrence, 'needs actual beauty more than bread.'

What he called 'the industrial problem' arose, he concluded, 'from the base forcing of all human energy into a competition of mere acquisition'. This debased and degraded culture had, it was claimed, virtually obliterated a world of beauty and taste.

Elizabeth Jenkins, in her biography of Jane Austen written some years before her essay on Martha Ray, describes the fragments of Georgian elegance that in the intervening decades have been overlain by layer upon layer of tastelessness. 'The eighteenth century was an age such as our imagination can barely comprehend,' she begins, 'weltering as we do in a slough of habitual ugliness, ranging from the dreary horrors of Victorian sham gothic to the more lively hideousness of modern jerry-building, with advertisements defacing any space that might be left unoffending blank.' Only occasionally will we see 'a house front, plain and graceful, with a fanlight like the half of a spider's web and a slip of iron balcony', or 'a tombstone with elegant letters composing, in a single sentence, a well-turned epitaph'. Her valedictory tone is that of Goldsmith's Deserted Village, whose sentiments she copies from an inscription on a 'china patch box':

> Ill fares the land, to hastening ills a prey,
> Where wealth accumulates, and men decay.

She sees this eighteenth-century accessory, 'a trivial little object devoted to a silly purpose', as a sign of the ubiquity of Georgian good taste. In the twentieth century, she explained, we can see only the remnants of what was once 'the common sight of everyday life', a 'plain elegance, uncompromising good taste' that 'surrounded . . . [the Georgians] with an almost monotonous completeness'.

For Jenkins the Georgian era was 'the last of those in English history which produced great works of art' and 'the most civilised era the world had ever seen'. Modern materialism has brought greater comfort, more leisure, and 'cheap sophisticated entertainment for the masses', but at a terrible price. In the 1930s 'the lower middle class, as it is the most considerable among consumers, dictates the canons of taste which, by their preponderating bulk, has corrupted and destroyed the standards of language, of architecture, of entertainment and of literature, which once prevailed'.

The villains in this story are not just the masters of capital and big business, but the politicians who support mass education and the press barons, journalists and publishers who feed a vitiated taste. Many critics felt that high culture could never flourish where there was compulsory education and general literacy. Hilaire Belloc, writing in the *New Statesman* in the spring of 1930, complained that 'the difference between the old England and the newer is that people have by now fallen into a habit of *perpetual* reading, which in the better days the great mass of English men and women did not'. A few years later Aldous Huxley went further: 'Universal education', he tartly remarked, 'has created an immense class of what I may call the New Stupid.' Against this democratic standardization of taste, critics like Clive Bell asserted the virtues of social and aesthetic distinction. 'All artists', he asserted in *Art* (1928), 'are aristocrats . . . the mass of mankind will never be capable of making delicate aesthetic judgements.'

Of course hostility to modern mass society had many outcomes, of which a reappraisal of the eighteenth century was only one. It could lead to radical politics – of the far left or the far right – and to different sorts of escape, including exile. Equally, there was more than one positive version of what the eighteenth century seemed to embody. If intellectuals on the left looked back to a pre-industrial time of organic communities rather than mechanized anonymity, their vision was not quite the same as conservatives whose commitment to Georgian styles covered an enduring commitment to social and economic inequality.

Ironically, the mass readership condemned by Leavis and Huxley appropriated their own version of the eighteenth century, which in the late 1920s and the 1930s became the preferred setting for the innumerable middle- and low-brow historical novels and romances that high-brow critics and modernists dismissed as the shallow and tawdry products of commercial publishing. In the 1920s Georgette Heyer published her first four Georgian romances, beginning with *The Black Moth* (1921) with its dashing highwayman, Jack Carstares, a kidnapped beauty, Miss Diana Beauleigh, and a wicked aristocrat, the Earl of Wyncham. The Bodley Head began to sell C. S. Forester's Hornblower books in the 1930s. Hugh Walpole's *Rogue Herries*, the first of the Herries Chronicle series and described by its publisher as mirroring 'the heart and pulse of eighteenth-century England', appeared in the same year as *The Chaste Mistress*. Seen from the inter-war period, and through the sepia fog of the Victorian era, Georgian England appeared remote, glamorous, outwardly firm in its public principles yet inwardly marked by noble feelings and high passion: the perfect setting for a torrid romance, thrilling action or a dynastic saga. This version of the eighteenth century, purchased at the railway bookshops of W. H. Smith, or borrowed from Mudie's or Boot's circulating libraries, grew ever more popular up to the Second World War and is with us still.

Apart from this renewed enthusiasm for eighteenth-century high society, particular circumstances in the late 1920s rekindled interest in the story of Martha Ray. In 1928 *The Times*, as part of a survey of art in the great houses of Britain, published an article on the paintings at Hinchingbrooke, which included a portrait of Martha Ray and one of her children. A dispute arose about the identity of Augusta Speed, Ray's only surviving daughter, and the then Earl of Sandwich, showing no embarrassment about his illegitimate relatives, published a moving letter from the fourth earl's correspondence that

THE NOVELS OF

Georgette Heyer

POWDER AND PATCH

The popular version of Georgian elegance: a fop, a booted horse-man and a couple in clean streets surrounded by elegant architecture on a Georgette Heyer dust jacket.

not only proved that Mrs Speed, the Contessa Viry, was Sandwich and Ray's daughter, but that he had loved her dearly. Three years before his death Sandwich had written to the Compte de Viry, asking that he forgive the marriage between Augusta and the Compte's son and no longer exclude them from his household. The fourth earl argued that manners in Britain were more liberal than elsewhere: 'In this country disparity of rank is not so much considered as else where.' No special stigma was attached to illegitimacy. 'We have before our eyes', he explained somewhat disingenuously, 'many examples of persons of the highest classes among us who have thought that they did not degrade themselves by marriage with a woman of merit although she was not legitimately born.' Pointing out that his daughter 'has had an education equal to that of the women of the first quality in England', Sandwich pleaded the case for tolerance and family forgiveness. At about the same time as he published this letter, the ninth earl of Sandwich also announced that he was going to erect a new plaque to the memory of Martha Ray in Elstree church.

These acts, at once chivalrous and enlightened, excited a flurry of correspondence in *The Times*. A number of letter-writers, all women, wrote to flesh out Martha Ray's story and to praise Lord Sandwich, whose conduct they felt would please all 'lovers of the eighteenth century'. The great-great-granddaughter of Basil Montagu's third wife, Zoe Procter, urged readers to look at Burgess's edition of *The Love Letters of Mr H. and Miss R.*; Mrs Percy Leake, writing from 'Monk Lewis's Chambers, Albany', retold Mrs Lewis's story about Martha Ray and the rose, describing Ray as 'that lovely and gentle person, Martha Ray, whose murder in Covent Garden Theatre caused much grief and consternation to others beside her patron Lord Sandwich'. But the longest contribution came from Constance Hagberg Wright herself. She treated Ray's story as a remote and obscure tale: 'It is possible that the sad and romantic story to which the Sandwich letters given in *The Times* today make allusion is known only to a few.' This is regrettable, she says, because 'seldom has a more touching episode occurred in the annals of England's high and well-born; seldom has an "unfortunate female" deserved more honour or received in her lifetime more sympathy and respect than Martha Ray, . . . until her early tragic death, the beloved mistress of the fourth Earl of Sandwich'. For Wright Ray is a person who was the virtuous embodiment of eighteenth-century aristocratic elegance, but who, though rightly loved and cherished, seen as talented and skilled, was always aware of her humble beginnings and her position as a demi-rep. 'In the charming portrait of her at Hinchingbrooke her looks are refined and composed, her dress (in the mode of Reynolds's period) is elegant, and her dark, simply arranged hair admirably set off by the soft blue of her gown.' But 'this girl who exchanged the counter of a draper's shop for the stately luxury of a splendid old house, was never allowed to forget the ban of the bend sinister'. For Wright the current Earl of Sandwich's recognition of the importance of Martha Ray was some recompense for the slights she received in her own lifetime.

We do not know if Wright had already begun work on *The Chaste Mistress* when she wrote to *The Times*, though, as her letter indicated, she had already visited Hinchingbrooke, a place which she clearly regarded with some affection. But in 1930 The Bodley Head published *The Chaste Mistress*, listing it along with a raft of novels and historical romances.

Wright's book relies, like many of its precursors, on Croft's *Love and Madness* and Cradock's *Memoirs*, but it also contains a number of important innovations. Foremost among these is her debt to women's romantic fiction of the time. Much of her tone, language, characterization and even some of the plot mirror the enormously popular work of such bestselling authors as E. M. Hull (author of *The Sheik*, published in 1919 and filmed in the following year), and Elinor Glyn, whose *Three Weeks* (1907) inaugurated the explicit expression of female sexual desire.

The heroines in these novels often embody a powerful contradiction: they are familiar with carnal pain and pleasure (Diane Mayo is repeatedly raped by the Sheik, the Balkan princess in *Three Weeks* seduces a young Englishman on what became the best-known sexual accessory of the day, a tigerskin-rug) yet somehow transcend their carnality by the purity of their feelings. Wright depicts Martha Ray as such a woman: the mistress of one man, the lover of another, but also a person of unsullied virtue. The oxymoron in Wright's title *The Chaste Mistress* places her book firmly in this tradition of female romance.

Ray's purity draws men to wish to possess her. Her 'trilling with the untutored sweetness of a skylark' brings her to Sandwich's attention in the milliner's shop. Later, when she sings at Hinchingbrooke, 'Her singularly sweet voice rose like a fountain to fall in crystal drops of melody. To some of the assembly, and to my lord in particular, it seemed as though the lost spirit of their youthful purity hovered over them.' She moves Sandwich to tears; he aches 'for her body and soul'. She has a similar effect on James Hackman. When, out riding with him, she agrees to sing for him in private, the promise sends him into a reverie: 'Amid the tremulous gladness of awakening Nature that spring morning he moved enraptured in a mist of happy imaginings, vague and inarticulate, heedless of all that stood between him and his barely formed desire.' His spirit soars with 'uncalculating ecstasy'.

The Chaste Mistress has little of the coyness that prompted Burgess's expurgations – somewhat surprising perhaps for the steamy 1890s – in *The Love Letters of Mr H. & Miss R.* Wright does not flinch from physical love. 'Soft, fresh lips' are kissed again and again, there are many passionate embraces, arms wrap firmly round waists and when Hackman and Ray spend the night together at the inn in Hockerill we are left in no doubt of the energy of their lovemaking. But these descriptions are repeatedly sublimated into transcendent, spiritual feeling, so that love becomes not only ennobling but almost a religious experience. As the doyenne of romantic fiction, Elinor Glyn, explained in her credo, *The Philosophy of Love* (1920), 'Being *in love* is merely a physical state of exaltation.' On the other hand, '*loving* is the merging of the spirit which at its white heat has glorified the physical instinct for re-creation into a godlike beatitude not of earth. Loving throbs with delight in the flesh; it thrills the spirit with reverence; it glorifies into beauty commonplace things.'

Thus when Sandwich first makes love to Ray not blood but 'ichor', the substance said to flow through the classical gods, 'filled his veins'. Love transmutes him into a sort of deity. When Ray gives herself up to her love for Hackman, she in turn is transformed into a celestial creature. 'Dead and gone', says Wright, 'was the Martha who loved dress and pretty ornaments, kept careful accounts, was piqued by petty slights, eager for the pleasures of Ranelagh and Vauxhall, for masquerades, for water-parties.' Love lifts her above prosaic life: 'She floated, lighter than gossamer, in a vast iridescent bubble that swelled out and out until its aerial dome vanished altogether from her sight, drawn up, like mists at dawn, into the illimitable heavens. Passion, pain, hope, despair, were as used garments out of which her soul had slipped.' And when she is finally in bed with Hackman: 'It had come, the longed-for, the impossible. Exquisite surrender . . . divine possession.'

This semi-spiritual language, which Q. D. Leavis condemned in her uncompromising *Fiction and the Reading Public* (1932) as 'tosh', pervades *The Chaste Mistress*, equating love both with a higher ethical state and with Christian sacrifice. We are made to feel that it is Ray's duty to obey her heart and her fate to pay the price for doing so. Indeed, this is true of all three protagonists, though Wright's focus is on Ray's suffering, so much more complex than that of the two men.

For Wright, Ray's problem is that she loves too much, not that she is too much loved. She first comes to love Sandwich and to win his love, and once the relationship is consummated, she dotes on him: 'His masterful wooing, his vivid personality and the love of music that was so strong in him had made him a prince of lovers in her eyes, not to be denied his will.' Then she loves her children, especially Basil, to whom she is tied by 'the oneness of spirit that sometimes exists between mother and son, and seldom, if ever, so strongly in any other relationship'. And, finally, she is drawn to love Hackman, despite her attempts to hold him back: 'the charm she had used to curb this young, hot passion had worked backwards and made him drunk with the heady wine of love. She, too, had sipped of it, seen visions, dreamed divinely.' She is impelled by a force she cannot control: 'Deep within her spirit, beyond the radius of will and reason, something had stirred, like the first throb of pre-natal life, and instinct told her it was perilous.' As she explains to Sandwich, 'I loved him in spite of myself. I could not hold back. It was too strong for me.'

When the affair with Hackman is exposed and Sandwich, in the presence of Ray's children, calls on her 'Make your choice!', it is clear that she is in no position to do so. Sandwich confronts her only because 'he perceived that Providence was about to play into his hands'. Both on this occasion, and in a later confrontation in which Sandwich says that if she leaves with Hackman she will never see her children again, it is impossible for Ray to overcome her maternal affections.

We are left with the picture of a woman who is pulled in every

direction by loves she cannot control. Wondering if her surrender to
Sandwich – 'I give in' – is motivated by 'mother-love, or altruism,
or cowardice', she concludes that 'wherever the fault lay, or the virtue,
it had mastered her'. Equally, she cannot stop loving Hackman, even
when she promises Sandwich that she will no longer see him. She
cannot let go and fantasizes about being rescued by her lover: 'Somewhere deep in her soul fluttered a faint, wild hope that he would
compel her to come to him, if only that they might die together.'
Even in the moment of her death she loves her killer. After Hackman
has fired the fatal shot she dies smiling at him: 'With a sweet bright
smile of supreme love and understanding still curving the beautiful
mouth, with hope and happiness deepening the warm hazel of her
eyes, Martha would have sunk to the ground but for the arm of her
companion.'

In *The Chaste Mistress* Martha Ray is a martyr to love who makes
the supreme sacrifice. Wright even compares her with Christ. Each
of Ray's offspring, she says, 'had been a thorn the more in her Calvary
crown of motherhood'. And, in case the analogy passed the reader
by, the book's final scene shows Ray as 'she who in her short life
knew the greatest variations of fortune and in whose character there
appeared strange contrasts of strength and weakness, but who, at her
weakest, had the strength to crucify herself'.

In the eighteenth-century accounts of Martha Ray's murder, Hackman was the slave to love, but in Wright's twentieth-century romance
the chaste mistress was the victim not just of her killer's violence
but of her own love. This entails subordination not just to love but
to men. As in many other romantic fictions, female desire is nurtured
in relationships of radical inequality, in which male dominance, privilege and authority thrive on female subordination, obedience and
deprivation. Wright repeatedly stresses that Ray is in thrall to the
Earl – 'Tempted, fascinated, awed, Martha must yield' – and that

much of his attraction stems from his power over her. Sandwich is invariably described as 'masterful'; in his absence Ray misses 'his commanding presence'. The affair with Hackman makes her aware of her subordination but gives her little more freedom than before. 'Oh,' she complains, stamping her foot, 'that I should be a toy, a slave, to be carried here, cast there, and do my master's bidding without power to resist!' But before too long she is replicating her subordination to Sandwich in her relations with Hackman: 'She found courage to belittle herself to him, that his love, high poised on the pinnacle of adoration, might sink of itself to earth and make its own quietus.'

Ray cannot act without men; all of her actions are constrained by her keeper, her lover and her son. When she suggests to Hackman that she break from Sandwich and begin a musical career, his veto of her plan dissolves her resolve. 'Strengthened by him she could have faced Lord Sandwich's certain displeasure; alone, the habits of obedience and submission, ingrained for fifteen, sixteen years, were like cords of silk, supple in appearance but, when put to the test, offering the resistance of steel.' It is as if she is held motionless by the magnetic force exerted by the two men. The plot cannot advance, nor the story go forward, except by an act of sacrifice. Yet even this is not willed by Martha Ray. She is betrayed by others, confined within the Admiralty and constantly watched so that she cannot send her final protestation of love to Hackman – a letter that declares the 'greatness' and 'hopelessness' of their love and offers him 'her assurance that she would ever love him and none but him should possess her to her death'. Deprived of this last missive, Hackman, 'befooled wretch', pulls the trigger. 'Love conquers death', Wright has Basil Montagu mutter at the end of the book, but in *The Chaste Mistress* it would be more accurate to say that a woman's love could not avoid it.

In telling the story of Martha Ray as a modern romance, Wright also introduced another new element into the story, transforming Lord Sandwich into a very different figure from the ruthless politician and unappetizing libertine depicted by his critics. She follows Cradock's more sympathetic portrait but goes much further, making Sandwich into a type of romantic hero, with a much larger role in the drama. She transforms his relationship with Ray into one of mutual love.

Sandwich's outward appearance remains daunting. Powerful, publicly ruthless and privately a man of steely determination, 'the habitual exercise of power joined to native arrogance gave force to his least whim'. Minions and servants respect him and tremble in his presence. But this is exactly what draws Ray to him. He is a natural ruler and leader of men, a true aristocrat, who can shake off the envious attacks of his enemies as 'the pricklings of a thousand pigmies'. 'My lord, like the true patrician that he was, could be on the easiest terms with one and all – artists, authors, musicians, players – without losing one fraction of his innate pride of birth.' At times the narrator of *The Chaste Mistress* shows even more interest and admiration than Ray in her aristocratic keeper, an effect that is reinforced by repeated reference to 'my lord', as if he were the narrator's lord as well as his mistress's.

Wright paints Sandwich as a proud aristocrat determined to uphold standards and abide by the social rules. He is an even more patrician – and intimidating – Mr Darcy. She is therefore concerned to depict him as a man of some probity. She excuses Sandwich's rakish reputation on the grounds that he bore 'the sore encumbrance' of a mad wife, and interprets his original interest in the sixteen-year-old Martha as affected by his musical interests rather than by sexual desire. She plays down Sandwich's libertinism, portraying him as reluctantly complicit in the male manners of the age. 'My Lord

Sandwich, though by no means such a "sad dog" as detractors would have us believe, was not too stately to chuck a pretty girl under the chin, nor so firm in virtue as to resist all overtures.' But, she adds, 'in a generation of hard drinkers he stood for sobriety; and while party leaders left their beds to attend debates unshaven and unprepared, he gave an example of punctuality and industry'. She portrays the attack on Wilkes as neither a personal betrayal nor a vendetta, but the reluctant act of a dutiful public servant who knows that, whatever the consequences, he has an obligation to obey his monarch.

In *The Chaste Mistress* Sandwich grows to love and desire Ray as her musical and social talents blossom. He is enamoured by her youth, the purity of her voice and the elegance of her manners. But he does not press his advances on her; he lets the relationship unfold. He risks the occasional kiss, but does not go further: 'Once he came upon her in one of the passages without her hearing him coming, took her in his arms in his masterful way and kissed her passionately.' As their intimacy ripens, so their love grows. Their mutual passion is released when Sandwich tells Ray that he is not going to leave her to take up the embassy in Spain, a position he was offered in 1763. Sandwich calls Ray into the library, where she is told to sit on a stool at his feet. 'She obeyed with a delicious thrill of fore-knowledge of that which was to come.' Sandwich announces his decision which, it is implied, is motivated by a reluctance to leave Ray behind. The scene ends with what for Sandwich is an act of mutual passion: 'the slim body of the girl he had drawn on to his knees, the soft, fresh lips he kissed and kissed again, all were his to make his own, not, he gloried to feel, out of obedience, but in responsive love'. Even when Ray starts the affair with Hackman the Earl, though angry, remains dignified and noble. He uses their children to try to keep Ray, but only because he loves her and her family.

The final verdict on Sandwich is offered by Basil Montagu when, years later, he visits his mother's grave and ruminates 'on the tragic triangle formed by his father, his mother and James Hackman'. He absolves all three from blame, seeing them as noble victims. He recognizes that his mother was torn apart by her conflicting affections. As for Hackman, 'who could refuse him pity? So fired by high ideals, so mocked by fate, so young to die.' But Montagu's father receives the most of his attention. He was, says Basil, a 'greatly maligned nobleman . . . tied to an insane wife from earliest manhood', a person who 'behaved with exceptional continence compared to many of his contemporaries, being constant in his love as in his friendships'. A devoted public servant and politician, he refused the fruits of power. 'Poor for his high position, when it would have been easy to become rich, his party had no more loyal partisan nor one on whom the fierce invectives of their opponents fell with more frequency.' In public he wore a tough carapace, but in private 'he was affectionate to his children, and . . . grieved increasingly for his lost Martha'. According to Basil all three protagonists have nobility – Sandwich by the way he fills his rank and calling; Ray because of her sacrifice; Hackman because of his ideals. But Sandwich occupies centre stage.

This rather unusual foregrounding of Sandwich – it is, after all, rare in a romance for light to be deflected from young lovers to the older man – is connected to another remarkable twist in Wright's plot, one which shows that, though much of what she wrote can be read as a female romance, it can also be interpreted as a plea to stand by an old order, a hierarchical, deferential society in which everyone knows their place.

The key to this story is Wright's identification of a new villain who is almost exclusively responsible for the romantic tragedy of Ray's death. Almost exclusively, but not quite, for Wright identifies two figures responsible for Ray's death. Unlike earlier writers, she does not make Caterina Galli the betrayer of Martha Ray; instead her husband is indicted in her place. He forges a letter in Ray's hand, telling Hackman that their love is over; and it is he, not Caterina, who hints to Hackman that Ray has a new lover. All the women, in this version of the story, are therefore lined up on the side of love.

But Signor Galli is a minor figure when compared to the real villain of *The Chaste Mistress,* Omai, Pacific islander and guest of the Earl of Sandwich who betrays Ray twice, once at Hinchingbrooke where he spots a lovers' tryst, and again in London, when he purloins a letter from Hackman to Ray, proving to Sandwich that the affair is not, as the Earl had thought, at an end.

Omai certainly spent a good deal of time with Sandwich and Martha Ray. As First Lord of the Admiralty and the sponsor of Cook's voyages, Sandwich was Omai's host, lodging him in the Admiralty, taking him to music festivals, sailing with him on naval inspections and entertaining him on three occasions among his guests at Hinchingbrooke. As Omai's lesson with Granville Sharp about the fifth Commandment shows, the Society Islander grew to know the family well. Shortly before Omai returned to the Pacific Sandwich wrote to his friend, the botanist and explorer Sir Joseph Banks, regretting the loss of his visitor, 'I . . . have grown so used to him, and have so sincere a friendship for him, from his very good temper, sense & general good behaviour.' Crucially for the story of James Hackman and Martha Ray, Omai had been staying at Hinchingbrooke during the winter of 1775 when the affair between the two of them supposedly began.

Wright was not the first writer to draw attention to Omai's presence. The Pacific islander had featured in the story of Hackman and Ray ever since Manasseh Dawes suggested in *The Case and Memoirs of James Hackman* that he had been the one who first alerted Sandwich to Hackman's pursuit of Ray. In *Love and Madness* Omai sees and senses Hackman and Ray's love, even though his poor English means that he cannot yet understand the lovers' whispered intimacies. 'I thought', writes Ray, 'the other day he caught our eyes conversing. Eyes speak a language all can understand.' On the one hand she feels sure that as a 'child of Nature' he will protect the lovers; on the other, despite his 'diverting' simplicity, he seems too curious about the couple. Croft has Omai using a mixture of signs and words to inform Sandwich of the intimacies between Ray and her admirer, but neither Dawes nor Croft suggests that his actions are motivated by anything more than curiosity and a desire to please his patron. Certainly there is none of the malignity that Wright ascribes to Omai in *The Chaste Mistress*. He is merely a minor actor – an exotic diversion – in the main plot and has no effect on the outcome of the story.

This is very much in tune with eighteenth-century views of Omai as an exotic curiosity and exemplary noble savage. Both press accounts and contemporary memoirs are full of anecdotes about his quiddities with language (calling horses 'great hogs', ice 'stone water', or a wasp 'a soldier bird'), his misapprehensions (confusing the juice of morello cherries with human blood) and his traditions (cooking mutton in a stone-filled pit). He was almost always viewed benignly. In Cradock's eyes, for example, Omai was 'naturally genteel and prepossessing', and most contemporary commentators remarked on his natural dignity and nobility, famously captured in his portrait by Reynolds in which the Pacific islander adopts the pose of the Apollo Belvedere. Frances Burney said of him that he seemed 'to shame Education, but his manners are so extremely graceful, and he is so polite, attentive, and easy, that you would have thought he came from some foreign court'. She and her family compared him favourably to Lord Stanhope, the son of Lord Chesterfield, the doyen of modern English manners. He even showed the refined sensibility of an English gentleman, weeping bitterly at a funeral: 'It was so painful a scene he could not see it finished, but, handkerchief before his face, got up and fled.'

Sir Joshua Reynolds's portrayal of Omai as noble savage and classical hero.

Those who met Omai professed to be charmed by him. He was also known, chiefly by those who were acquainted with him only through press reports, as the embodiment of the free sexuality that had so shocked and fascinated English society since accounts of the Edenic paradise of Tahiti were published after Cook's first voyage. (When Charlotte Hayes staged her Tahitian evening in her brothel in King's Place, she was playing on the reputation of the South Seas as a place of uninhibited sexual freedom.) Omai's presence in the drawing rooms and closets of the aristocracy spread rumours of liaisons and conquests, and Sandwich's enemies used these stories to attack the Earl and aristocratic morals in general. In 1776 Sandwich's old adversary George Kearsley published a long poem, *Omiah's* [sic] *Farewell; inscribed to the Ladies of London*. 'The novelty of his figure', Kearsley wrote, 'drew much attention upon him, and more particularly from women of quality, for with many of them he was intimate and familiar.' He followed this innuendo with false professions of regret that it should ever have been made in the first place. 'Is it not cruel', he asked, 'that such generous politeness to a stranger should have such illiberal insinuations put on it?' But, he continued, 'scandal will be predominant, if a dove and a raven of the blackest hue are publicly together, nor will it lose its circulation, while the horn of the News-Post can blast it abroad ... I have a higher opinion of my fair countrywomen, than to think they would be so condescending; and yet philosophy cannot reconcile the depravity of female inclinations.'

Kearsley's critique was general but it pointed particularly to Sandwich and Ray. Sandwich, he reported, 'has always honoured him [Omai] with a peculiar attention', and Omai, in return, 'has not been ungrateful in his particular attentions to his Lordship's family'. Anecdotes about him at Hinchingbrooke were 'as trivial as possible, and unworthy of repetition; his animal powers were his best, and those he used with freedom and success'.

We do not know if Wright knew of these eighteenth-century stories about Omai, but she certainly demonized his sexuality, transforming a curious child of nature or a noble savage into a modern-day Caliban. He is not only Ray's betrayer but a creature who inspires loathing as the very embodiment of 'cunning and lust'. 'He is so dark as to be nearly black,' Ray tells Hackman, 'and I cannot tell you how much revulsion I feel towards him, though I do my utmost to conceal it. He is like a cat, that will often go to those who it knows by instinct dislike it. Either it is my fancy or he does so haunt me.' The point is reinforced by Wright's third-person narrator. In a box at the Drury Lane Theatre with Omai, 'Martha was uneasy at his proximity and painfully aware of a disagreeable odour from his person that had forced itself on her consciousness at their first meeting, and which no distilled perfume was able to dissemble'. Omai is repeatedly compared to an animal. He has 'wild-beast eyes'; he is 'apt as a dog to read his master's mood', in a dream he appears as a serpent. What Ray fears most is his animal touch. 'Once', Ray tells Hackman, 'he fingered my dress, which made me like to retch.' In the theatre, 'All at once she felt the touch of fingers on the nape of her bare neck, and a sensation of horrified disgust raced through her nerves. She recoiled, shuddering, and at the same moment saw, in the mirror of her fan, the face of Omai distorted with rage.' On another occasion, when she is asleep and dreaming of her freedom, Omai steals a letter from her, and Ray awakens, to find him 'staring at her, his coarse, spatulate fingers touching the laces of her tucker'.

Such crude racial and sexual fears which were, of course, prominent in the 1930s, sustain the conflict between purity and danger, civilization and barbarism, love and lust that runs through Wright's narrative. Omai's purpose is to play up the nobility of its protagonists. Sandwich's natural ability to command contrasts with Omai's fawning submission to his will. Hackman's good looks counter Omai's ugliness. (Wright contrasts his coarse 'spatulate fingers' with Hackman's 'well-kept hands of a man of refinement', with their 'long tapering fingers that are taken to denote artistic tastes'.) And the romantic and maternal purity of Ray's love – she is, after all, the chaste mistress of the book's title – is set against Omai's crude lust.

But Omai is also – as his physical intrusion upon Ray makes clear – a threat. Ray loathes Omai not just for his appearance but because he renders topsy-turvy the social rules she must abide by. 'She, who was the mother of the Montagus, must submit to social exclusions, humiliating condescensions, barriers innumerable, and must endure daily association with a savage on equal terms and show civility where she felt repulsion, while he, the savage, was welcomed by the proudest hostesses.'

Ray's sense of injustice about this disparity is the key to the breakdown in her relationship with Sandwich, and to her willingness to continue to respond to Hackman's protestations of love. Friends of Sandwich had flirted with her, but she had never been disloyal, 'nor might young Hackman's ardour have found reward but for ulterior events. A cloud had risen between herself and her lord – at first no bigger than a man's hand, but a portent of storm – with the advent of Omai, the Otaheitan.'

Omai was, in Wright's hands, much in request with 'certain ladies of fashion who chose to call him prince, gave himself the airs of a person of *ton* and strutted about London in the velvets and lace provided for him'. The servants at Hinchingbrooke love Ray because 'she never overstepped her position', while they despise Omai: 'He was generally styled "the dirty nigger" and by none disliked more heartily than by old James, my lord's devoted negro attendant, who considered it beneath him to wait at table on a brother darkie.' So Omai's intrusion – his threat to the natural order of things – occurs because of the adulation of the sort of women who shunned Martha

Ray at Hinchingbrooke and because Sandwich makes the one fatal error of inviting Omai into the bosom of his family. The welcome accorded him contrasts with the failure to appreciate Ray's true nobility.

In *The Chaste Mistress* Ray is like the heroine of Disraeli's *Sybil: or, The Two Nations*. Ostensibly a common girl, she turns out to be of distant noble blood. Some people, comments Wright, have doubted whether Martha Ray, 'so refined in features, so talented and with so much the air of good breeding', could be the offspring of her reputed father. Perhaps her mother had been a nobleman's mistress. But this is of no great matter because 'it is not extremely uncommon for a child of low birth to revert in mind and person to the type of some anonymous noble ancestor'. Buried deep in Ray's ancestry is the source of her virtue and refinement. Ray embodies the old nobility that she willingly passes on to Sandwich, whose stock is threatened by degeneration. His closeness to their children is partly because he realizes that he now had 'two sons in whose veins ran no septic menace', unlike the Earl's legitimate children, tainted by the madness of Lady Sandwich.

The survival of a strong, natural social order, based on rank and race, Wright seems to be saying, depends on a sort of social eugenics, in which those who are the leaders of society learn to choose and recognize those who have 'natural' nobility, if not noble social rank. In this way, natural leadership will be strengthened, a way of life preserved. But the way of life this novel was defending was not associated with a picturesque, verdant, rural England of great houses and pretty thatched cottages, as in other conservative jeremiads of the 1920s and 1930s. Rather it was a matter of blood and breeding, the perpetuation of conservative leadership and the codes it lived by. As a romantic heroine, Ray dies for love, a noble and aristocratic emotion, as in any romantic story from Tristan and Isolde onwards.

And as the embodiment of nobility, she is done to death by dangerous and dark forces, her killing a portent that all is not right in the world. The portrayal of Omai, though filled with racial (and racist) disgust, is not so much a specific racial and social type (how could a Society Islander threaten the beleaguered landed classes of the early 1930s?) as a general embodiment of savagery knocking for admission to the halls of civilization.

The Chaste Mistress seems curiously outside time and place. Despite the detailed descriptions of Georgian finery and the walk-on parts of well-known eighteenth-century literary figures, the action might as well take place in the ancient or medieval world, the mountain forests of central Europe or the deserts of Arabia – anywhere, in fact, where heroic romance might be imagined to flourish. The characters are little more than bundles of extreme feeling, bereft of psychological depth; they swoop and soar but lack substance. All that matters is the plot.

It is quite different in Elizabeth Jenkins's *Ten Fascinating Women*, who all possessed 'to a rare degree that elusive, often undefinable quality – fascination'. She puts Martha Ray alongside powerful women like Queen Elizabeth, Sarah Duchess of Marlborough, and the Duchess of Lauderdale, free spirits and literary courtesans like Becky Wells and Harriet Wilson, muses like Rosamund Clifford and Mary Fitton, and literary ladies like the nineteenth-century Lady Blessington and Elizabeth Inchbald. Her subjects are either public figures of great character and power, women writers who had received less attention than Jenkins thought their due, adventurers who used their sexual and social charms to defy convention, or women whose misfortunes made them the subject of scandal, myth or literary legend. Jenkins's interest is in character. What was it about these women that made them the objects of fascinated love, admiration, fear, hatred or contempt?

Like *The Chaste Mistress*, Jenkins's story of Ray is largely derived from Croft's *Love and Madness* – as mediated by Burgess – and from Cradock's *Memoirs*. And just as in Wright, the relationship between Sandwich and Ray is one of dominance and submission. Sandwich is described as ruthless in professional matters and with 'an emotional callousness which made him formidable', while Ray is 'timid'. 'She had no self-confidence in her dealings with him', but nevertheless she has a powerful hold on his affections. Her meekness was the very quality that drew him to her: 'It may well have been one of her charms in Lord Sandwich's eyes, accustomed as he had been to the boldness of trollops and the assurance of women of fashion.'

Jenkins never suggests, however, that the relationship between Sandwich and Ray blossomed into an ardent love affair. On the contrary, she portrays Martha's feelings as governed by prudence. 'She had never had a passion for Lord Sandwich, but she had considerable affection for him and a great respect. She owed to him the things that made her life interesting. He was kind to her, and to someone who had not been born to it, it meant something to be treated with the deference that was considered due to a woman under Lord Sandwich's protection.'

This world of making-do is suddenly upset by Hackman's arrival. Ray, ever prudent, tries to place obstacles in the way of their meeting, but she is overpowered by his ardour: 'Her own emotions were never as deeply stirred as Hackman's, but his youth and passion created a feeling which she had never known before.' As the affair develops Ray's anxieties increase: 'The lyrical rapture of the opening was past, but it gave place, not to a calmer state of mind and a more mundane sense of pleasure, but to a relentless, driving impulse.' Hackman had only one end in view – marriage – but for Ray the situation was far more complex: 'She loved him both passionately and tenderly and her personal happiness would have been secured by a marriage with him. But whereas Hackman had one idea in his head and one only, she had several matters of great difficulty to consider. The security of her children was the first.'

Wright's novel sees this conflict as a heroic struggle between sexual and maternal love. Jenkins's account is more mundane and psychologically complex, linking Ray's timidity to her acute consciousness of her weakness vis-à-vis Sandwich. Jenkins, as we have seen, saw the eighteenth century as an age of great refinement and artistic creativity, but she was also well aware of its deep inequality. Not only in her essay on Ray, but in her biographies of Henry Fielding, Caroline Lamb and Jane Austen she reminded her readers that the intimate circles of great literature and art, exquisite artefacts and costume were surrounded by swathes of poverty, illness and abjection.

Ray may have presided at Lord Sandwich's table and sung in the hall at Hinchingbrooke, but Jenkins will not let us forget that she began life as a working girl. 'She had never lost the remembrance of her humble origins,' she says, 'the poverty of her home with her disreputable father and her anxious, burdened mother, nor of that insight into the inferno of the London slums which no girl who had worked for five years in Clerkenwell could have failed to gain.' She feared returning to the world from which she had been plucked.

Her worries were compounded by her fears for her children. As Jenkins pointed out, 'if she had been married to Sandwich, she would have had no claim on the children except what he allowed', but because they were illegitimate, 'the possession of the children was entirely hers, and so was the responsibility. If their father chose to turn them off, the law as it then stood could not have helped her.' Hackman could probably have provided something towards their upkeep, but Ray had unpaid debts and Sandwich 'might pursue the lovers with hatred'. He could ruin Hackman's prospects in the army and prevent Ray from singing on the stage.

Jenkins focuses on the terrible, practical dilemma she faces. 'Martha Ray was confronted, inescapably, with a choice of two actions: either would entail the most extreme agitation: the dismay and terror of leaving Lord Sandwich, the anguish of finally rejecting James Hackman.' The crisis is not with the murder but in the agony of Ray's choice. Nor is the reader offered the reassurance of any resolution. According to Jenkins, we do not know how or if Ray ever resolved the conflict. Caterina Galli's betrayal and Hackman's pistol leave us with an open verdict. All we know is that Ray was 'unusually troubled'.

Jenkins ends on a romantic note, describing the tombstone by the path in Elstree churchyard with its inscription 'Sacred to the memory of Martha Ray, died 1779' erected by the ninth earl of Sandwich. 'The neighbourhood is famous today for the manufacture of synthetic romance. Do any of the stories it has produced compare with hers?' But Jenkins's version of Ray's life was not the sort of romance that could be made into a sentimental film. She describes a woman's dilemma, prompted less by her own passion than by the exigencies of being kept by an older man and loved by a younger one. The care with which Jenkins clearly renders historical context has the paradoxical effect of making Martha Ray and her problems seem more 'real' and pressing, more in tune with the sorts of decisions that young women might have faced in mid-twentieth-century society. Her account complements the novels she wrote in the 1940s and 1950s – including her best-known fiction, *The Tortoise and the Hare*, written at the same time as *Ten Fascinating Women* – which explore the problems faced by women.

Like her nineteenth-century predecessors, Jenkins is a moralist who applies a universal, trans-historical morality to her material. But whereas Victorian commentators read moral qualities into individual actions – murder, living in 'sin', adultery – Jenkins is concerned with moral character and personality, the response of individuals to the choices they are often unwillingly forced to confront because of prevailing social codes, particularly those that legislate that men and women live different lives by different values. Neither in the biographies nor in her novels does she offer an explicit critique of this double standard, which is portrayed 'realistically' as something that must be negotiated rather than challenged and removed. But she does assert (in a way reminiscent of F. R. Leavis) the moral power of literature: its ability to teach the ways of the world and how to respond to them, and also its importance for women as a way of escaping from or going beyond their conventional role. This vision unites her fiction and biography in a single, sympathetic humanism, with roots Jenkins sees in eighteenth-century culture. Martha Ray's terrible death is not a sentimental story, a tale of madness, an anecdote for the times, a female romance or the result of a failing social order; it is an opportunity for moral reflection.

CHAPTER 10

——— ❧ ———

History and Telling Stories

THOUGH THE MURDER of Martha Ray by James Hackman was recounted in many forms, including biography, fiction, and medical case-book, we have yet to identify any one version of their story that claims to be a work of history. Sir Herbert Croft and Constance Hagberg Wright, a century and a half apart, called theirs a 'true story', and Gilbert Burgess claimed that the Hackman–Ray correspondence were 'documents', though he was concerned with their universal appeal, their 'human interest' (today a rather debased term), rather than their historical specificity. Nineteenth-century commentators, more cautiously, called the incident an 'anecdote', as Thackeray did in *The Four Georges*, which he was careful to describe, not as history, but as 'Sketches of Manners, Morals and Court Life'. Perhaps Horace Walpole was right. As he commented a few days after Ray's murder, 'I do not love tragic events *en pure perte*. If they do happen I would have them historic. This is only kin to history, and tends to nothing.'

How can such an isolated incident find a place in the pattern of history? What broader effects did it have, beyond its impact on the main protagonists? Is it, in fact, the stuff of history? Would it not be better filed with those 'strange but true' stories that fascinate, amuse, or repel but hardly instruct their readership?

Though I don't preclude putting the incident in the category of the esoteric or exotic (but I would want to consider the forces that lay behind such a decision), I do want to treat the story of Hackman and Ray as history. Just as I have explored the motives behind the different stories about their case, so I want to end my story by uncovering the reasons for my doing so. For my larger purpose in writing this book has been to respond to the different ways in which our answers to E. H. Carr's famous question, 'What is history?' have changed over the last thirty years.

The sources of Hackman and Ray's exclusion from history lie in the nineteenth century's ideas about what were proper objects of historical inquiry. As we have seen, in the first half of the century writers like Macaulay and Croker were repelled by the intrusion of private life and sentiment into the historical record. This powerful feeling that historical research should confine itself to public affairs and the actions of great men was institutionalized (and reinforced) with the emergence of modern academic history in the 1860s and 1870s. The establishment of the Public Record Office in 1866, the foundation of the Royal Historical Society (1868), and the publication of the first Historical Manuscripts Commission report on privately held documents (1870), were the immediate precursors of the Oxford School of Modern History ('modern' meaning since the fall of Rome) and the Cambridge History Tripos, which brought academic history as developed by Leopold von Ranke and his followers in Germany to Britain.

This Victorian history sought to apply the rules of evidence to historical documents to reveal 'what actually happened', in Ranke's famous phrase. Central to its purpose was *Quellenforschung* – the distinction between potentially misleading secondary materials and primary sources, *original* documents, whose critical evaluation was the touchstone of historical truth. But what counted as an original historical document – what ended up in the Public Record Office and in the pages of the reports of the Historical Manuscripts Commission – was material of a very particular kind. National record keeping and archiving were devoted to sources that cast light on the political history and public life of the English nation: documents from the departments of state and the organizations of local government, family papers of the landed classes, the archives of statesmen and politicians. What counted as history was primarily political. J. R. Seeley, a key figure whose memory is perpetuated in the undergraduate history library at Cambridge that bears his name, wrote: 'History is not concerned with individuals except in their capacity as members of a state. That a man in England makes a scientific discovery or paints a picture is not in itself an event in the history of England. Individuals are important in history in proportion not to their intrinsic merit, but to their relation to the state.' The dominance of this claim never became clearer than when it finally came under attack. As G. R. Elton, the Cambridge historian who offered the most robust defence of political history, put it in 1968, 'All forms of history that have existed, exist now, or may yet come to exist belong to the world which the political historian inhabits.'

This emphasis on politics and the state was in line with the object of teaching history in the universities, which was to shape the sensibility and vision of a (male) ruling elite. Seeley made it crystal clear: 'Our university is, and must be, a great seminary of politicians.' Nevertheless, history was not seen as being directly instrumental; on the contrary, it was to be studied 'for its own sake'. The nineteenth-century historian J. R. Green put it this way: history 'was looked upon as no special or definitive study, but as part of that general mass of things, which every gentleman should know'. The practice of history – empirical, pragmatic, committed to the study of legislative institutions, successive monarchs, and ministries – would shape the moral vision and codes of conduct of magistrates and civil servants, both at home and in the empire. As my old teacher, Sir Herbert Butterfield, put it, 'I happen to think that history is a school of wisdom and statesmanship.'

But academic political history, even in the Victorian age, never held total sway over the historical imagination. Popular history, with its interest in 'olden times', and a long-standing antiquarian tradition, nurtured by the rural clergy of the Church of England, was as concerned with manners and morals as with politics, and as inquisitive about ordinary people and their lives as about the intrigues of the great. The topographical works (including those that used Hackman's crime to flesh out the sins of Covent Garden), histories of crime and tales of the evils of the Georgian age, together with the scrapbooks in which Victorians pasted old newspaper clippings, handbills, and every sort of printed ephemera, made up the archives and history of everyday life that was studiously ignored at the universities. Occasionally scholars like J. R. Green in his popular *History of the English People* and H. T. Buckle in his *History of Civilisation in England* wrote histories that were broader in scope and appeal, but by and large there was a wide gulf between these works and the scholarship of university dons.

The roots of such popular history were antiquarian and literary; its greatest inspiration and avatar was not a historian but a Scottish lawyer, antiquarian, poet, and novelist: Sir Walter Scott. During the nineteenth century two different forms of realism – history and the (often historical) novel – divided the territory of human experience. Academic history dealt with reason, policy, public affairs, the outward world of the state and politics; fiction portrayed family life, the world of towns, villages and neighbourhoods, examined inner feeling, emotion, private life, love and passion. Part of the appeal of the historical novel, and of the antiquarian researches on which it was often based, was that it blended the two genres, though real-life historical characters in such fiction rarely occupied centre stage. Biography and memoirs – often the sources for historical writing but not to be confused with the real thing – uneasily occupied a no-man's land somewhere between history and fiction. They might deal with the stuff of history, but they were dangerously subjective and personal.

Fiction and memoirs threatened history by nurturing an uncritical sympathy between the reader and people in the past, by seeming to detract or distort the real story of politics and nation, and by breaking down the distinction between the public realm and private life that political historians were so determined to insist upon. They also played fast and loose with 'the facts'. Not surprisingly, academic historical writing has almost always expressed a deep suspicion of both genres, and has repeatedly defined itself against 'fiction'. For many years, then, historians have distinguished both the content and the form of history from the partial insights of the memoir-writer and the creative suppositions of imaginative literature.

The effects of these distinctions are obvious in the stories that I have told. The Earl of Sandwich, aristocrat, public figure, and government minister, is a figure of the historical record: his family papers catalogued by the Historical Manuscripts Commission, his official papers published by the Naval Records Society, his life remembered and recorded by such friends as Joseph Cradock, and the subject of two excellent historical biographies, whose chief concern is with assessing his contribution to eighteenth-century politics and the fortunes of the Georgian navy. We have a historical record of his life, punctuated of course by the occasional gap, yet largely complete. Though much criticised, he is obviously a figure who deserves a place in 'history'. Contrast his story with that of Ray and Hackman. She flits in and out of the historical record – an evanescent if glittering figure in the Admiralty, occasionally mentioned in the same breath as political corruption, thrust posthumously into the public eye, and then plunged into obscurity. Ray only has a voice in her story thanks to the letters that her keeper conserved in his family archive. Similarly, James Hackman flies in and out of history: his fame may have lasted longer than Andy Warhol's notorious fifteen minutes, but after a few weeks of notoriety he left little more to posterity than two letters, a sheaf of newspaper reports, and a perfunctory account of his trial. The lives of Ray and Hackman turned on the events of 7 April 1779, which, traumatic though they were, made up only one minor incident in Sandwich's long public career.

But the literary afterlife of Ray and Hackman eclipses that of Sandwich. True, he carried the nickname 'Jemmy Twitcher', from John Gay's *Beggar's Opera*, to his grave; but only in Constance Hagberg Wright's *Chaste Mistress* did he play anything more than a minor role. First Hackman, and then Ray, becomes the chief protagonist in the story.

Is there any way that we can begin to break down the contrasts – between history and imaginative literature, politics and private life – that have governed how we tell this story? By considering how historical writing has changed over the last thirty years I believe we can gain some insight into this problem.

In the 1960s the so-called new social history, though it sometimes claimed to be using a new method, eloquently argued that historians should expand their subject-matter to include not just politics, the economy, and ideas, but also society – by which was meant all members of society. Poor mantua-makers like Ray as well as rich men like Sandwich, madmen like Hackman as well as the sane, women and children as well as men, the local as well as national, private as well as public life – all fell within the ambit of the social historian. The aims of this new sort of history were neatly encapsulated in a special issue of *The Times Literary Supplement* devoted to

'New Ways in History' in April 1966. Essays by such luminaries as Keith Thomas, E. P. Thompson, and Eric Hobsbawm laid out an agenda that would be followed (with some radical modifications) over the next twenty years.

As the *TLS* essays make clear, the impulses behind this new history were at once technocratic and democratic. Many of its supporters – this was especially true of Keith Thomas in his essay 'The Tools and the Job' – wanted to put history into the camp of the social sciences, to replace a rather amateurish, narrative method with one shaped by the techniques of anthropology, sociology, social psychology, and demography. Its aims were inclusive and comprehensive, covering society in its entirety. Employing these more rigorous and scientific approaches, it was felt, would create not just better history, but enable history to contribute to a better future. History was to be part of Harold Wilson's 'white heat of the technological miracle'. Though Thomas himself did not follow this route, his analysis led to quantification and enumeration, and to the desire to create panoramic landscapes of the past shaped by what was to become 'social science history'.

This technocratic impulse, with its tacit managerial aspirations, sat uneasily with the democratic desire to produce a mainstream history that was 'intelligible and attractive to the layman', that answered 'the questions about history which ordinary people wanted answering'. The aim was to connect a new sort of history, tackling questions that were relevant to a new public beyond the academic world of scholars and students. Subject and audience were one, a people's history, a popular history, what Thompson called 'history from below'. History, in this view, should not concern itself only with remote elites or with high politics, but with ordinary people and everyday lives. The key concept was 'experience', not just of individuals but also of the many and often conflicting groups that make up any society. Historians who adopted this approach sought historical truth, but rejected the view that science was the means by which it could be achieved. They encouraged emotional sympathy and identification with various groups in the past in order to understand (and perhaps change) their position in contemporary society. And they laid great emphasis on recovering the voices of those, such as women and the poor, who had previously been silenced, excluded from history. Not only were they to be brought back into history, but they were to be given a part in its making. Their aims were famously laid out in the opening of Edward Thompson's *The Making of the English Working Class* – with his call 'to rescue the poor stockinger, the Luddite cropper, the "obsolete" handloom weaver, the "utopian" artisan, and even the deluded follower of Joanna Southcott, from the enormous condescension of posterity'.

This sort of historical writing was not new – indeed, in Britain it had a proud pedigree, as Thompson acknowledged, in the Fabian, socialist, and Marxist work of Sidney and Beatrice Webb, R. H. Tawney, G. D. H. Cole, Donna Torr, and H. L. Morton. With the emergence of the highly politicized new social groups of the 1970s and 1980s, this was diversified to include race, gender, and sexual orientation. This scholarship was passionate and committed, and depended for much of its effect on dramatic historical narrative. It might be scientific in the socialist sense of embodying a theory of historical change, but, as Edward Thompson – its greatest practitioner of the 1960s and 1970s – clearly demonstrated, it was resolutely literary and rhetorical in form.

Tensions and differences between these two views of history – one scientific, objective, and technocratic, the other engaged, subjective, and political – were at first obscured by their shared commitment to destroy a common enemy, the narrative political history that had dominated teaching in British schools and universities. This vision of history and its purposes had begun to break up in the 1960s and 1970s when the British empire was in terminal decline and, as higher education expanded, the social and gender composition of universities changed. The critics of old political history won a memorable victory – not with a decisive battle but through a long, and strongly resisted, campaign of attrition. The old orthodoxy enshrined in the curricula was successfully toppled; historical writing was immeasurably enriched. Academic history became a house of many mansions, a pluralist rather than a unitary discipline. It became possible to explore many realms of social experience, to write about the marginal and dispossessed, women and children, the criminal and insane, the irrational and obscure, the private and the intimate, and to have such studies taken seriously.

Yet the new subject-matter of history posed problems for its scholarly practitioners. Was it possible to conform to the rather rigorous protocols of traditional historical method – the construction of a true account based on facts – when dealing with such intangibles as the passions, or was a new method or understanding of historical inquiry required? Often this issue was said to be one about sources: where was love to be found in the state papers? how did historians find documents that yielded evidence of these new subjects? Neither the archives (built up by nation states to preserve national documents and the papers of significant public figures, almost invariably men) nor the methods of history were attuned to writing about the emotions, intimacy, gender, childhood, households, or indeed almost any aspect of everyday life, with the possible exception of certain sorts of work. The best (most plausible, most real) versions of this world were literary fictions by the likes of Dickens, Zola, Flaubert, Tolstoy, Manzoni, and Upton Sinclair.

In the last thirty years the historian's archive has changed. Personal and familial correspondence like that between Sandwich and Ray have achieved a new prominence. Old records, especially criminal proceedings and account books, have been used for their insights into everyday life, and the determined search for more personal materials – diaries, journals, and love letters – has uncovered a large cache of documents either overlooked by or concealed from earlier generations of professional historians.

But the problem of pursuing historical characters out of the public arena and into their closets and bedrooms, of recovering their inner feelings as well as their manifest actions, was never a purely technical or evidentiary problem, as the proponents of the second revolution in historical studies were quick to point out. The power of great novelists to convey a sense of the real lay not, after all, in their pursuit of factual accuracy expressed in an objective voice, but in their passionate and partial engagement or capacious sympathy, their power to evoke a vision which, through its very singularity and subjectivity, convinced readers, as Sir Herbert Croft wished to do, that the story they told was real. Was it possible for the historian, attempting to depict a new sort of historical landscape, to use the literary artifice of the novelist and yet retain the discipline's scrupulous scholarly standards?

Lurking behind this question, as a number of critics were quick to point out, was that of historians' claims to objectivity. In the wake of the new social history came a new set of issues, raised not so often within the fraternity of historians (though there was the odd mole in the profession) as by philosophers, literary critics, and social theorists. They all, in their different ways, questioned the cardinal assumptions and self-descriptions of most historians. It doesn't much matter whether we call these critics post-structuralist, post-modernist, sceptic, relativist, or constructivist (terms of abuse as well as description); what counts is that they mounted a formidable challenge.

Historians claimed to tell a true story of past events, one that conformed to and rendered coherent a body of historical facts. Historical interpretation was judged by this conformity and coherence. History was 'out there' waiting to be discovered, just as Sherlock Holmes used his forensic skills to find clues to explain a mystery like the theft and smashing of the six busts of Napoleon. And just as Holmes's revelation that their destruction was explained by the jewel secreted in one of them, which showed that other explanations were false or fictitious, so the right historical interpretation rendered others invalid, because they were less in accord with 'the facts'.

Not so, said the historians' critics: facts have no existence independent of a structure or pattern that gives them the status of facts, just as events have no existence as events except in relation to other events that tell a story. History is made, not found; it is the artefact of the historian, not a natural object awaiting discovery. There is therefore not one history but many, as many as there are historians. Different stories were told with different ends in view, a position that accorded with the burgeoning varieties of history written in the 1970s and 1980s. The analogy between the historian and detective was not complete: Holmes's account was true to its purpose, to catch and convict the thief, but other stories also accorded with the same facts, and could also be told about the busts – a history, for instance, of Victorian furnishing or collecting, or of the English cult of Napoleon. Conan Doyle did not discuss these – they never shaped his narrative, which was fashioned by the genre he worked in, the detective story.

It followed from this that history ceased to be an imperious subject looking down on the events of history and became part of history itself. A historian's work was bounded by time and place; its preoccupations, methods, and prejudices were of its time, emerging from a particular historical context. History itself should be treated historically, for there was no reason why historians should historicize everything but themselves.

Writing history involves selecting, organizing, and presenting facts, and in doing so there is always a narrative, implied or explicit. Since narratives have their covert codes and messages conveyed in their very form and language, historians should attend to the medium as much as the message, critics said. More precisely, they should stop pretending that the medium did not affect the message. Perhaps the medium was the message or, as the historian Hayden White put it, the content the form.

If these critics were right, how could fact and fiction, history and imaginative literature, be distinguished? Where did it leave the historian devoted to his craft? In practice, it did not much change the situation. The new social historians had had an enormous impact on historical practice, but the effect of what is sometimes (rather unhappily) called the linguistic turn was much more limited. Historians became more interested in language and form, especially in the concepts they used; they became more interested in and self-conscious about the history of the historical profession; they tried, sometimes successfully, to write history from several points of view, and they began to ask about the history of such notions as 'fact', 'fiction', and 'history'. Mostly, however, history professors invited a speaker on the new heresy to a seminar, lost their temper, and went back to business as usual. When a card-carrying member of the profession like Simon Schama experimented with the genres of history and fiction in *Dead Certainties* (1991) he was shrilly condemned for deserting the historian's true calling.

Elsewhere in the literary world the response to the blurring of the line between history and fiction, facts and the imagination, was far more positive. Engaged, sympathetic biography, pioneered by Michael Holroyd, practised with such élan by Richard Holmes, and pushed in new directions by women biographers, explicitly identified the author with his or her subject. Historical novels, very much a revived genre of recent years, flamboyantly advertise their scholarly research and verisimilitude. An entire genre of journalism, first developed by Truman Capote but which has flourished since the 1960s, makes the author both protagonist and reporter of the story. Such writing often makes explicit what historians have sometimes wished to conceal – that what we see depends on our point of view – but treats this as a positive benefit rather than a failing.

Similarly, it seems to me important to recognize that recent reflection on the nature of historical scholarship has offered historians an opportunity to develop new forms of historical writing. The recent attempt to rethink the practice of historians, in other words, is a challenge not a threat. And it is in this spirit that I have written this book, partly as a certain kind of new history but also as an experiment, to see if it will work. I deliberately forswore an approach that set out to recover the truth about events between 1775 and 1779, though I, as much as anyone, wonder about what lay behind the miasma of news, rumour, and information that circulated after Martha Ray's death. It would be nice to know more about the nature and conduct of James Hackman's relations with Ray and with the Earl of Sandwich. But if there had been material to give us this information, neither the accounts I have discussed here, nor the book itself, would ever have been written.

And I did not want to treat all subsequent accounts of the affair merely as sources of facts or evidence. Historians often depict this work as an anatomizing of the past – stripping away layers of flabby misapprehension and misinterpretation to reveal the naked truth. But this process of dissection involves a lot of ripping and tearing: facts that historians think are relevant are torn out of their context and transplanted to the 'true' story. Victory is achieved at the price of the mutilation of all others. The primacy of history over other ways of representing the past legitimates the dismembering of other genres in order to create a dominant cyborg, justified because it is 'true'.

I took what I considered a less invasive alternative. I tried to treat these accounts as stories or narratives with their own histories – not as databases of facts. The significance of each individual account – whether novel, anecdote, or essay – lay not in what it told us about James Hackman, Martha Ray, and the Earl of Sandwich, but in what it told us about the relationship between itself and the events of 1779, the connection between the past it was describing and its present. To understand this, you have to understand its conventions of representation – its genre; but you also have to move further. Hence my attention, not just to the form and content of each individual story, but to the teller, the medium of expression, the audience (imagined or otherwise), and to the underlying assumptions both about feeling and about the history of a particular era.

This approach produces a punctuated history, not a continuous narrative, one marked by a particular series of moments when the story was told once again. The continuity, such as it is, lies in the transmission of versions of the story – its embodiment in the strange figure of Basil Montagu, or the republication of *Love and Madness* by Gilbert Burgess in the 1890s. The narrative is inevitably evanescent, a series of snapshots, not a saga.

Evanescent, yes, but innocent, no. I may have tried to distance myself from the historian as anatomist, choosing facts from other narratives to create his own, but my own story cannibalizes many other ones. The historian cannot escape from providing a master narrative made up of others; all that he or she can do is expose it in order to invite criticism or acceptance. Writing history is a part of history. Yet it is this and more – both a historical and a literary act, which our writing should explore and display rather than overlook and conceal.

293

NOTES

Place of publication is London unless otherwise stated.

CHAPTER 1

Page 9:
'strong legs . . . in the navy': *The Early Journals and Letters of Fanny Burney*, ed. Lars E. Troide and Stewart J. Cooke, 3 vols (Oxford, 1988–94), ii, 189.
'your Lordship . . . learned to dance': Joseph Cradock, *Literary and Miscellaneous Memoirs*, 4 vols (1828), iv, 166.
'I am sure . . . street at once': Ibid., 165–6.

Pages 9–11:
'I have never . . . a public man': N. A. M. Rodger, *The Insatiable Earl: A life of John Montagu, fourth Earl of Sandwich 1718–1792* (1993), 80.

Page 11:
'Universally admitted . . . as well as dispatch': N. A. M. Rodger, *The Admiralty* (Lavenham, Suffolk, 1979), 74.
'he rose at an early hour . . . breakfast': Rodger, *The Insatiable Earl*, 163.

Page 12:
'I am fatigued to death . . . thirteen hours': Ibid.

Page 13:
'The situation of our affairs . . . hanging over us': Sandwich to North, 15 October 1779, *The Private Papers of John, Earl of Sandwich, First Lord of the Admiralty*, ed. G. R. Barnes and J. H. Owen (4 vols, Naval Records Society, 1932–8), ii, 179.

Page 15:
'was out of . . . in his possession': Sandwich Mss 55c/9.
Hackman left disappointed . . . wish to believe: Galli depositions, Sandwich Mss 55c/3.
'not what we . . . to every beholder': 'Genuine Narrative of the Life of the late Miss Ray; with several anecdotes relative to the Reverend Mr Hackman', *Westminster Magazine* (April 1779), 172.

Pages 15–16:

'a second Cleopatra . . . apt to think Chimerical': *The Cumberland Letters: Being the correspondence of Richard Dennison Cumberland and George Cumberland, between the years 1771 and 1784*, ed. Clementina Black (1912), 228.

Page 18:

It seems likely . . . press of Admiralty business: See Cradock, *Literary and Miscellaneous Memoirs*, i, 145, for his surprise that Sandwich was not with the two women.

Page 20:

'*My Dear Frederick*': printed, inter alia, in *Gentleman's Magazine* (April 1779), 213.

'O! thou dearer to me . . . Adieu!': *The Case and Memoirs of the late Rev. James Hackman* (1779), 29–30.

He seems to . . . brandy and water: *General Advertiser* (20 April 1779).

Page 21:

'who seemed somewhat distressed . . . hold of his arm': *General Advertiser* (17 April 1779).

'the sudden assault . . . face': *Personal Recollections of the Life and Times, with extracts from the Correspondence, of Valentine Lord Cloncurry* (Dublin, 1849), 39.

'came round behind her . . . blows than by the ball': Horace Walpole to Lady Ossory, 9 April 1779, *Horace Walpole's Correspondence*, ed. W. S. Lewis (48 vols, New Haven and Oxford, 1937–83), vol. 33, 100. This account closely follows the report in *London Evening Post*, 10 April 1779.

'beating himself . . . kill me!"': *London Evening Post* (10 April 1779).

Page 22:

'two very pretty girls . . . amorous play': James Boswell, *London Journal 1762–1763*, ed. Frederick A. Pottle (1950), 264.

'he came up . . . the Master of the Tavern': *General Advertiser* (17 April 1779).

'What devil could induce . . . whom he had sent for': Sandwich Mss 55c/17.

Pages 22–3:

'upon the miserable . . . *now was happy!*': *General Advertiser* (15 April 1779).

Page 23:

'You know that I forbade . . . borne anything but this".': Cradock, *Literary and Miscellaneous Memoirs*, i, 145–6.

'all was confusion and astonishment': Cradock, *Literary and Miscellaneous Memoirs*, i, 146.

Galli had fainted . . . in Sandwich's coach: *Gazetteer* (12 April 1779).

Pages 23–4:
'For gods sake . . . sent to prison': Sandwich Mss 55c/1.

Page 24:
'in order to . . . wanton, idle curiosity': *General Advertiser* (12 April 1779).
'From the agonizing . . . Magistrate could proceed': *General Advertiser* (12 April 1779).
'he wished for . . . Misery he laboured under': *St James's Chronicle* (10 April 1779).
That same afternoon . . . guarded Ray's body: *General Advertiser*, (13 April 1779).

Pages 24–5:
'owned that they never saw . . . fracture': *Morning Post* (10 April 1779).

Page 25:
That day all . . . into mourning clothes: *General Advertiser* (13 April 1779).
'so that property . . . in her coffin': *Gazetteer* (13 April 1779).
'My Dear Galli . . . immediately to me': Ray to Galli, 30 March 1779, Sandwich Mss 55a/17.
'has disturbed his . . . mind for ever': *General Evening Post* (13 April 1779).

Pages 25–6:
'upon his word . . . rejected': Sandwich Mss 55c/3.

Page 26:
'He is desirous . . . soon as possible': Sandwich Mss 55c/4.
'you can't think . . . life is concerned': quoted in Rodger, *The Insatiable Earl*, 108.

Pages 26–7:
'I am clearly of opinion . . . ever since': Sandwich Mss 55c/7.

Page 27:
'to avail himself . . . of temporary insanity': *Morning Post* (12 April 1779).
The trial came on: see the official transcript, *The Whole Proceedings on the King's Commission of the Peace, Oyer and Terminer and Gaol Delivery for the City of London and also the gaol delivery for the County of Middlesex; held at the justice hall in the Old Bailey On 4ᵗʰ April 1779 and the following days being the fourth session in the Mayoralty of the Rt. Hon. Samuel Plumbe, taken in shorthand by Joseph Gurney, Number IV part 1* (1779) and the reports in *The Genuine Life, Trial and Dying Words of the Reverend James Hackman* (1779); *London Evening Post* (15–17 April 1779); *Gazetteer* (17 April 1779); *St James's Chronicle* (15–17 April 1779); *London Chronicle* (15–17 April 1779); *General Advertiser* (17 April 1779); *General Evening Post* (17 April 1779).

'I always know . . . Mr Wilkes does': *The Yale Edition of the Private Papers of James Boswell: The Laird of Auchinleck, 1778–1782*, ed. Joseph W. Reed (New York, 1977), 85, 85n.

Page 28:
'*mains serrees*': Ibid', 85.
'he came into . . . trying hour of death': *Gazetteer* (20 April 1779).

Page 29:
'No . . . Very ill': *Boswell: The Laird of Auchinleck*, 93.
'Having been placed . . . over on each side': Henry Angelo, *Reminiscences*, 2 vols (1828–30), ii, 192.

Pages 29–30:
'Soon after the doors . . . age, sex or distinction': *Daily Advertiser* (21 April 1779).

Page 30:
'It is understood . . . I ever shall be': *The Private Papers of John, Earl of Sandwich*, ii, 257.
'No-one . . . your domestic felicity': Sandwich Mss 55 c/31.
'From what I have heard . . . irreproachable' Sandwich Mss 55c/27.

Pages 30–1:
'I am sorry . . . your situation': *The Private Papers of John, Earl of Sandwich*, ii, 249.

Page 31:
'You have suffered much . . . rest of mankind': Law Reynolds to Sandwich, 20 April 1779, Sandwich Mss 55c/37.
'Enemies . . . wicked and arbitrary': Sandwich Mss 55c/33.

Pages 31–2:
'where the portrait . . . my leave': Cradock, *Literary and Miscellaneous Memoirs,* I, 146–7.

Page 32:
'one of the company . . . left the room': Cradock, *Literary and Miscellaneous Memoirs,* I, 147.

Page 33:
'sorry to inform . . . any way': Sandwich Mss 55c/17.
'whatever . . . to the public': Ibid.
'I am ill . . . live in the world': Sandwich Mss 55c/11.
'I cannot assist myself . . . always help me': Sandwich Mss 55c/15.

Page 35:
The flow of information: *The Diary of a Country parson, the Reverend James Woodforde, 1758–1803*, ed. John Beresford (5 vols, Oxford, 1924–31), I, 249–50.

CHAPTER 2

Page 39:

'A blackguard being . . . of the trial': *The Yale Editions of the Private Papers of James Boswell: The Laird of Auchinleck, 1778–1782*, ed. Joseph W. Reed (New York, 1977), 85.

Page 40:

'A sentiment . . . rent with anguish!': James Boswell, quoted in *Public Advertiser* (19 April 1779), *The Laird of Auchinleck*, 86.

When a false . . . correct the story: Ibid. 93–5.

'Among these . . . number and authenticity': Johann Wilhelm von Archenholz, *A Picture of England: Containing a description of the laws, customs, and manners of England* (2 vols, Dublin, 1789), ii, 42.

'for every letter . . . transmitted to the paper': Robert Haig, *The Gazetteer 1735–1797* (Carbondale, Illinois, 1960), 156.

Page 41:

'The general run . . . sent into the world': *Literary Liberty Considered; in a Letter to Henry Sampson Woodfall* (1774), 16–17.

Page 42:

'The Political Controversy . . . unpitied to the Pillory': *An Essay on the Art of News-Paper Defamation, in a letter to Mr William Griffin, publisher and printer of the Morning Post, a master of that art.* By C. D. Piguenit (1775), 2–3.

Pages 42–4:

'inventing, adding and . . . brains can suggest': *London Magazine*, xlvi (1777), 230.

Page 44:

In 1781 he . . . living for himself: Sir John Fortescue (ed.), *The Correspondence of King George the Third*, 6 vols. (1927), v, 149, 471.

'Ld. SANDWICH'S Morning Post': Lucyle T. Werkmeister, *The London Daily Press, 1772–1792* (Lincoln, Nebraska, 1963), 118.

Page 45:

'There is certainly . . . that requires explanation': *Gazetteer* (20 April 1779).

Pages 45–6:

'Besides many other . . . this extraordinary transaction': Ibid.

Page 46:

'That Miss Ray . . . she had promised': Ibid.

'it is certain . . . committing the crime': Ibid.

'In short . . . form an opinion': Ibid.

Pages 46–7:

'Upon Enquiry into . . . fatal to himself': *St James's Chronicle* (21 April 1779).

Page 47:
'both sides of the question': *Gazetteer* (20 April 1779).
'is desirous to . . . he wishes for': quoted in George Martinelli, *Jemmy Twitcher. A Life of the Fourth Earl of Sandwich 1718–1792* (1962), 171.
'Mr H has . . . and was rejected': Sandwich Mss 55c.

Page 48:
'he lays the whole on Galli': Martinelli, *Jemmy Twitcher*, 171.
'It was Miss . . . to the lady': *London Chronicle* (13 April 1779), *General Evening Post* (13 April 1779), *Gazetteer* (12 April 1779).

Pages 48–9:
Joseph Cradock later . . . look at the stars': Cradock, *Literary and Miscellaneous Memoirs*, i, 140–1.

Page 49:
'The earl of . . . which it afforded': *Voyage performed by the late Earl of Sandwich round the Mediterranean in the Years 1738 and 1739. Written by himself, to which are prefixed, Memoirs of the Noble Author's Life, by John Cooke, M.A.* (1799), xxxii.
'Few houses were . . . every one was at ease': Charles Butler, *Reminiscences of Charles Butler Esq.*, 3rd edn, 2 vols (1822), i, 74.
Charles Burney . . . him a headache: *The Letters of Dr. Charles Burney*, ed. Alvaro Ribeiro, 4 vols (Oxford, 1991), i, 237.
'The lady's . . . intercourse whatever since': *General Evening Post* (8 April 1779).

Page 50:
'Lord Sandwich says . . . had entirely disappointed': *General Advertiser* (9 April 1779).
'his visits became . . . forbidden the house': *General Evening Post* (10 April 1779).

Pages 50–1:
'The unfortunate Mr . . . to every body': *General Advertiser* (16 April 1779).

Page 51:
'descended from a . . . catastrophe on Wednesday night': Same report, *London Evening Post* (10 April 1779); *Gazetteer* (10 April 1779).
'Mr Hackman, so . . . Delicacy of Sentiment': *St James's Chronicle* (10 April 1779).
'As his manners . . . all his own': *St James's Chronicle* (15–17 April 1779); see Boswell in *Laird of Auchinleck*, 87.
'the lovely victim': *London Chronicle* (8 April 1779).
'irreproachable in her . . . legal Marriage ceremony': *St James's Chronicle* (10 April 1779).

Page 52:

'the memory of . . . of every imputation': *General Evening Post* (13 April 1779).

'under the protection of the noble Peer': *St James's Chronicle* (10 April 1779).

'Her person was . . . on the Harpsichord': Ibid.

'She was also . . . in the Family': Ibid.

'was never suspected . . . strict fidelity': *General Evening Post* (10 April 1779).

'strictness of motherly attention': *London Chronicle* (8 April 1779).

'Miss Ray made . . . lost a tender mother': *General Advertiser* (19 April 1779), *General Evening Post* (14 April 1779).

Page 53:

'There was scarce . . . her through life': *London Chronicle* (8 April 1779).

'all ranks of . . . lost its edge': *General Advertiser* (9 April 1779).

'to describe in . . . head and heart': *General Advertiser* (9 April 1779).

Page 54:

'Is there any . . . most bloodily assassinated?': *Morning Post* (12 April 1779).

'We are assured . . . by his death"': Cf. *London Chronicle* (13 April 1779), *London Evening Post* (8 April 1779).

'inconsolable . . . this unmans me"': *London Evening Post* (10 April 1779).

'deplorable . . . his dearest friends': *Gazetteer* (9 April 1779).

Page 55:

'From [Ray's] having . . . of his Friendship': *St James's Chronicle* (8 April 1779).

'the common passions of Humanity': PHILANTHROPIST in *St James's Chronicle* (10 April 1779).

'let us endeavor . . . to the Phaenomenon': Ibid.

Page 56:

'The public . . . of his mistress': *London Evening Post* (14 April 1779).

'the many thousand . . . of despotism': Ibid.

'man who, by . . . with murdered blood': Ibid.

'we should not . . . any previous warning': Ibid.

'We should rather . . . as she did': Ibid.

'had the wretched . . . grave in peace': Ibid.

Page 57:

'unfortunate': *London Evening Post* (15–17 April 1779); *Gazetteer* (17 April 1779); *St James's Chronicle* (15–17 April 1779); *London Chronicle* (15–17 April 1779); *General Advertiser* (17 April 1779); *General Evening Post* (17 April 1779).

'delicacy of sentiment': *St James's Chronicle* (10 April 1779).

Page 58:
'No quality of . . . to our own': David Hume, *A Treatise of Human Nature* (1739–40), ed. L. A. Selby-Bigg, 2nd edn, rev. P. H. Niddich (Oxford, 1978), 316.
'that peculiar structure . . . and passing events': *The Monthly Magazine* quoted in Markman Ellis, *The Politics of Sensibility. Race, Gender and Commerce in the Sentimental Novel* (Cambridge, 1996), 5.

Pages 58–9:
'it may be . . . and others' misfortunes?': *Man a Paper for Ennobling the Species*, no. 43 (22 October 1755), 4.
'The *nervous system* . . . more exquisite pleasure': Thomas Trotter, *A View of the Nervous Temperament; being a practical enquiry into the increasing prevalence, prevention and treatment of those diseases*, 2nd edn (Newcastle, 1807), 25.
'How much soever . . . with sentiment': Cradock, *Literary and Miscellaneous Memoirs*, i, 63.
'Sensibility . . . of my virtue': *Lady's Magazine* quoted in Ellis, *The Politics of Sensibility*, 7.

Page 60:
'derives its efficacy . . . brought to feel': Hugh Blair quoted in John Dwyer, *Virtuous Discourse. Sensibility and Community in late eighteenth century Scotland* (Edinburgh, 1987), 59.
'It is from . . . the real character': Mark Salber Phillips, *Society and Sentiment. Genres of Historical Writing in Britain, 1740–1820* (Princeton, New Jersey, 2000), 44.
'an *Epic* in lower Life': quoted in R. F. Brissenden, *Virtue in Distress. Studies in the Novel of Sentiment from Richardson to Sade* (1974), 101.

Page 61:
'I not only . . . of my soul': Joseph Boruwlaski, *Memoirs of the Celebrated Dwarf* (1788), 71.

CHAPTER 3

Page 63:
'It seems to . . . Mistress or Friend': *Thraliana: The Diary of Mrs. Hester Lynch Thrale (later Mrs. Piozzi) 1776–1809*, ed. Katharine C. Balderston, 2 vols (2nd edn, Oxford, 1951), i, 384.
'the strangest thing . . . if she will': *Thraliana*, i, 385–6.

Page 64:
'For the last . . . a shocking murder': Horace Walpole to Sir Horace Mann (17 April 1779) in *The Yale Edition of Horace Walpole's Correspondence*, ed. W. S. Lewis, 48 vols (Oxford, 1983), xxiv, 459.
'I found Miss . . . occupied everybody': Lady Ossory to George Selwyn

(17 April 1779) in *George Selwyn and his Contemporaries*, ed. John
Heneage Jesse, 4 vols (1844), iv, 75.
'the topic of conversation': see inter alia *London Evening Post* (10 April
1779).
'Now, upon the . . . understand it': Horace Walpole to Lady Ossory
(9 April 1779), in *The Yale Edition of Horace Walpole's Correspondence*,
xxxiii, 98.

Page 65:
'the man is . . . distresses of others': Samuel Richardson quoted in
Brissenden, *Virtue in Distress*, 4.
'From the agonizing . . . could proceed': *London Chronicle* (8 April 1779).

Pages 65–6:
'His manifest . . . .wished to die': Ibid.

Page 66:
'he sank into . . . words to paint': *London Evening Post* (8 April 1779).
'quite composed, and . . . becoming fortitude': Ibid.
'His sighs and . . . of human nature': Ibid.
'The very humane . . . pale of reason?': *General Advertiser* (13 April
1779).
'the tear of . . . *of the deed*': *General Evening Post* (13 April 1779).

Page 67:
'was wonderfully touching': Lady Ossory to George Selwyn (17 April
1779) in *George Selwyn and his Contemporaries*, iv, 75.
'The prisoner by . . . conducted himself': *London Chronicle* (17 April 1779).
'The behaviour . . . denied his pity': Ibid.

Pages 67–8:
'However we may . . . the unhappy *criminal*': *London Evening Post*
(17 April 1779).

Page 68:
'He might have . . . rent with anguish!': James Boswell, quoted in *Public
Advertiser* (19 April 1779), *The Yale Editions of the Private Papers of James
Boswell: The Laird of Auchinleck, 1778–1782*, ed. Joseph W. Reed (New
York, 1977), 85–6.
'glorious': Lady Ossory to George Selwyn (17 April 1779) in *George
Selwyn and his Contemporaries*, ed. John Heneage Jesse, iv, 78.
'He behaved with . . . perfect resignation': quoted in *George Selwyn and
his Contemporaries*, iv, 84.
'he collected his . . . a contrite heart': *Gazetteer* (20 April 1779)
'He behaved as . . . a situation': Ibid.

Page 69:
'He repeated that . . . of his Saviour': Ibid.

Page 70:
'the curiosity which . . . of callousness': *The Hypochondriack. Being the Seventy Essays of the Celebrated Biographer, JAMES BOSWELL, appearing in the LONDON MAGAZINE, from November 1778 to August 1783, and here first reprinted*, ed. Margery Bailey, 2 vols (Stanford, 1928), ii, 282.
'We all desire . . . to enter them': Adam Smith, *The Theory of Moral Sentiments*, ed. D. D. Raphael and A. C. Macalfie (Oxford, 1976), Part VII, IV, 28.

Page 71:
'Natural to destroy . . . cannot have': Boswell, *Laird of Auchinleck,* 79.
'Natural to <shoo>t mistress': Boswell, *Laird of Auchinleck*, 92.
'Let those whose . . . a dreadful act': Boswell, *Public Advertiser* (19 April 1779), see Ibid., 86.

Page 72:
'Hackman's case . . . melancholy situation': Boswell in *St James's Chronicle* (15–17 April 1779), see Ibid., 88–9.

Page 73:
The tenth and . . . appeared in early June: Copies survive of all but the third edition according to the *Eighteenth-Century Short Title Catalogue*.
'his deportment was . . . course of his trial': *The Case and Memoirs of the Late Rev. Mr James Hackman* (1779), 10–11.

Page 75:
'What tho' I . . . were in my soul': *Miscellanies, in Prose and Verse, on Various Occasions, by the author of several anonymous, well-received pieces* (1776), 14.
Dawes claimed to . . . before the notorious case: *Gazetteer* (6 May 1779).

Page 76:
'Mr Hackman was . . . Satisfaction in his power': *St James's Chronicle* (15–17 April 1779).
'the following pages . . . amiable and fair character': *Case and Memoirs*, v.
'I think it necessary . . . with my own name': Newspaper cutting in the British Library copy of the *Case and Memoirs*, C 39 f.16.

Page 77:
'There being some . . . catch the penny of curiosity': *Gazetteer* (5 May 1779).
'The Rope . . . poor Hackman's fate': *Public Advertiser* (2 June 1779).
Dawes complained bitterly about this attack to Henry Woodfall in a letter published in the *Public Advertiser* three days later.
'revelling in all . . . stolen bliss': *Case and Memoirs*, 2, 31.
'the indulgencies she . . . gratification': Ibid., 3.
'they corresponded in . . . by every post': Ibid., 3–4.

Page 78:
   '(whether under the . . . with it longer': Ibid., 4.
   'That Miss Reay . . . more dear to her': Ibid., 4–5.
   'originated on that . . . his wretched mind': Ibid., 29–31.
   'with one other . . . cancel': Ibid., 29.

Pages 78–9:
   'I know you . . . on my living': Ibid., 30.

Page 79:
   'For God's sake . . . but death or you': Ibid., 6–7.
   'in the presence . . . described by words': Ibid., 21.
   'he concluded it . . . to die together': Ibid., 7–8.
   'momentary phrenzy [sic]': Ibid., 19, 12.
   'It is the . . . act that kills': Ibid., 17.
   'that he did not . . . destroy himself *only*': Ibid., 19.
   'a felonious action . . . of mind': Ibid., 20.

Page 80:
   'as he was . . . assassins and murderers': Ibid., 21.
   'hurried him, when . . . were living': Ibid., 27.
   'he has fallen . . . according to law': Ibid. (4th edn), 6.
   'he was a . . . Poor Hackman!': Ibid. (8th edn). 16.
   'imprudence, impolicy . . . rank, and fortune': Ibid., 32.

Page 81:
   'had he been . . . been so criminal': *St James's Chronicle* (15 April 1779).
   'entreating him . . . happier as they were': Ibid. (7th edn), no pagination.

Pages 81–2:
   The author of . . . her undeservedly': Anon to Miss Galli, Enclosure 1, with Edwina Galli to Sandwich (17 May 1779), Sandwich Mss 55c/12.

Page 82:
   'said to her . . . *bless you Galli*': Ibid.
   'She will not . . . of her name': Ibid.
   'she was out of town': Ibid., Enclosure 1, 2nd letter (13 May 1779).

Page 83:
   'His capital crime . . . preferable to life': Ray's case was first advertised on 9 June.
   'The passion of . . . an arbitrary way': Dawes, *Case and Memoirs* (8th edn), 2.

Pages 83–4:
   'as an unhappy . . . eternity with him': See the 'Address' of the 7th edn, in Ibid., 4.

Page 85:
'It is much ... of a valuable member': *The Case and Memoirs of Miss
Martha Reay, to which are Added Remarks, by way of Refutation on the Case
and Memoirs of the Rev. Mr Hackman*, (1779), 32.
'Thus in an ... laboured to traduce': Ibid. 11.

Page 86:
'Author, and Inventor ... Luxuriant imagination': Ibid., 45.

CHAPTER 4

Page 88:
'Two fiends with ... the love of gain': William Preston, *Seventeen
Hundred and Seventy-Seven; or, A picture of the manners and character of the
age. In a poetical epistle from a lady of quality* (1777), 17.

Page 89:
'Ye Gods! ... the siege of *Troy*': Edward Thompson, *The Meretriciad* (6th
edn, revised and corrected with large additions, 1765).

Page 90:
'The man who ... character of the nation': *The Memoirs of Miss
Arabella Bolton. Containing a genuine account of her seduction, and the
barbarous treatment she afterwards received from the Honourable Colonel
L—l, the present supposed M—r for the county of Middlesex*, 2 vols (1770), i,
xiii.

Page 91:
'went into his Lordship's keeping': See for instance *London Evening Post*
(7, 10 April 1779).
'the scene of ... your hoary licentiousness': *Four Letters from the Country
Gentleman, on the Subject of the Petitions* (1780), 21.

Page 92:
'as you are ... proving your youth': Martinelli, *Jemmy Twitcher*, 39.
The poorest girls ... taverns and brothels: James Boswell, *London
Journal 1762–1763*, ed. Frederick A. Pottle (1950), 49, 52.

Page 93:
There were clusters ... Streets in Westminster: Randolph Trumbach,
*Sex and the Gender Revolution. Volume One: Heterosexuality and the Third
Gender in Enlightenment London* (Chicago, 1998), especially 116–18,
120–2, 130, 144, 155, 157, 163, 182 for an excellent account of the
sex industry to which I am heavily indebted.
'One would imagine ... near at hand': Cited in Hugh Phillips,
*Mid-Georgian London. A topographical and social survey of central western
London about 1750* (1950), 142.

Pages 93–4:

'Then Your Lordship . . . all at once': The woman wrote about the incident to Sandwich in the summer of 1779, Sandwich Mss 54a/22.

Page 94:

'a Mansion where . . . *Bagnio* in Leicester Fields': *Authentic and Interesting Memoirs of Miss Ann Sheldon; (Now Mrs. Archer). A lady who figured, during several years, in the highest line of public life, and in whose history will be found, all the vicissitudes, which so constantly attend on women of her description. Written by herself*, 4 vols (1788), i, 136.

(Many of these . . . with their patrons.): *The History of the Human Heart; or, The adventures of a young gentleman* (1749); reprinted 1885, Rochester series of reprints, no. 4, 103–5.

Page 95:

'she throws [them] . . . peruse them': Sandwich Mss 54a/45. The letters themselves are Sandwich Mss 54a/42–44.

Page 96:

'the females remained . . . of the spectators': *Nocturnal Revels; or, The History of King's-Place, and other modern nunneries . . . by a monk of the order of St Francis*, 2 vols (1779), ii, 25–7.

(She was first . . . many other occasions.): *Authentic and Interesting Memoirs of Miss Ann Sheldon*, i, 110, 121; iv, 80, 88–9.

'The time of . . . than distinct orbs': Trumbach, *Sex and the Gender Revolution*, 211.

'not long in town': *Nocturnal Revels*, ii, 20.

Pages 96–7:

Certainly the press . . . by a nobleman: *Covent Garden Magazine*, ii (1774), 273.

Page 97:

'the poor girl . . . luckily procured him': Ibid.

She was later . . . £70 for her: *Authentic and Interesting Memoirs of Miss Ann Sheldon*, i, 172–4.

'well known in . . . and private gentlemen': Ibid., iv, 107.

Page 98:

'I suppose madam . . . at your door': Ibid., i, 198.

'who wishes to . . . for his seraglio': Ibid., iv, 107.

'the garret was . . . a negro wench': Ibid., ii, 169; iv, 202, 206–8.

Page 99:

'these *stale commodities* . . . take them off': *The Honest London Spy: Discovering the base and subtle intrigues of the Town* (1724), 3.

'you know that . . . with its goodness': *Genuine Memoirs of the Celebrated Miss Maria Brown* (1766), 100, 137.
'I'll have you . . . is her own': *The Honest London Spy*, 10–11.

Page 100:
'there were seldom . . . contained in it': *The Genuine Memoirs of Miss Faulkner* (1770), 38, 60, 63, 70.
'excuse this appearance . . . study to please': Sandwich Mss 54a/56, 7 August. Anonymous, presumably to Sandwich.
'the Marquis was . . . of a Virgin': *Authentic and Interesting Memoirs of Miss Ann Sheldon*, i, 57.

Pages 100–1:
'now he is . . . trouble of pursuing': *Town and Country Magazine*, i (1769), 178.

Pages 103–4:
'he had a . . . their lordships': Quoted in Adrian Hamilton, *The Infamous Essay on Woman or John Wilkes Seated between Vice and Virtue* (1972), 107.

Page 104:
'Awake, my Fanny . . . Pricks to scan': Ibid., 213.
'they do not . . . a public man': Rodger, *The Insatiable Earl*, 80.
'Notwithstanding Lord Sandwich's . . . on that subject': Horace Walpole to Lord Hertford (18 November 1763) in *Horace Walpole's Correspondence*, xxxviii, 232.

Page 105:
'the wicked even affirm . . . out of company': Horace Walpole to Horace Mann (17 November 1763), Ibid., xxii, 185.
'The blasphemous book . . . as is incredible': Horace Walpole to Lord Hertford (25 November 1763), Ibid., xxxviii, 243.

Pages 105–6:
'Of these men . . . of the people': Quoted in Hamilton, *The Infamous Essay on Woman*, 105; see also the postscript to Wilkes's *North Briton*, no. 46.

Page 106:
'with more hypocrisy . . . a professed Methodist': Horace Walpole, *Memoirs of the Reign of King George III*, ed. G. F. Russell Barker, 4 vols (1894), i, 247.

Page 107:
'I scarce ever . . . blasphemy and bawdy': Hamilton, *The Infamous Essay on Woman*, 9; Edward Gibbon, *Memoirs of my life and writings*, ed. A. O. J. Cockshut and Steven Constantine (Keele, 1994), 136.
'these morals he . . . make his fortune': Ibid.
'had the divine gift of lewdness': *The Life of John Wilkes Patriot. An*

Unfinished Autobiography (1955), 34. He also added: 'All her sensibility seemed to have reference to one favourite spot'. This is a reprint of British Museum manuscript Add. Mss 30865.

'At an early . . . universal Condemnation': *The Historical and the Posthumous Memoirs of Sir Nathaniel William Wraxall, 1722–84*, ed. H. B. Wheatley (1884), i, 399.

'the most abandoned Man of the Age': Wilkes, *Letter to the Electors of Aylesbury*,

Page 109:

'LOTHARIO, holding Honour . . . seek for fame': Charles Churchill, *The Candidate* (1764), 15.

'Search Earth, search . . . to his mind': Ibid., 19.

'Come Jemmy Twitcher . . . her only child': Edward Thompson, *The Courtesan and the Meretriciad* (1765), 14–15.

Pages 109–10:

'His licentious mode . . . George the Third': Wraxall, *The Historical and the Posthumous Memoirs*, i, 400.

Page 110:

'His Fortune, which . . . open to seduction': Ibid.

'His enemies, who . . . of the Admiralty': Ibid., 401.

'as Names and minute . . . deep impression': Ibid., 401–2.

Pages 110–11:

'The cellars were . . . objects were provided': Charles Johnstone, *Chrysal, or the adventures of a guinea* (3rd edn, 1767), iii, 233.

Page 111:

'covered with emblems . . . explanation': Ibid., 234–5.

'painted with the pourtraits . . . imagination': Ibid.

'even the most . . . horrid occasion': Ibid.

'loose songs and gross lewdness': Ibid., 238.

During one of . . . summon Lucifer: Ibid., 240.

'Spare me, . . . half a sinner': Ibid., 243

'he exerted all . . . into ridicule': Ibid., 248.

Page 112:

In 1789, when . . . talking to him: Mary Driscall to Sandwich, 4 September 1789, Sandwich Mss 54a/23.

'she is a . . . be in keeping': Ibid., 54a/63.

Fanny Denton from . . . own wicked thoughts: Ibid.,53/113.

Pages 114–15:

'I don't excuse . . . distracts me': Ibid., 53/30.

Page 115:

'My sorrows and . . . in life': Ibid., 53/32.

'far be it . . . here and hereafter': Ibid.

Page 116:
'As I find . . . troublesome to you': Ibid., 53/27.
'you have made . . . least concern': Ibid.
'Your Lordship likewise . . . to my prejudice': Ibid., 53/31.
But she died . . . of society: Ibid., 53/37.

CHAPTER 5

Page 120:
'A friend to . . . her own name': Ibid., 55b/12.
'It is very . . . reputable families': Ibid.
'I make no . . . more resentment': Ibid., 55b/13.
'As you are . . . our musical meetings': Cradock, *Literary and Miscellaneous Memoirs*, i, 117–18.

Pages 120–1:
'When Lords turn . . . praising his mistress': Ibid., iv, 167.

Page 121:
Omai remarked . . . was delighted: *Memoirs of Granville Sharp, Esq. Composed from his own manuscripts, and other authentic documents in the possession of his family and of the African Institution. By Prince Hoare* (1820), 150–2.

Pages 121–2:
'Thus it is . . . woman to his bed': Ibid., 150.

Page 122:
'Give me rhyme . . . of the DEMI-REP!': Edward Thompson, *The Demi-Rep* (2nd edn, 1765), 9.
'Where Matrimony veil's . . . the name of Wife': Ibid., title page.
'This Town's infested . . . them up within': Ibid., 14.

Page 123:
'The Ladies pick . . . their dying Swains': Edward Thompson, *The Meretriciad*, in *The Courtesan and the Meretriciad*, 45.
'Rotten or sound . . . simile might suit': Edward Thompson, *The Courtesan. By the author of the Meretriciad* (3rd edn, 1765), 37.

Pages 124–5:
'It will readily . . . some modest Women': Article signed and dated 'ADOLESCENS. Inner Temple, 9 April 1775', *St James's Chronicle* (April 1775).

Page 125:
'A Man rises . . . other features': Ibid.
'makes him unfit . . . of Painful Reflections': Ibid.

'I take care . . . the Scandalous Magazine': Oliver Goldsmith, *She Stoops to Conquer*; Friedman, *Works of Goldsmith*, v, 150.
'A LADY on . . . beholds the Interview': *Town and Country Magazine* (1781), frontispiece.

Page 126:
  'have so peculiarly . . . all others': Ibid.
  'Mirror to Vice . . . a just Medium': Ibid.

Page 127:
  'her wit and sprightliness': The account of Sandwich and Ray is from the *Town and Country Magazine* (November 1769), 561–4.

Pages 127–8:
  According to this . . . loses her honour: Ibid., 561–3.

Page 128:
  'She calmly submitted . . . of the profession': Ibid., 562.
  'gave her a . . . amorous passion': Ibid.
  'a loose idea . . . her mind': Ibid., 562.
  'A girl of . . . of his sex': Ibid., 563.
  'When Miss Ray . . . of the waiters': Ibid., 564.

Page 129:
  'Till at last . . . loathsome weed away': Ibid., 562.
  'A female who . . . by necessity': Ibid., 564.
  'She often sings . . . his satisfaction': Ibid.
  'In a word . . . of her lover': Ibid.

Page 130:
  'Every one of . . . particularly Signora Fr-si': *Town and Country Magazine* (1779), 180.
  'It was a rule . . . in that predicament': Ibid.
  'her person was . . . peculiarly harmonious': Ibid.

Page 131:
  'a woman of . . . female in Europe': *Nocturnal Revels*, i, 250.
  Not content with . . . his bloody deed: Ibid., 247–9.

Page 132:
  'Illicit love now . . . of incontinent beauty': The reprint, used here, of Jackson's original essay was included as a preface to the Dublin (1780) edition of *Love and Madness, A Story too True*, a work I discuss at length in chapter 6; see xiv.
  'If probable conjecture . . . a modern courtesan': *Love and Madness: A Story too True* (Dublin, 1780), xvi.

Pages 132–3:
  'are generally uniform . . . and their occupations': Ibid., xvii.

Page 133:
'possess that degree . . . of our nature': Ibid.
'men, skilled in . . . of their possessor': Ibid.
'virtue mourns . . . sensibility and beauty': Ibid.
'may be classed . . . of their admirers': Ibid. xvi.

Page 134:
'That little ogling . . . they cannot do': *The Midnight Spy; or, A view of the transactions of London and Westminster, from the hours of ten in the evening, till five in the morning* (1766), 80, 113.
'twice for what . . . could not do': Ibid., 121; Edward Thompson, *The Meretriciad* (6th edn, 1766), 14.
'more flexible to . . . and vigorous lover': Captain Charles Walker, *Authentick Memoirs of the Life Intrigues And Adventures of the Celebrated Sally Salisbury. With true characters of the most considerable gallants* (1723), 73.
'her amours offered . . . of their fortune': Miss Ambross, *The Life and Memoirs of the Late Miss Ann Catley, the Celebrated Actress. With biographical sketches of Sir Francis Blake Delaval, and the Hon. Isabella Pawlet* [1789], 40.
'who by her . . . cleanly made': Edward Thompson, *The Meretriciad*, in *The Courtesan and the Meretriciad*, 6th edn (1765), 40.

Pages 134–5:
'Of all the . . . for pleasure too': Ibid., 30.

Page 135:
'she is the . . . their fortunes': *The Modern Atlantis; or, The devil in an air balloon* (1784), 54, 58.
'The manners of . . . fraud and avarice': Ibid.

Pages 135–6:
'If a man . . . of her benefactor': *The Midnight Spy*, 141–2.

Page 136:
'This life of . . . round of deception': Ibid., 141.
'I know it . . . themselves created': *Authentic and Interesting Memoirs of Miss Ann Sheldon*, iii, 143.

Pages 136–7:
Hugh Kelly's *Memoirs* . . . to her fiancé: For the dangers of the period between betrothal and marriage see *The Lady's Magazine*, iv (1773), 176.

Page 137:
'She . . . she was actually undone!': *Memoirs of a Magdalen; or the History of Louisa Mildmay, by Hugh Kelly, Esq.* 2 vols. (1782), i, 17–18.
'the same warmth . . . with every body else': Ibid.

Page 138:
'The character left . . . to be exhausted': *Love and Madness* (Dublin, 1780), xvii–xviii.

'motives of mere . . . heart and person': Ibid.
He even believed . . . secrets of state: Ibid., xxi.

Page 139:

'amassed immense riches . . . half-pay officers': *Town and Country Magazine* (October 1769), 505.
Nancy Parsons was . . . Duke of Grafton: Horace Bleakeley, *Ladies Fair and Frail. Sketches of the demi-monde during the eighteenth century* (1909), 112.
'There was no office . . . executed and secured': *The Genuine Memoirs of Miss Faulkner*, 309–10.
'it is impossible . . . *much better grace*': Ibid., 284.

Page 140:

'the pandar of your own vices': [Israel Pottinger], *The Duenna: A comic opera, in three acts* (1776), 35. Jackson cites this as a source for his view that Ray uses her wiles for political and financial gain.
'I must now . . . men of merit': Ibid., 38.
'an acquaintance of . . . Mrs Margaret Ray': *The evidence, (as taken down in court) in the trial wherein the Rt. Hon. John, earl of Sandwich was plaintiff, and J. Miller, defendant, before William, Lord Mansfield, and a special jury, in the court of King's Bench, July 8, 1773* (1774), 32.
But the favourable . . . gaining naval promotion: Sandwich Mss 55b/20, 21.

Page 141:

'Our misfortunes . . . of her disappointment': George Forster, *A Letter to the Right Honourable the Earl of Sandwich*, in Thomas et al., *A Voyage Round the World*, appendix D, 792.
'as to the . . . had your share': Sandwich Mss 55d/6.

Page 142:

'if I own to . . . a ridiculous being': Quoted in Rodger, *The Insatiable Earl*, 189.
'You cannot want . . . converted into brothels': Sandwich Mss, 55c/25.
'We all know . . . dropping a tear': Ibid.
'For shame . . . two common prostitutes': Ibid.

Page 143:

'with dialogue of . . . the late unfortunate ——': Ibid., 54b/1.
'Nothing can be . . . more rich, profuse': Edward Thompson, *The Demi-Rep. By the author of the Meretriciad* (2ⁿᵈ edn, 1766), 10.
'fine buckles . . . in upon me': *Authentic and Interesting Memoirs of Miss Ann Sheldon*, i, 183.
'I received from . . . enamoured little knight': Ibid.

Page 144:

'His carriage . . . of *Hyde Park*': Ibid. 183–4.
'Hug, embrace and . . . a new gown': Sandwich Mss 55b/15.
'It was I . . . care of herself': Sandwich Mss 55b/2.

Pages 144–5:
'would never take . . . along with it': Ibid., 55b/3.

Page 145:
He added that . . . to Covent Garden: Ibid.
'I believe with . . . way of life': Ibid.
'Dear Lord Sandwich . . . of sincere love': Ibid., 55a/7.

Page 146:
'Till now . . . myself in time': Ibid., 55a/8.
'I must beg . . . an affection for': Ibid., 55a/10.
'Your reply was . . . things to you': Ibid.

Pages 146–7:
'I have not . . . taking the book': Sandwich to Loudoun (22 October 1772) in Huntingdon Library Loudoun Papers 9203.

Page 147:
'set me at . . . expectation elsewhere?': Ibid.
'she has pressed . . . such an idea': Ibid.
'giving way to . . . at this event': Ibid.
'She upbraided me . . . for Mrs Walker': Ibid.
Unfortunately for Sandwich . . . they had children: See, for instance, examples cited in Lawrence Stone, *The Family, Sex and Marriage in England, 1500–1800* (1977), 531–2.

Pages 147–8:
'I am sorry . . . of children': Sandwich Mss 55b/10.

Page 148:
'From all I . . . but Your Lordship': Ibid.
'All I wrote . . . every point properly': Ibid., 55a/13.

Pages 148–9:
'the power of . . . see [the will]': Ibid., 55b/9.

Page 149:
Sandwich appeared to . . . even in death: See, amongst others, *London Evening Post* (10 April 1770).
'Miss Ray made . . . any possible contingencies': *London Evening Post* (13 April 1779).

CHAPTER 6

Page 151:
'There are many . . . of foolish women': Cited in Haig, *The Gazetteer 1735–1797*, 166.

Page 152:
'Throw yourself once . . . splendor and importance': *Four Letters from the Country Gentleman, on the Subject of the Petitions* (1780), 24.

'Many other favours . . . matter that occurs', explained the editor of the *St James's Chronicle* in March 1780: *St James's Chronicle* (11 March 1780); *Morning Chronicle* (20 March 1780).

But not even politics: For an excellent re-evaluation of *Love and Madness* see Max Novak, 'The Sensibility of Sir Herbert Croft in *Love and Madness* and the "Life of Edward Young"', *The Age of Johnson* 8 (1997), 187–207.

Page 153:

'taken from the . . . and fair character': *Case and Memoirs* (8th edn), iii.

'This day is . . . Oreoonoko [sic]': *Morning Post* (3 March 1780); *London Evening Post* (14 March 1780); *St James's Chronicle* (11 March 1780); *Gazetteer* (16 March 1780); *Morning Chronicle* (10 March 1780); *Whitehall Evening Post* (9 March 1780).

Pages 153–4:

The play was . . . had been executed: Thomas Southerne, *Oroonoko*, ed. Max Novak and David Rodes (1977), xvi; *The London Stage; Part 5, 1776–1800*, vol. i, ed. Charles Beecher Hogan (Carbondale, Illinois, 1968), 253.

Page 154:

'I must assist you,/And since it is the common cause of both,/'Tis just that both be employed in it./Thus, thus 'tis finished, and I bless my fate/That where I lived, I die, in these loved arms': Southerne, *Oroonoko*, v, 275–8.

Page 155:

'as the dreadful . . . horror and pity': *London Evening Post* (1 April 1780).

'beyond all doubt . . . the English language': Ibid.

'Had Hackman's passion . . . of each other': *Morning Chronicle* (4 April 1780); *Gazetteer* (10 April 1780).

Page 156:

It is not . . . priced at 5s. 6d.: Haig, *The Gazetteer*, 223.

Love and Madness . . . early nineteenth century: John Bowyer Nichols, *Illustrations of the Literary History of the Eighteenth Century,* 8 vols (1858), V, 216–18.

'every syllable which . . . made Hackman relate': In Thomas Warton, *An Enquiry into the Authenticity of the Poems Attributed to Thomas Rowley* (1782), 113.

Pages 156–8:

'The LVIIth Letter . . . only is true': *Love and Madness* (1786), 339.

Page 158:

Nearly fifteen years . . . of the text: Sir Herbert Croft, *Chatterton and 'Love and Madness'. A letter from Denmark, to Mr Nichols, editor of the Gentleman's Magazine* (1800), 15.

'These papers . . . of a heart': *Love and Madness*, 204.
'We cannot bear . . . we like him': Ibid., 38.
'of their authenticity . . . to be conjurors': *Monthly Review*, 62 (1780), art. 40.
'with regard to . . . descriptive and affecting': *Town and Country Magazine* (April 1780), 211.

Pages 158–9:
'In this age . . . published trial record]': *Gentleman's Magazine*, I (1780), 287.

Page 159:
'to avoid hurting . . . to be Fiction': Cited in A. D. McKillop, *The Early Masters of English Fiction* (Lawrence, Kansas, 1956), 42.

Page 161:
Croft's claim to . . . the English Poets': Material on Croft's life, unless otherwise indicated, is from his entry in the *Dictionary of National Biography*.
He was a . . . tyranny of democracy: Herbert Butterfield, *George III, Lord North and the People 1779–80* (1949), 247–8.

Pages 163–4:
Many accounts of . . . nearly two volumes: *Trials for Adultery: or, the History of Divorces, by a Civilian*, 7 vols (1779). Another bookseller published Cumberland's embarrassing and jejune love letters, one of which Hackman quotes in *Love and Madness*, xxx.

Page 164:
'You once said . . . to be married': *Love and Madness*, 41.
'notwithstanding the dear . . . are my wife': Ibid., 44.
"Torture shall not . . . regiment in Ireland: Ibid., 44, 49.

Pages 164–5:
'persist in your . . . share your earnings': Ibid., 73, 65.

Page 165:
'for God's sake! . . . or ten letters': Ibid., 74.
'at the hazard . . . to your prayers': Ibid., 100–2.
'What a struggle! . . . my bosom; then . . .': Ibid., 136.

Page 166:
'To my little . . . in the scales': Ibid., 4.

Pages 166–7:
'Observe – when I . . . than lose you': Ibid., 31–2.

Page 167:
'Inconsistent being! . . . like a child': Ibid., 32.
'Be a man . . . Join your regiment': Ibid., 62.

Page 168:
'Suppose *he* [Sandwich] . . . scale of gratitude?': Ibid., 3.
'The same coloured . . . a certain signal': Ibid., 42.

Pages 168–9:
Hackman tries to . . . the lovers' fate: Ibid., 33–4.

Page 169:
'I protest, I . . . life without her': Ibid., 65–6.
'Nonsense, to say . . . such a story': Ibid., 73–4.
'with *an advice . . . spite of me*': Ibid., 93–5.

Pages 169–70:
'Oh love, love . . . devils, hell-hounds!': Ibid., 123.

Page 170:
Discussing the notorious . . . act of madness: Ibid., 225–62. For the Smiths' case, see Michael Macdonald and Terence R. Murphy, *Sleepless Souls. Suicide in early modern England* (Oxford, 1990), 157–9, 319–21.
'If you will . . . rage too fiercely': *Love and Madness*, 265–6.
'As yet the . . . depths of destruction': Ibid., 267.

Page 171:
'The stream of . . . arm of despair': Ibid., 201.
'a miserable business . . . ungrateful woman': Ibid., 223–4.
'The torture of . . . too exquisitely': Ibid., 224.
'Often, very often . . . propriety of suicide': Ibid.

Pages 171–2:
'Could my countrymen . . . of mental torture': Ibid., 296–7.

Page 172:
'Werther was clearly . . . much better man': Ibid., 286.
'blunting the edge . . . shocking example': In Warton, *An Enquiry into the Authenticity of the Poems Attributed to Thomas Rowley*, 113.
(He even sent . . . that gave offence.): Sandwich Mss 55d/10: Herbert Croft to the Earl of Sandwich, 22 September 1786.
'effort of genius . . . and atrocious example': Charles Moore, *A Full Enquiry into the Subject of Suicide. To which are added (as being closely connected with the subject) two treatises on dueling and gaming*, 2 vols (1790), ii, 155.

Page 173:
Chatterton's fame rested . . . chronicles about Bristol: The story is best followed in E. H. Meyerstein, *A Life of Thomas Chatterton* (1930), ch. xix.
'If it should . . . will be disarranged': Warton, *An Enquiry into the Authenticity of the Poems Attributed to Thomas Rowley*, 7–8.

Page 175:
'The original of . . . of the Publisher': See, for instance, *London Evening Post* (14 March 1780).

Pages 175–6:
Like a number . . . such accomplished verse: *Love and Madness*, 125.

Page 176:
'it is but . . . *his inventive genius*': Warton, *An Enquiry into the Authenticity of the Poems Attributed to Thomas Rowley*, 123.
To equate such . . . was a misapprehension: *Love and Madness*, 139.
'Most readily I . . . trait of greatness': Ibid., 140.

Pages 176–7:
'They who do . . . not this strange?': Ibid., 27.

Page 177:
'That fertile genius . . . with the story': Ibid., 32–3.

Pages 177–8:
(The point was . . . forgeries of Chatterton.'): *Gentleman's Magazine* (June 1780), 287.

Page 178:
'Is Macpherson's name . . . be the same?': *Love and Madness*, 138–9.
'he knew no . . . or assist him': Ibid., 147.
'steeped to the lips in poverty': Ibid., 237.
'one of the starved children of genius': Croft uses the term twice: Ibid., 199–200, 224.
'living to all . . . memory of Fame': Ibid., 237.
'in his own . . . fame and eternity': Ibid., 233.
Thus, on the . . . friend Samuel Johnson: Ibid., 225.

Page 179:
'His spirits was . . . times exceeding chearfull': Ibid., 145.
'appeared to have something wonderful about him': Ibid., 191.
As a reader . . . to Samuel Richardson: *The Correspondence of Samuel Richardson* (4 vols, 1804), IV, 30.

Page 180:
'I take it . . . the reader': *Love and Madness*, 104.
'what visions have . . . from my hand': Ibid., 66.
'Well, my M—— . . . appear in print': Ibid., 248.

Page 181:
'which continued for . . . to reprint it': George Borrow, *Celebrated Trials, and Remarkable Cases of Criminal Jurisprudence*, 6 vols (1825), v, 1.
'The editor cannot . . . have been genuine': Ibid., 28.

Page 182:
The Love Letters . . . his authorial role: Rodger, *The Insatiable Earl*, 123:
'There is no doubt that the letters as then published contained numerous passages added by the editor to bolster his argument in an

unrelated literary dispute. The modern editor of the correspondence, however, believed the letters, stripped of their additions, to be genuine. They certainly had a good provenance and contain nothing which is obviously impossible.'

and a recent . . . eighteenth-century punishment: V. A. C. Gatrell, *The Hanging Tree: Execution and the English people, 1770–1868* (Oxford, 1994), 275, 282–4.

CHAPTER 7

Pages 184–5:
'The natural effect . . . its object'; 'us prefer . . . by a rival'; 'wherever passion is . . . horrid deeds'; 'The use to . . . restrain it': quoted in *St James's Chronicle* (15 April 1779).

Page 185:
'The unfortunate Mr . . . dreadful deed'; 'talked about Miss . . . ever of her'; 'A line . . . has lov'd".': *The Genuine Life, Trial, and Dying Words of the Reverend James Hackman* (1779), 9.
'supposed to have . . . his execution': *Public Advertiser* (5 May 1779).

Page 186:
'Driven by Love . . . maddest Gale': *Public Advertiser* (5 May 1779).
'the third stage . . . sentimental love': Erasmus Darwin, *Zoonomia: or, The laws of Organic Life*, 2 vols (1794–6), ii, 365.
'Love . . . and Effects': Joseph Mason Cox, *Practical Observations on Insanity*, 2nd edn (1806), 31–2.

Pages 187–8:
'laws of organic life'; 'distinguishes mankind . . . of nature'; 'described in its . . . and poets'; 'who have not . . . romance writers'; 'is supposed . . . felicity'; 'alleviates the pain . . . it into pleasure'; 'as when it . . . possess himself'; 'counteracted . . . philosophy'; 'When a lover . . . of the playhouse': Erasmus Darwin, *Zoonomia: or, The laws of Organic Life* (1794–6), ii, 363–5.

Pages 188–9:
'as the ambition . . . moderate the other': Trotter, *A View of the Nervous Temperament*, 31.

Pages 189–90:
'How far delicacy . . . of behaviour': David Hume, 'Of the Delicacy of Taste and Passion', in *Essays, Moral, Political and Literary*, ed. Eugene F. Miller (Indianapolis, 1987), 603. This quotation did not appear in all eighteenth-century editions of the essay.
(Female patients confined . . . four to one): Helen Small, *Love's Madness. Medicine, the Novel and female Insanity 1800–1865* (Oxford University

Press, 1996), 33 and more generally Roy Porter, 'Love, Sex and Madness in Eighteenth-Century England', *Social Research*, vol. 53 no. 2 (summer 1986), 211–42.

Page 190:

'Earth has no . . . a woman scorn'd': Erasmus Darwin, *Zoonomia: or, The laws of Organic Life* (1794–6), ii, 365.

Page 191:

'I write merely . . . the first carrier': See Mark L. Reed, *Wordsworth. The Chronology of the early years 1770–1799* (Cambridge, Mass., 1967), 224, for the circumstances and dating of Wordsworth's acquisition of *Zoonomia*.

The case fascinated . . . both of them: Erasmus Darwin, *Zoonomia: or, The laws of Organic Life* (1794–6), iv, 68–9.

Page 192:

'No more I know . . . Oh misery!': *Lyrical Ballads: Wordsworth and Coleridge*, ed. R. L. Brett and A. R. Jones (1991), 75, lines 155–65, 199–202.

Wordsworth's use of . . . of good taste. For the following discussion I have relied on James H. Averill, *Wordsworth's Poetry of Human Suffering* (Ithica, 1980), esp. 167–78; Mary Jacobus, *Tradition and Experiment in Wordsworth's Lyrical Ballads* (Oxford, 1976), 240–50; Jerome Christensen, 'Wordsworth's Misery, Coleridge's Woe: Reading "The Thorn", *Papers in Language and Literature*, 16 (1980), 268–86.

Page 193:

(Indeed, because of . . . of his debt.): Stephen Gill, *Wordsworth: A Life* (Oxford, 1989), 116.

Through Montagu . . . in north Dorset: Ibid., 91–3.

Page 194:

'My child was . . . with his sister': Dove Cottage Wordsworth Mss, Basil Montagu Mss 526 Notebook, 12.

'I consider . . . of my life': Gill, *Wordsworth: A Life*, 91.

'God bless you . . . were most valuable': Dove Cottage Wordsworth Mss, To WW (17 February 1840).

'He is . . . pleasure': *The Letters of William and Dorothy Wordsworth: The Early Years, 1787–1805*, ed. E. De Selincourt, revised, C. L. Shaver, 2nd edn (Oxford, 1967), Dorothy Wordsworth to Mrs John Marshall (7 March 1796), 166.

'extremely petted from . . . to cry': Dorothy Wordsworth to Mrs John Marshall (19 March 1797), Ibid., 180.

Page 195:

'He is quite . . . fearless boy': Dorothy Wordsworth to Mrs John Marshall (7 March 1796), Ibid., 166.

'the flowers . . . the road etc': Dorothy Wordsworth to Mrs William Rawson (13 June & 3 July 1798), Ibid., 222.

'is quite well . . . a little devil': William Wordsworth to Revd Francis Wrangham (7 March 1796), Ibid., 168.

(One of the . . . Basil's mendacity.): *Lyrical Ballads: Wordsworth and Coleridge*, ed. R. L. Brett and A. R. Jones (1991), 285.

'We teach him . . . make him happy': *The Letters of William and Dorothy Wordsworth*, Dorothy Wordsworth to Mrs John Marshall (19 March 1797), 180.

'a very . . . child': Dorothy Wordsworth to Mrs William Rawson (13 June & 3 July 1798), Ibid., 222.

'day after day . . . been starved': Dove Cottage Wordsworth Mss, Basil Montagu Mss 526 Notebook, 43.

Page 196:

'my repugnance . . . civil things': Ibid., 95.

'hectic flush': Dove Cottage Wordsworth Mss, WLMS A/Montagu (1 October 1809).

'Wm and Basil . . . a stunted thorn': *Journals of Dorothy Wordsworth*, ed. E. De Selincourt, 2 vols (1941), i, 13.

'experiments': *Lyrical Ballads: Wordsworth and Coleridge*, 7.

'to ascertain . . . endeavour to impart': Ibid., 241.

Page 197:

'infinite complexity . . . and pleasure': Ibid., 258.

'the fluxes and . . . of our nature': Ibid., 247.

'the spontaneous . . . powerful feelings': Ibid., 246.

'describes and imitates . . . action and suffering': Ibid., 256.

'in the . . . of men': Ibid., 241.

'the degrading . . . outrageous stimulation': Ibid., 249.

'eternal talking of . . . delicious tears': Averill, *Wordsworth and the poetry of human suffering*, 22.

Page 198:

'to exhibit some . . . on the mind': *Lyrical Ballads: Wordsworth and Coleridge*, 288.

'The poem . . . of the story': Ibid., 8.

'The Reader . . . prone to superstition': Ibid., 288.

' 'Tis three feet . . . two feet wide': *Lyrical Ballads: Wordsworth and Coleridge*, 70–8, line 33.

'a wretched thing forlorn': Ibid., line 9.

'the wretched woman': Ibid., line 68.

Page 199:

'But wherefore to . . . wind may blow?': Ibid., lines 100–4.

'I cannot tell . . . no one knows . . .': Ibid., lines 89–90.

We are told . . . envelops the story: Ibid., lines 115–33, 134, 138, 149, 173, 214.
'No more I . . . that ever knew': Ibid., lines 155–8.
'But kill a . . . think she could': Ibid., lines 223–4.
'many swear . . . with Martha Ray': Ibid., lines 173–6.

Pages 199–200:
'It was my . . . is swayed': Ibid., 288.

Page 200:
'I looked around . . . on the ground': Ibid., 70–8, lines 192–8.
Wordsworth did not . . . the 1800 edition: Ibid., 287–8.
'Old Farmer Simpson': Ibid., 70–8, line 149.

Page 201:
'I did not . . . Oh misery!': Ibid., lines 199–203.
'I never heard . . . she is there': Ibid., lines 98–9.
'Perhaps when you . . . tale may trace': Ibid., lines 109–10.

Page 202:
'I cannot tell . . . Oh misery!': Ibid., lines 243–53.
'author should have . . . tiresome himself': Review by Southey in *The Critical Review*, 2nd ser., xxiv (October 1798), 197–204.
'it is not . . . dulness and garrulity': Coleridge, *Biographia Literaria*, ed. Nigel Leask (1997), 207.
'I wd rather . . . botanic garden': Henry Crabb Robinson, *The Correspondence of Henry Crabb Robinson with the Wordsworth Circle*, ed. Edith Morley, 2 vols (Oxford, 1927), i, 44.

Page 203:
'real and substantial action and suffering': *Lyrical Ballads: Wordsworth and Coleridge*, 256.

CHAPTER 8

Page 205:
'Who would be . . . murdered mother?': Basil Montagu, 'The Pleasure of the Fine Arts', *Essays and Selections* (1837), 335.

Page 206:
'I have for . . . comfort through life': Quoted in Eliza Meteyard, *A Group of Englishmen (1795 to 1815): Being records of the younger Wedgwoods and their friends* (1871), 120–1.
'I attached myself . . . to your father': *Memoirs of the Life of Sir James Mackintosh*, ed. Robert James Mackintosh, 2 vols (1835), 153; and also cf. 151.
'fond of playing the patron': *Henry Crabb Robinson on Books and their Writers*, ed. Edith J. Morley, 3 vols (1938), i, 171.

'He expressed nothing . . . destroyed [in France]': Margaret Crum, *The Life of Basil Montagu* (Oxford University M.Litt. thesis, 1954), 45.

Page 207:
'It makes almost . . . on the subject': Hazlitt, *Works*, xix, 243.
'from a desire . . . lives of culprits': Ibid., iii, 199.
Whether because of . . . secure its prevention: Ibid., xix, 244.

Page 208:
'I have a . . . produced upon one': Crum, *The Life of Basil Montagu*, 212.

Page 209:
On a long . . . *Liber Amoris*: W. M. Thackeray, *The Letters and Private Papers*, ed. G. N. Ray, 4 vols (Cambridge, Mass., 1945–6), ii, 245.
'I love him very much': Quoted in Crum, *The Life of Basil Montagu*, 43.
'As for the state of his mind . . . heard of Philosophy': Quoted in Ibid., 88.
Basil was one . . . the poet's death: Ibid., 88, 162–3.
'he was a . . . ostentation and pretence': Ibid., 178.
'an honest-hearted-goose': Thomas Carlyle to John A. Carlyle (30 November 1824), in *The Collected Letters of Thomas and Jane Welsh Carlyle*, eds. C. R. Sanders and K. J. Fielding, 4 vols (Duke, North Carolina, 1970), iii, 211; see also *Life of Basil Montagu*, 197.
'curious strain of sentimentality': *Life of Basil Montagu*, 213.
'The manners, at . . . in modern society': Ibid., 179.
'his usual fidelity . . . art of forgetting': William Wordsworth to Francis Wrangham, 12 July [1807], *The Letters of William and Dorothy Wordsworth. The Middle Years. Part 1: 1806–1811*, ed. Ernest de Selincourt, revised by Mary Moorman (Oxford, 1969), 154.

Page 210:
His cavalier attitude . . . his closest friends: There is a good summary of his complex financial relations with Wordsworth in Crum, *Life of Basil Montagu*, appendix 2.
He was always . . . of legalized injustice': Ibid., 164.
'My boy's asleep . . . as I wish': Meteyard, *A Group of Englishmen*, 117.
'the Preservation of . . . of the Understanding': *Life of Basil Montagu*, 233.
'He was a lover of all quiet things': Thomas Carlyle to James Lewis (26 October 1825), in *Collected Letters of Thomas and Jane Welsh Carlyle*, iii, 399.
'The foundation of . . . love and duty': Montagu, *Essays and Selections*, 184.

Page 212:
'Good middle stature . . . highly tragic way!': Thomas Carlyle, *Reminiscences*, ed. Charles Eliot Norton, 2 vols (1887), ii, 128.
Leigh Hunt, accompanying . . . he exclaimed: *The Autobiography of Leigh*

Hunt with Reminiscences of friends and contemporaries, and with Thornton Hunt's introduction and postscript, ed. Roger Ingpen, 2 vols (1903), i, 2.
'[His mother] pretty . . . hanged for it': Carlyle, *Reminiscences,* ii, 126.
'a loose foolish . . . not worth reading': Ibid., 248–9.

Page 213:
'tragical scene': Leigh Hunt, *The Town,* 2 vols (1848), ii, 157.
'According to . . . had educated her': Ibid.
'Sir Herbert's book . . . considered apocryphal': Ibid., 160.
'Upon the whole . . . retaining her heart': Ibid., 167.
'the great cause . . . love stories': Ibid.
'not as a bad-hearted . . . and passionate': Ibid.
'The truest love . . . know of passion': Ibid.

Page 214:
After cards Cradock . . . examine the heavens: Cradock, *Literary and Miscellaneous Memoirs,* i, 140–1.

Page 215:
'had been printed fifty times before': See *Quarterly Review,* xxxv (January & March 1827), 152.
'I can attest . . . on public decorum': Cradock, *Literary and Miscellaneous Memoirs,* iv, 166, 168.
Most of the . . . lost my Love', was sung after supper: Ibid., i, 146–7.
'the first attraction': Ibid., 117.

Pages 215–16:
'Her voice was . . . most difficult description': Ibid., 118.

Page 216:
'was so assiduous . . . of the evening': Ibid., iv, 167.
'I need not . . . delicate a subject"': Ibid., i, 143.
'as her voice . . . the Opera-house': Ibid., 144.

Page 217:
'in which Miss . . . sung so enchantingly': Ibid., iv, 172.
'I sincerely . . . deeply lamented': Ibid.,iv, 172.
'the affair of . . . many enquiries': Ibid., i, lvi.
'The account of . . . to the author': See *Gentleman's Magazine* (March 1826), 237.

Page 218:
'the ordinary gossip . . . the drawing room': See *London Magazine,* new ser., iv (April 1826), no. xvi, 562.
'Now Madam . . . to the state': Horace Walpole to Lady Ossory (8 April 1779), in *The Yale Edition of Horace Walpole's Correspondence,* xxxiii, 98.

Page 219:
'Is not the . . . understand it': Horace Walpole to Lady Ossory (9 April 1779), Ibid., 101.

'I do not . . . tends to nothing': Horace Walpole to Lady Ossory (6 May 1779), Ibid.
'It is very . . . a kept mistress!': Ibid.
'It just sets . . . critical moment': Ibid.
'might as well . . . Covent Garden': Ibid.

Pages 219–20:
'The history of . . . despatch her too': Revd Dr Warner to George Selwyn, quoted in *George Selwyn and his Contemporaries*, ed. John Heneage Jesse, 4 vols. (1843–4), iv, 67–8.

Page 220:
'How much you have missed!': Countess of Ossory to Selwyn, Ibid., 75.
'in order to give . . . friends everywhere': Earl of Carlisle to Selwyn, Ibid., 85.
'a genteel, well-made . . . four and twenty': Warner to Selwyn, Ibid., 96.

Page 221:
'You get up . . . for a shilling': W. M. Thackeray, *Cornhill Magazine* (1860), ii, 263; see also John Heneage Jesse, *The Edinburgh Review*, CLXI (July 1844), 12.
'the very prince of gossips': Hazlitt on Walpole, quoted in *Horace Walpole: The Critical Heritage*, ed. Peter Sabor (1987), 187.

Page 222:
'The conformation of . . . his serious business': Macaulay on Walpole, Ibid., 312–13.
'awful debauchery . . . dissoluteness': Thackeray, *Cornhill Magazine*, ii, 261.

Page 223:
'so different . . . important struggles': Mary Berry, 'Advertisement to the Letters Addressed from Lord Orford to the Miss Berrys', *England and France: a comparative view of the social conditions of both countries* (2 vols, 1844), ii, 146.
'A very few . . . of the world': *Cornhill Magazine*, ii, 1.
'the old society . . . courtly splendours': Ibid., 257.
'[here] we have . . . enough': Ibid., 260.
'great unacknowledged . . . and beauty': Ibid., 262.

Page 224:
'it has brought . . . park at home': Ibid., 261.
'We can have . . . and his supper': Ibid., 260.
'palace of Nebuchadnezzar': Ibid., 258.
'I fancy that . . . the Red Indian': Ibid., 259.
'It was the . . . of social life': Ibid., 260

Page 225:
'The legends about . . . they passed by': Ibid., 263.

'was forced into . . . and idler': Ibid., 262.
'slipped Lord North's . . . their ruffles': Ibid., 260.
'The only palliation . . . of his contemporaries': Jesse, *The Edinburgh Review* (July 1844), 6.

Page 228:
'was an event . . . at that period': *The Life and Correspondence of M. G. Lewis: With many pieces in prose and verse never before published*, ed. Margaret Baron-Wilson, 2 vols (1839), i, 19.
'was vulgar . . . its circumstances': See *Blackwood's Edinburgh Magazine* (February 1844), no. 55, 179.
'The shame . . . to honourable feelings': Ibid.
'merely the work of an assassin': Ibid., 180.
'The clear case . . . going on foot': Ibid.

Page 229:
'We are happy . . . highly satisfactory': Jesse, *The Edinburgh Review* (July 1844), 38.
'No prime minister . . . attend cock-fights': Ibid.

Page 233:
'unhappy passion . . . to his country': William Jackson, *New and Complete Newgate Calendar; or, Malefactors Universal Register*, 8 vols (1812–18), vi, 21.
'There are some . . . case before us': Ibid., 1.
'Miss Reay . . . humble station': Ibid., 18.
'unhappy, irregular, and ungovernable passion': Ibid.

Page 235:
'The comparison of . . . of the other': Camden Pelham, *The Chronicles of Crime; or the New Newgate Calendar, being a series of memoirs and anecdotes of notorious characters who have outraged the laws of Great Britain from the earliest period to the present time* (1841), vii.
'Those dreadful and . . . of the people': Ibid.
'In the year . . . were little safer': *The New Newgate Calendar* (5 March 1864), no. 20.

CHAPTER 9

Page 240:
The story almost . . . detail or accuracy: John Doran, *Saints and Sinners; or, In church and about it*, 2 vols. (1868), ii, 139–41.
They quarrelled over . . . the Newgate Calendars: See, for example, *Notes and Queries*, ser. 7, vi, 87, 212–13.

Page 241:
'I have been . . . is permissible nowadays': Gilbert Burgess, *The Love Letters of Mr H. & Miss R. 1775–1779* (1895), xv.

Burgess also inserted . . . narrative' were missing: Ibid.
'the result of a momentary impulse': Ibid., 150.

Page 243:
'Miss Ray seemed . . . in spirits': M. G. Lewis, *The Life and Correspondence of M. G. Lewis*, 2 vols (1839), i, 19.
'return as soon . . . over': Ibid., 20.
As she got ready . . . leaves on the ground'.): Ibid.

Page 244:
Even more than . . . on Lord Sandwich: Ibid., 22–3.
'rigidly punctilious': Ibid., 19.
'cold, selfish, and formal': Ibid., 26.
She would never . . . negative bounty': Ibid., 23–4.
'Mastered by a . . . to absolute frenzy': Ibid., 25.

Pages 244–5:
'The effect which . . . pensiveness and melancholy': Ibid., 26.

Page 245:
'No record of . . . such a romance': Burgess, *The Love Letters of Mr H. & Miss R.,* xvi.
'convinced that such . . . and Miss Reay': Ibid.
'The story and . . . of strong interest': Ibid.

Page 246:
'It is not . . . protests from him': Ibid., vi.
'He clumsily put . . . of the volume': Ibid., viii.
'The enormous success . . . claiming this portion': Ibid., xiv.

Page 247:
'Full of hope . . . events that followed': Ibid., 143.
'he must have . . . man's *billets-doux*': E. H. Lewis, 'Are the Hackman–Reay Love Letters Genuine?', *Modern Language Notes*, x, 8 (1895), 456–7.

Pages 247–8:
'The letters that . . . true Hackman style': Ibid., 459.

Page 248:
'protestations of love . . . speedy marriage': Ibid., 456.
'nobody ever gave . . . that of Hackman': Ibid., 463.
'the awful eloquence . . . by expressing it': Ibid., 463–4.

Page 249:
Surviving portraits of . . . a baffling hiatus': Constance Hagberg Wright, *The Chaste Mistress* (1930), v.

Page 250:
'We believe that . . . its pathetic interest': Ibid.

She complained that . . . have invented them': Elizabeth Jenkins, 'Martha Ray', in *Ten Fascinating Women* (1955), 15.
'It is not . . . and James Hackman': Ibid.
Thus she inferred . . . quite remarkable: Ibid.

Page 252:
an edition of . . . *Casanova in England* (1923): See J. W. Lambert and Michael Ratcliffe, *The Bodley Head 1887–1987* (1987), 179–80.

Page 253:
'give his advice . . . preservation or publication': Ibid., 181.

Pages 253–4:
'The great crime . . . of mere acquisition': D. H. Lawrence, 'Then disaster looms ahead', *Architectural Review* LXVIII (1930), 47.

Page 254:
'The eighteenth century . . . and men decay': Elizabeth Jenkins, *Jane Austen: A Biography* (1938), 9.
She sees this . . . almost monotonous completeness': Ibid.

Pages 244–5:
For Jenkins the . . . which once prevailed': Ibid., 10.

Page 255:
'the difference between . . . women did not': Hilaire Belloc, quoted in the *New Statesman* (29 March 1930), 808.
'Universal education . . . New Stupid': Aldous Huxley, quoted in John Carey, *The Intellectuals and the Masses* (1992), 16.
'All artists . . . aesthetic judgements': Clive Bell, *Art*, ed. J. B. Bullen (Oxford, 1987), 242, 261.

Page 258:
'In this country . . . quality in England': Sandwich to Viry, Sandwich Mss 56b.
'that lovely and . . . patron Lord Sandwich': *The Times* (15 October 1928).

Page 260:
'trilling with . . . a skylark': Wright, *The Chaste Mistress*, 4.
'Her singularly sweet . . . over them': Ibid., 20–1.
She moves . . . and soul': Ibid., 22.
'Amid the tremulous . . . uncalculating ecstasy': Ibid., 62.

Pages 260–1:
Wright does not . . . their lovemaking: Ibid., 24, 145.

Page 261:
As the doyenne . . . commonplace things': Elinor Glyn, *The Philosophy of*

Love (1920) cited in Rachel Anderson, *The Purple Heart Throbs the sub-literature of love* (1974), 266.

Thus when . . . his veins': Wright, *The Chaste Mistress*, 24.

'Dead and gone . . . her soul had slipped': Ibid., 183.

And when she . . . divine possession': Ibid., 145.

'tosh': Quoted in Q. D. Leavis, *Fiction and the Reading Public* (1932), 181; see also 23, 67–8, 130–6, 226.

Page 262:

'His masterful wooing . . . denied his will': Wright, *The Chaste Mistress*, 27–8.

'the oneness of . . . any other relationship': Ibid., 190.

'the charm she . . . it was perilous': Ibid., 111.

'I loved him . . . strong for me': Ibid., 112.

'Make your choice! . . . into his hands': Ibid., 114–15.

Page 263:

'I give in': Ibid., 191.

'mother-love . . . had mastered her': Ibid. 202.

'Somewhere deep in . . . might die together': Ibid.

'With a sweet . . . of her companion': Ibid., 211.

'had been a . . . crown of motherhood': Ibid., 115.

'she who in . . . crucify herself': Ibid., 219.

'Tempted, fascinated, awed . . . yield': Ibid., 8.

Page 264:

'masterful': Ibid., 17.

'his commanding presence': Ibid., 23.

'Oh . . . power to resist!': Ibid., 66.

'She found courage . . . its own quietus': Ibid., 175.

'Strengthened by him . . . resistance of steel': Ibid., 170.

'Love conquers death': Ibid., 219.

Page 265:

'My lord, . . . pride of birth': Ibid., 174.

'the sore encumbrance': Ibid., 6.

Pages 265–6:

'My Lord Sandwich . . . punctuality and industry': Ibid., 14.

Page 266:

'Once he came . . . kissed her passionately': Ibid., 17.

'She obeyed with . . . was to come': Ibid., 24.

'the slim body . . . in responsive love': Ibid.

Page 267:

'on the tragic . . . James Hackman': Ibid., 108.

'who could refuse . . . young to die': Ibid., 215.

'greatly maligned . . . his lost Martha': Ibid.

Page 268:
> He forges a . . . a new lover: Ibid., 197–200.
> 'I . . . have grown . . . general good behaviour': Quoted in E. H.
> McCormick, *Omai. Pacific Envoy* (Auckland and Oxford, 1977), 131.

Page 269:
> 'I thought', writes . . . about the couple: *Love and Madness*, 7.
> 'naturally genteel and prepossessing': Cradock, *Literary and Miscellaneous Memoirs*, iv, 179.
> 'to shame . . . up and fled': Frances Burney to Samuel Crisp (1
> December 1774), *The Early Journals and Letters of Fanny Burney*, ed. Lars
> E. Troide, 2 vols (Oxford, 1990), ii, 60, 62–3.

Page 271:
> 'as trivial as . . . freedom and success': *Omiah's Farewell; inscribed to the Ladies of London* (1776), ii–iii.

Page 272:
> 'cunning and lust': Wright, *The Chaste Mistress*, 85.
> 'He is so . . . so haunt me': Ibid., 74.
> 'Martha was uneasy . . . able to dissemble': Ibid., 76.
> 'wild-beast eyes': Ibid., 78.
> 'Once . . . like to retch': Ibid., 75.
> 'All at once . . . distorted with rage': Ibid., 77.
> 'staring at her . . . of her tucker': Ibid., 187.

Page 273:
> 'well-kept hands . . . denote artistic tastes': Ibid., 53.
> 'She, who was . . . the proudest hostesses': Ibid., 84.
> 'nor might young . . . the Otaheitan': Ibid., 84.
> 'certain ladies of . . . provided for him': Ibid., 148.
> 'He was generally styled . . . a brother darkie': Ibid., 108.

Page 274:
> 'so refined in . . . noble ancestor': Ibid., 49.
> 'two sons . . . septic menace': Ibid., 48.

Page 276:
> 'an emotional callousness . . . women of fashion': Jenkins, 'Martha Ray',
> 11–13.
> 'She had never . . . Sandwich's protection': Ibid., 13.
> 'Her own emotions . . . known before': Ibid., 15.
> 'The lyrical rapture . . . driving impulse': Ibid., 19.

Pages 276–7:
> 'She loved him . . . was the first': Ibid., 20.

Page 277:
> 'She had never lost . . . failed to gain': Ibid., 13.
> 'if she had been . . . could not have helped her': Ibid.

Page 278:
'Martha Ray was . . . rejecting James Hackman': Ibid., 24.
'unusually troubled': Ibid.
'Sacred to the . . . compare with hers?': Ibid., 35.

CHAPTER 10

Page 280:
'I do not love . . . tends to nothing': Horace Walpole to Lady Ossory,
9 April 1779, *The Yale Edition of Horace Walpole's Correspondence*, xxxiii,
101.

Page 281:
The establishment of the Public Record Office: Philippa Levine, *The
Amateur and the Professional: Antiquarians, Historians and Archaeologists in
Victorian England, 1838–1886* (Cambridge, 1986), chapter 5.

Page 282:
'History is not concerned . . . relation to the state': J. R. Seeley, *Lectures
and Essays* (1870), 296.
'All forms of history . . . historian inhabits': G. R. Elton, *Political
History: Principles and Practice* (1970), 160.
'Our university . . . politicians': Seeley, *Lectures and Essays*, 299.
'was looked upon . . . should know': quoted in John Kenyon, *The History Men.
The Historical Profession in England since the Renaissance* (2nd edn, 1993), 170.

Page 283:
'I happen to think . . . statesmanship': Ibid, 278. Butterfield is echoing
Seeley.
Popular history: Peter Mandler, *History and National Life* (2002), 23–32.

Page 285:
The aims of this new sort of history: 'New Ways in History', *Times
Literary Supplement* (7 April 1966), 275–310.

Page 286:
'The Tools and the Job': Ibid., 275–6.
'intelligible . . . wanted answering': Ibid, 276, 275.

Page 287:
'to rescue . . . condescension of posterity': E. P. Thompson, *The Making
of the English Working Class* (1963), 12.

INDEX

Abbreviations in subentries: H is James Hackman, R is Martha Ray, S is 4th Earl of Sandwich

Abingdon, Mrs 126
Admiralty 11–12
advertisements 38
Ainsworth, William Harrison 236, 238
Almon, John 44, 74
American war 12–13
Ancaster, Lord 143
Anderson, Mary 27
Angelo, Henry 29
Annesley, Arthur 95
Anson, Lord 122
aristocratic libertinage 94–8, 99–101, 106–7, 110–11
Arne, Thomas 18

Baddeley, Sophia 19, 144
bagnios 94
Baker, Nanny 92
Balding, Mr 25
Banks, Sir Joseph 119
Barré, Colonel 126
Bate, Henry 42, 44
Bates, Joah 119
bawds 97–9
Beard, John 144
Bedford, Duchess of 33
Bell, Clive 255
Bellamy, George Anne 90, 126, 139
Belloc, Hilaire 255
Berkeley, Miss 142

Berry, Mary 222–3
Bickerstaff, Isaac 18
Bickerton, Sir Richard 119
biographies 284, 291
Blackstone, Sir William 27, 28, 67
Blair, Hugh 60, 159
Blandy, Richard 22, 27
Bleackley, Horace 252
'Blessell, Anna De' 98
Bodley Head 252
Bolton, Arabella 89–90
Booth, Frederick 16, 27, 28, 40, 68, 76, 246
Borrow, George 181, 233
Boswell, James
    H's trial and execution 27, 28, 29, 63, 68
    The Hypochondriack 70
    newspaper correspondent 39–40
    prostitutes 92
    Public Advertiser 71
    Shakespeare Tavern 22
    St James's Chronicle 72, 81, 184–5
    view of H 51
Bristol, Lord 14, 30, 44
brothels 93, 94–6
Brown, Hannah 231
Brown, Maria 99
Buckle, H.T. 283
Bulwer Lytton, Edward 236, 238

Dawes's account 78–9, 82–3
execution 28–9
and Galli 15
historical record 285
letters 20, 25
magistrate, appears before 24,
  65–6
press views of 50–1, 56
public fascination with 71
public speculation over motives
  45–6, 64–5
and R 16, 20, 21, 25, 48–9
suicide attempt 20–1
suicide note 20, 79
trial 27–8, 66–7
and Walsingham 47
Halifax, Lord 90, 98, 102, 126
Hardwicke, Lord 30
Harrington, Lord 101
Haslewood, Joseph 182
Hawkesworth, John 119
Hayes, Charlotte 94, 95, 96, 271
Hazlitt, William 207, 208, 209,
  212
'Hermitage, Polly' 95
Heyer, Georgette 256
Hiberian Magazine 132
Hinchingbrooke 49, 120, 146, 256,
  268
historical documents 282
historical novels 256, 283–4, 291–2
historical record 288–9
history 5, 7, 281–93
Hobsbawm, Eric 286
Hogarth, William 238
Hollinworth, Mr 12
Holmes, Richard 291
Holroyd, Michael 291
The Honest London Spy... 88
Horsham, Mrs 98
Howarth, Henry 27
Hull, E.M. 259
human sciences 58
Hume, David 58, 189
Hunt, Leigh 208, 212–14

Huntingdonshire society 120
Huxley, Aldous 255

inquest (R's) 24–5
insanity 186
insanity pleas 67

Jackson, Christopher 132–3, 138
Jackson, William 232, 233
James (S's servant) 23
Jarvis, Mr 24
Jenkins, Elizabeth 4, 182, 249, 250,
  254–5, 275–9
Jesse, John Heneage 219–20
Johnson, Samuel 63, 174
Johnstone, Charles 110–11
Jones, Miss 97
journalism 292
journalists 38–9

Kearsley, George
  Case and Memoirs (Dawes) 74, 232
  demi-reps 135
  *Love Letters of Mr H. and Miss
    R.* (Burgess) 246
  Love and Madness (Croft) 152,
    155, 156, 175
  Omai 271
Kelly, Hugh 136–7
Kemble, Frances 207, 208
Kennedy, Margaret 16, 18
Keppel, Augustus 13, 14, 122
Kidgell, Revd. 103

Lady's Magazine 59
Lamb, Charles 207, 208
Lane, John 252–3
Lawrence, D.H. 253–4
Lawrence, Herbert 144
Leake, Mrs Percy 258
Leavis, F.R. 253
Leavis, Q.D. 261
legal reform 207
Lennox, Lady Sarah 126
Lester, Sir Peter 143